THE ENVIR

ACTION

'The Phrase "health of the environment" is not a literary convention. It has real biological meaning, because the surface of the earth is truly a living organism. Without the countless and immensely varied forms of life that the earth harbours, our planet would be just another fragment of the universe with a surface as drab as that of the moon and an atmosphere inhospitable to man.'

René Dubos, from the chapter *Limits of Adaptability*

IS OUR ENVIRONMENT TO BE DEALT WITH IN THESE TERMS, OR IS IT TO BE HANDED OVER TO CEASELESS, UNTHINKING DEVELOPMENT BY THOSE WHO THINK ONLY OF WHAT IT COULD YIELD TO THEM TODAY?

There is now a generation in Britain, in the world, which is demanding better answers to this question, and to many more about our environment. They speak out in this book with an urgency born of the realization that time is running out. They are joined by those who have long warned that our reckless devotion to head-long development will threaten our very existence. At most we have this decade to deal with some of the problems. In many cases we have already damaged the environment beyond repair.

The real turning point in the battle to save what is left and rebuild what we can is at hand for each of us in our own community, and the information and suggestions in *The Environmental Handbook* can become the source for our efforts. Read it and look around. There is a Britain – indeed, a planet – that needs your help . . .

We nominate the following themes which, properly varied, may persuade good people to change course:

(1) *Man needs more time to learn.* In the week of creation (using *Genesis* time) man arrived only three minutes before midnight on the sixth day. The world had worked quite well without him all the previous week.

(2) *Progress does not need ever-increasing speed*, whether it be in air travel; in using up coal, oil, and gas; in polluting the air; or in broadcasting poisonous chemicals the environment cannot cope with.

(3) *There are limits.* We cannot keep on doubling anything. We cannot let technology grind up the last natural beauty and wilderness before we turn around to repair our damage. As rational beings we can turn around sooner, while there is still natural beauty and wildness around us, serving purposes we may one day be wise enough to understand.

(4) *In diversity is strength.* Biological wealth and stability are dependent upon complexity. For example, had we somehow simplified the New Forest to chestnuts only, the immediate advantages might have been numerous, but a chestnut blight could have wiped the landscape clean of trees. The lesson is unheeded too often. We can learn it now.

(5) *Man can remember his greater attribute.* Through the ages he has aggressively manifested his territoriality, to which there are limits. He has less often shown his capacity to love, the one resource that increases with use.

Conclusion

Thoreau put it all in one question: 'What is the use of a house if you haven't got a tolerable planet to put it on?'

The push for a tolerable planet is on!

THE ENVIRONMENTAL HANDBOOK

ACTION GUIDE FOR THE UK

Edited by John Barr

Introduction by Kenneth Allsop

This handbook was based on the American
Environmental Handbook edited by Garrett De Bell
for Friends of the Earth in The United States

A BALLANTINE/FRIENDS OF THE EARTH BOOK
published in association with
PAN BOOKS LTD. 33 TOTHILL ST. LONDON S.W.1

First published in United Kingdom 1971.

ISBN 0 345 02137 1

© Friends of the Earth 1971

Printed by Cox & Wyman Ltd,
London, Reading and Fakenham

Additional Copyright ©

FRIENDS OF THE EARTH was founded in 1969 in America and in 1970 in the United Kingdom. It is a non-profit-making organization created to undertake aggressive political and legislative activity aimed at restoring an environment misused by man, and at preserving the Earth's remaining wilderness. FOE invites your participation.

> We seek a renewed stirring of love for the earth; we urge that what man is capable of doing to the earth is not always what he ought to do; and we plead that all people here, now, determine that a wide, spacious untrammelled freedom shall remain as living testimony that this generation, our own, had love for the next.

David R. Brower

Address:
Friends of the Earth,
8 King Street,
London, WC2.
Telephone: (01) 836 0718

CONTENTS

INTRODUCTION BY KENNETH ALLSOP

The Environmental Handbook is a consumer's guide to the full range of methods available for the extinction of the human race and life at large on this planet, a death-*Which*. Or it is the blueprint for an ecological Sentinel System: the final ABM defence network against the incoming technological missiles bringing instant apocalypse. It depends how you read it and how you use it. It depends, in the ultimate resort, whether you can hang on to a stubborn optimism that man can still save himself by the skin of his last tooth; or whether, falling back under the blows – so powerful, so pervasive – against the fabric of existence, you conclude that it is all beyond hope and recovery.

What I have to say may not chime with the thematic message which is that, grave though the predicament is, it is soluble. You will see that, after the sombre and frightening recital of pan-denominational crises which beset the world – pollution, over-population, exhaustion of natural resources and the curiously ignored but actually escalating likelihood of nuclear cinderization by peradventure – there comes an upbeat coda. In the third part of this book are the lists of action groups and amenity commandos, exposition of strategy and tactics, explanation of legislation for the enactment of which citizens of consciences and good will can and must agitate.

It is a THEM and US situation. THEY are governments, industrial complexes, corporations public and private, monolithic officialdom and orthodox 'hardened' authority in its modern central executive form. Although they are strong, cynical, ruthless and psychopathically suicidal (the message goes), WE are greater in number and finer in spirit. Given the energy and determination, the meek shall thwart the caparisoned brutes and yet inherit a sweeter earth.

That is not a view I personally can confidently back. I WANT TO SEE THIS BOOK REACH THE BIGGEST POSSIBLE READERSHIP BECAUSE I CALCULATE THAT IT IS STILL WORTH MAKING A LONG-SHOT BET ON AN OUTSIDE CHANCE THAT THE FORE-GOING MAY BE TRUE AND REALIZABLE. Yet I can, in honesty, only put down my reading of the dilemma and how I interpret it, and declare that it is with profound pessimism.

I want to essay a thought which is not contained in the following pages and which conflicts with the thematic call to arms to vanquish the pig-greedy and the purblind and the vandals, and so win the battle for survival of the decencies. It is this. I believe that we have to face the fact that the trouble we are in is even uglier than that thenceforth described. I believe that we must understand that there is a grimmer prospect than catastrophe – adaption. I am far from certain that those on the side of US who have written and who may read this book have the capability of stopping or slowing the destruction. Furthermore I think it is possible that THEY may stay on course and may also stay intact. It may be that WE, and our concepts of quality and beauty and harmony, are obsolescent and doomed to extinction.

I have read a chillingly terrible reference to the discovery in the dead waters of Lake Erie – an American cesspool of chemical effluent and human sewage – a 'new strange mutant of carp which actually lives off the poisons in the water'. Our generation of campaigners feels anguish that the countryside and its marvellous multiplicity of life is under siege and succumbing; our aesthetic is that of the greenwood and birdsong and space and solitude. I think we must recognize that we may be on to a loser and that the enemy's ingenuity may be able to dispense with that archaic and romantic traditional idyll, and not necessarily perish as a result. I think we must reckon on there being fewer on our side than we imagine, that the human race is also producing its mutant carp which can live off poison.

Not long ago a journalist in a great British newspaper

wrote that he would like to see the countryside cemented over from end to end. From Governor Reagan of California came the observation that 'If you've seen one redwood tree, you've seen 'em all.' The President of US Steel made his position clear: he doesn't believe in 'clean water for its own sake'. Loutishly flippant or barbarously stupid, such remarks come from de-natured men, and it would be a mistake to underestimate their numbers or to fail to weigh that this is the uttered outlook of a vast bulk of the population who are conditioned to a treeless, neon-lit, profit-geared environment – indeed, to whom that environment is more 'natural' than that which conservationists take as their criterion.

Professor Colin Buchanan has made the point: 'There could be a real change of values. People could begin to say, "Well, we rather *like* an element of danger in the streets; we like traffic noise, it is somehow involved with the excitement of city life; we do not at all object to the squalor and untidiness." ' Implicit in most ecological arguments is the assumption that common to most people is an attachment to and a longing for the idealized countryside of Constable and Cobbett. That may be shaky ground. If we are effectively to preserve something of that old coherence and pattern, I suggest that it can be done only by taking account of a very different scale of standards: at their most scientifically articulated those of, for instance, Unilever and Buckminster Fuller and Athelstan Spilhaus and Constantinos Doxiadis.

Unilever are already experimentally producing lycine, 'woven synthetic fibre as meat substitutes': i.e. plastic food. Fuller, father of the geodistic dome, sees Utopia as his Dymaxion World, in which crystalline megacities will be encased in polyester fibreglass. Spilhaus, too, believes that the looming urban concentrations must go under giant translucent domes: stews under Pyrex lids. Doxiadis is even more dramatically prophetic. He looks to the ecumenopolis, or universal city, an ecosystem of engine cells for human occupation: Britain will be one supercity stretching on stilts across the North Sea.

Of course, within these glittering 'dynamic communities' feeding on plastic hamburgers will be recreational zones, rolled in like shop window grass. Is that the alternative? Perhaps there is no alternative but that. Therefore I feel that we should be aware that we may be combating more than antique sewage disposal by boorish town councils and 'planners' who get orgasmic highs from building flyovers across Georgian squares.

The contributors to this important symposium, a brains trust of some of the best minds now studying the pathology of ecological injury, each matter-of-factly lays on the line the present circumstances in his particular field. Sensationalism is neither employed nor needed to bring home to us the fast approaching crisis in which options are rapidly dwindling.

Yet my own estimate is that, in total, they still do not convey the enormity of the danger. We know that today's problems are appallingly complicated – they may be worse than we suppose. What we take to be immutable values, temporarily embattled, may be an eroded crust collapsing under our feet. The mutant carp may be breeding.

Kenneth Allsop

PART ONE:
THE MEANING OF ECOLOGY

Two inches of topsoil may be the creation of a thousand years.

Garth Christian
from *Tomorrow's Countryside*

Can he who has only discovered the value of whale-bone and whale-oil be said to have discovered the true uses of the whale? Can he who slays the elephant for his ivory be said to have seen the elephant? No, these are petty and accidental uses. Just as if a stronger race were to kill us in order to make buttons and flageolets of our bones, and then prate of the usefulness of man. Every creature is better alive than dead, both men and moose and pine-trees, as life is more beautiful than death.

Henry David Thoreau
Journal, 1st November, 1853

When we try to pick out anything by itself we find it hitched to everything else in the universe.

John Muir
from *My First Summer in the Sierra*, 1911

The Historical Roots
of Our Ecological Crisis

Lynn White, Jr

from *Science*

A conversation with Aldous Huxley not infrequently put one at the receiving end of an unforgettable monologue. About a year before his lamented death he was discoursing on a favourite topic: Man's unnatural treatment of nature and its sad results. To illustrate his point he told how, during the previous summer, he had returned to a little valley in England where he had spent many happy months as a child. Once it had been composed of delightful grassy glades; now it was becoming overgrown with unsightly brush because the rabbits that formerly kept such growth under control had largely succumbed to a disease, myxomatosis, that was deliberately introduced by the local farmers to reduce the rabbits' destruction of crops. Being something of a Philistine, I could be silent no longer, even in the interests of great rhetoric. I interrupted to point out that the rabbit itself had been brought as a domestic animal to England in 1176, presumably to improve the protein diet of the peasantry.

All forms of life modify their contexts. The most spectacular and benign instance is doubtless the coral polyp. By serving its own ends, it has created a vast undersea world favourable to thousands of other kinds of animals and plants. Ever since man became a numerous species he has affected his environment notably. The hypothesis that his fire-drive method of hunting created the world's great grasslands and helped to exterminate the monster mammals of the Pleistocene from much of the globe is plausible, if not proved. For six millennia at least, the banks of the lower Nile have been a human artifact rather than the swampy African jungle which nature, apart from man, would have

3

made it. The Aswan Dam, flooding 5,000 square miles, is only the latest stage in a long process. In many regions terracing or irrigation, overgrazing, the cutting of forests by Romans to build ships to fight Carthaginians or by Crusaders to solve the logistics problems of their expeditions, have profoundly changed some ecologies. Observation that the French landscape falls into two basic types, the open fields of the north and the *bocage* of the south and west, inspired Marc Bloch to undertake his classic study of medieval agricultural methods. Quite unintentionally, changes in human ways often affect non-human nature. It has been noted, for example, that the advent of the motor car eliminated huge flocks of sparrows that once fed on the horse manure littering every street.

The history of ecologic change is still so rudimentary that we know little about what really happened, or what the results were. The extinction of the European aurochs as late as 1627 would seem to have been a simple case of overenthusiastic hunting. On more intricate matters it often is impossible to find solid information. For a thousand years or more the Frisians and Hollanders have been pushing back the North Sea, and the process is culminating in our own time in the reclamation of the Zuider Zee. What, if any, species of animals, birds, fish, shore life, or plants have died out in the process? In their epic combat with Neptune have the Netherlanders overlooked ecological values in such a way that the quality of human life in the Netherlands has suffered? I cannot discover that the questions have ever been asked, much less answered.

People, then, have often been a dynamic element in their own environment, but in the present state of historical scholarship we usually do not know exactly when, where, or with what effects man-induced changes came. As we enter the last third of the twentieth-century, however, concern for the problem of ecologic backlash is mounting feverishly. Natural science, conceived as the effort to understand the nature of things, had flourished in several eras and among several peoples. Similarly there had been an age-old accumulation of technological skills, sometimes growing

4

rapidly, sometimes slowly. But it was not until about four generations ago that Western Europe and North America arranged a marriage between science and technology, a union of the theoretical and the empirical approaches to our natural environment. The emergence in widespread practice of the Baconian creed that scientific knowledge means technological power over nature can scarcely be dated before about 1850, save in the chemical industries, where it is anticipated in the eighteenth century. Its acceptance as a normal pattern of action may mark the greatest event in human history since the invention of agriculture, and perhaps in nonhuman terrestrial history as well.

Almost at once the new situation forced the crystallization of the novel concept of ecology; indeed, the word *ecology* first appeared in the English language in 1873. Today, less than a century later, the impact of our race upon the environment has so increased in force that it has changed in essence. When the first cannons were fired, in the early fourteenth century, they affected ecology by sending workers scrambling to the forests and mountains for more potash, sulphur, iron ore, and charcoal, with some resulting erosion and deforestation. Hydrogen bombs are of a different order: a war fought with them might alter the genetics of all life on this planet. By 1285 London had a smog problem arising from the burning of soft coal, but our present combustion of fossil fuels threatens to change the chemistry of the globe's atmosphere as a whole, with consequences which we are only beginning to guess. With the population explosion, the carcinoma of planless urbanism, the new geological deposits of sewage and garbage, surely no creature other than man has ever managed to foul its nest in such short order.

There are many calls to action, but specific proposals, however worthy as individual items, seem too partial, palliative, negative: ban the bomb, tear down the hoardings, give the Hindus contraceptives and tell them to eat their sacred cows. The simplest solution to any suspect change is, of course, to stop it, or, better yet, to revert to a romanticized past: make those ugly petrol stations look like Anne

5

Hathaway's cottage or (in America's Far West) like ghost-town saloons. The 'wilderness-area' mentality invariably advocates deep-freezing an ecology, whether San Gimignano or the High Sierra, as it was before the first Kleenex was dropped. But neither atavism nor prettification will cope with the ecological crisis of our time.

What shall we do? No one yet knows. Unless we think about fundamentals, our specific measures may produce new backlashes more serious than those they are designed to remedy.

As a beginning we should try to clarify our thinking by looking, in some historical depth, at the presuppositions that underlie modern technology and science. Science was traditionally aristocratic, speculative, intellectual in intent; technology was lower-class, empirical, action-oriented. The quite sudden fusion of these two, towards the middle of the nineteenth century, is surely related to the slightly prior and contemporary democratic revolutions, which, by reducing social barriers, tended to assert a functional unity of brain and hand. Our ecological crisis is the product of an emerging, entirely novel, democratic culture. The issue is whether a democratized world can survive its own implications. Presumably we cannot unless we rethink our axioms.

THE WESTERN TRADITIONS
OF TECHNOLOGY AND SCIENCE

One thing is so certain that it seems stupid to verbalize it: both modern technology and modern science are distinctly *occidental*. Our technology has absorbed elements from all over the world, notably from China; yet everywhere today, whether in Japan or in Nigeria, successful technology is Western. Our science is the heir to all the sciences of the past, especially perhaps to the work of the great Islamic scientists of the Middle Ages, who so often outdid the ancient Greeks in skill and perspicacity: al Ráizi in medicine, for example; or ibn-al-Haytham in optics; or Omar Kháyyám in mathematics. Indeed, not a few works of such geniuses seem to have vanished in the original Arabic and to survive only in medieval Latin translations that helped to

6

lay the foundations for later Western developments. Today, around the globe, all significant science is Western in style and method, whatever the pigmentation or language of the scientists.

A second pair of facts is less well recognized because they result from quite recent historical scholarship. The leadership of the West, both in technology and in science, is far older than the so-called scientific revolution of the seventeenth century or the so-called industrial revolution of the eighteenth century. These terms are in fact outmoded and obscure the true nature of what they try to describe – significant stages in two long and separate developments. By AD 1000 at the latest – and perhaps, feebly, as much as 200 years earlier – the West began to apply water power to industrial processes other than milling grain. This was followed in the late twelfth century by the harnessing of wind power. From simple beginnings, but with remarkable consistency of style, the West rapidly expanded its skills in the development of power machinery, laboursaving devices, and automation. Those who doubt should contemplate that most monumental achievement in the history of automation: the weight-driven mechanical clock, which appeared in two forms in the early fourteenth century. Not in craftsmanship but in basic technological capacity, the Latin West of the later Middle Ages far outstripped its elaborate, sophisticated, and aesthetically magnificent sister cultures, Byzantium and Islam. In 1444 a great Greek ecclesiastic, Bessarion, who had gone to Italy, wrote a letter to a prince in Greece. He is amazed by the superiority of Western ships, arms, textiles, glass. But above all he is astonished by the spectacle of waterwheels sawing timbers and pumping the bellows of blast furnaces. Clearly, he had seen nothing of the sort in the Near East.

By the end of the fifteen century the technological superiority of Europe was such that its small, mutually hostile nations could spill out over all the rest of the world, conquering, looting, and colonizing. The symbol of this technological superiority is the fact that Portugal, one of the weakest states of the Occident, was able to become, and to remain for a century, mistress of the East Indies. And we must remember that the technology of Vasco da Gama and Albuquerque was built by pure empiricism, drawing remarkably little support or inspiration from science.

In the present-day vernacular understanding, modern science is supposed to have begun in 1543, when both Copernicus and Vesalius published their great works. It is no derogation of their accomplishments, however, to point out that such structures as the *Fabrica* and the *De revolutionibus* do not appear overnight. The distinctive Western tradition of science, in fact, began in the late eleventh century with a massive movement of translation of Arabic and Greek scientific works into Latin. A few notable books – Theophrastus, for example – escaped the West's avid new appetite for science, but within less than two hundred years effectively the entire corpus of Greek and Muslim science was available in Latin, and was being eagerly read and criticized in the new European universities. Out of criticism arose new observation, speculation, and increasing distrust of ancient authorities. By the late thirteenth century Europe had seized global scientific leadership from the faltering hands of Islam. It would be as absurd to deny the profound originality of Newton, Galileo, or Copernicus as to deny that of the fourteenth century scholastic scientists like Buridan or Oresme on whose work they built. Before the eleventh century, science scarcely existed in the Latin West, even in Roman times. From the eleventh century onward, the scientific sector of occidental culture has increased in a steady crescendo.

Since both our technological and our scientific movements got their start, acquired their character, and achieved world dominance in the Middle Ages, it would seem that we cannot understand their nature or their present impact upon ecology without examining fundamental medieval assumptions and developments.

MEDIEVAL VIEW OF MAN AND NATURE

Until recently, agriculture has been the chief occupation even in 'advanced' societies; hence, any change in methods

8

of tillage has much importance. Early ploughs, drawn by two oxen, did not normally turn the sod but merely scratched it. Thus, cross-ploughing was needed and fields tended to be squarish. In the fairly light soils and semi-arid climates of the Near East and Mediterranean, this worked well. But such a plough was inappropriate to the wet climate and often sticky soils of northern Europe. By the latter part of the seventh century after Christ, however, following obscure beginnings, certain northern peasants were using an entirely new kind of plough, equipped with a vertical knife to cut the line of the furrow, a horizontal share to slice under the sod, and a mouldboard to turn it over. The friction of this plough with the soil was so great that it normally required not two but eight oxen. It attacked the land with such violence that cross-ploughing was not needed, and fields tended to be shaped in long strips.

In the days of the scratch-plough, fields were distributed generally in units capable of supporting a single family. Subsistence farming was the presupposition. But no peasant owned eight oxen: to use the new and more efficient plough, peasants pooled their oxen to form large plough-teams, originally receiving (it would appear) ploughed strips in proportion to their contribution. Thus, distribution of land was based no longer on the needs of a family but, rather, on the capacity of a power machine to till the earth. Man's relation to the soil was profoundly changed. Formerly man had been part of nature; now he was the exploiter of nature. Nowhere else in the world did farmers develop any analogous agricultural implement. Is it coincidence that modern technology, with its ruthlessness towards nature, has so largely been produced by descendants of these peasants of northern Europe?

This same exploitive attitude appears slightly before AD 830 in Western illustrated calendars. In older calendars the months were shown as passive personifications. The new Frankish calendars, which set the style for the Middle Ages, are very different: they show men coercing the world around them – ploughing, harvesting, chopping trees, butchering pigs. Man and nature are two things, and man is master.

These novelties seem to be in harmony with larger intellectual patterns. What people do about their ecology depends on what they think about themselves in relation to things around them. Human ecology is deeply conditioned by beliefs about our nature and destiny – that is, by religion. To Western eyes this is very evident in, say, India or Ceylon. It is equally true of ourselves and of our medieval ancestors.

The victory of Christianity over paganism was the greatest psychic revolution in the history of our culture. It has become fashionable today to say that, for better or worse, we live in 'the post-Christian age'. Certainly the forms of our thinking and language have largely ceased to be Christian, but to my eye the substance often remains amazingly akin to that of the past. Our daily habits of action, for example, are dominated by an implicit faith in perpetual progress which was unknown either to Greco-Roman antiquity or to the Orient. It is rooted in, and is indefensible apart from, Judeo-Christian teleology. The fact that Communists share it merely helps to show what can be demonstrated on many other grounds: that Marxism, like Islam, is a Judeo-Christian heresy. We continue today to live, as we have lived for about 1,700 years, very largely in a context of Christian axioms.

What did Christianity tell people about their relations with the environment?

While many of the world's mythologies provide stories of creation, Greco-Roman mythology was singularly incoherent in this respect. Like Aristotle, the intellectuals of the ancient West denied that the visible world had had a beginning. Indeed, the idea of a beginning was impossible in the framework of their cyclical notion of time. In sharp contrast, Christianity inherited from Judaism not only a concept of time as nonrepetitive and linear but also a striking story of creation. By gradual stages a loving and all-powerful God had created light and darkness, the heavenly bodies, the earth and all its plants, animals, birds, and fishes. Finally, God had created Adam and, as an afterthought, Eve, to keep man from being lonely. Man named all the animals, thus establishing his dominance over them. God planned all of this explicitly for man's benefit and rule: no item in the physical creation had any purpose save to serve man's purposes. And, although man's body is made of clay, he is not simply part of nature: he is made in God's image.

Especially in its Western form, Christianity is the most anthropocentric religion the world has seen. As early as the second century both Tertullian and Saint Irenaeus of Lyons were insisting that when God shaped Adam he was foreshadowing the image of the Incarnate Christ, the Second Adam. Man shares, in great measure, God's transcendence of nature. Christianity, in absolute contrast to ancient paganism and Asia's religions (except, perhaps, Zoroastrianism), not only established a dualism of man and nature but also insisted that it is God's will that man exploit nature for his proper ends.

At the level of the common people this worked out in an interesting way. In antiquity every tree, every spring, every stream, every hill had its own *genius loci*, its guardian spirit. These spirits were accessible to men, but were very unlike men; centaurs, fauns, and mermaids show their ambivalence. Before one cut a tree, mined a mountain, or damned a brook, it was important to placate the spirit in charge of that particular situation, and to keep it placated. By destroying pagan animism, Christianity made it possible to exploit nature in a mood of indifference to the feelings of natural objects.

It is often said that for animism the Church substituted the cult of saints. True; but the cult of saints is functionally quite different from animism. The saint is not *in* natural objects; he may have special shrines, but his citizenship is in heaven. Moreover, a saint is entirely a man; he can be approached in human terms. In addition to saints, Christianity of course also had angels and demons inherited from Judaism and perhaps, at one remove, from Zoroastrianism. But these were all as mobile as the saints themselves. The spirits *in* natural objects, which formerly had protected nature from man, evaporated. Man's effective monopoly on

11

spirit in this world was confirmed, and the old inhibitions to the exploitation of nature crumbled.

When one speaks in such sweeping terms, a note of caution is in order. Christianity is a complex faith, and its consequences differ in differing contexts. What I have said may well apply to the medieval West, where in fact technology made spectacular advances. But the Greek East, a highly civilized realm of equal Christian devotion, seems to have produced no marked technological innovation after the late seventh century, when Greek fire was invented. The key to the contrast may perhaps be found in a difference in the tonality of piety and thought which students of comparative theology find between the Greek and the Latin churches. The Greeks believed that sin was intellectual blindness, and that salvation was found in illumination, orthodoxy – that is, clear thinking. The Latins, on the other hand, felt that sin was moral evil, and that salvation was to be found in right conduct. Eastern theology has been intellectualist. Western theology has been voluntarist. The Greek saint contemplates; the Western saint acts. The implications of Christianity for the conquest of nature would emerge more easily in the Western atmosphere.

The Christian dogma of creation, which is found in the first clause of all the Creeds, has another meaning for our comprehension of today's ecologic crisis. By revelation, God had given man the Bible, the Book of Scripture. But since God had made nature, nature also must reveal the divine mentality. The religious study of nature for the better understanding of God was known as natural theology. In the early Church, and always in the Greek East, nature was conceived primarily as a symbolic system through which God speaks to men: the ant is a sermon to sluggards; rising flames are the symbol of the soul's aspiration. This view of nature was essentially artistic rather than scientific. While Byzantium preserved and copied great numbers of ancient Greek scientific texts, science as we conceive it could scarcely flourish in such an ambience.

However, in the Latin West by the early thirteenth century natural theology was following a very different bent. It

12

was ceasing to be the decoding of the physical symbols of God's communication with man and was becoming the effort to understand God's mind by discovering how his creation operates. The rainbow was no longer simply a symbol of hope first sent to Noah after the Deluge: Robert Grosseteste, Friar Roger Bacon, and Theodoric of Freiberg produced startlingly sophisticated work on the optics of the rainbow, but they did it as a venture in religious understanding. From the thirteenth century onward, up to and including Leibnitz and Newton, every major scientist, in effect, explained his motivations in religious terms. Indeed, if Galileo had not been so expert an amateur theologian he would have got into far less trouble: the professionals resented his intrusion. And Newton seems to have regarded himself more as a theologian than as a scientist. It was not until the late eighteenth century that the hypothesis of God became unnecessary to many scientists.

It is often hard for the historian to judge, when men explain why they are doing what they want to do, whether they are offering real reasons or merely culturally acceptable reasons. The consistency with which scientists during the long formative centuries of Western science said that the task and the reward of the scientist was 'to think God's thoughts after him' leads one to believe that this was their real motivation. If so, then modern Western science was cast in a matrix of Christian theology. The dynamism of religious devotion, shaped by the Judeo-Christian dogma of creation, gave it impetus.

AN ALTERNATIVE CHRISTIAN VIEW

We would seem to be headed towards conclusions unpalatable to many Christians. Since both *science* and *technology* are blessed words in our contemporary vocabulary, some may be happy at the notions, first, that, viewed historically, modern science is an extrapolation of natural theology and, second, that modern technology is at least partly to be explained as an occidental, voluntarist realization of the Christian dogma of man's transcendence of, and rightful mastery over, nature. But, as we now recognize, somewhat

13

over a century ago science and technology – hitherto quite separate activities – joined to give mankind powers which, to judge by many of the ecologic effects, are out of control. If so, Christianity bears a huge burden of guilt.

I personally doubt that disastrous ecologic backlash can be avoided simply by applying to our problems more science and more technology. Our science and technology have grown out of Christian attitudes towards man's relation to nature which are almost universally held not only by Christians and neo-Christians but also by those who fondly regard themselves as post-Christians. Despite Copernicus, all the cosmos rotates around our little globe. Despite Darwin, we are *not*, in our hearts, part of the natural process. We are superior to nature, contemptuous of it, willing to use it for our slightest whim. To a Christian a tree can be no more than a physical fact. The whole concept of the sacred grove is alien to Christianity and to the ethos of the West. For nearly two millennia Christian missionaries have been chopping down sacred groves, which are idolatrous because they assume spirit in nature.

What we do about ecology depends on our ideas of the man–nature relationship. More science and more technology are not going to get us out of the present ecologic crisis until we find a new religion, or rethink our old one. The beatniks, who are the basic revolutionaries of our time, show a sound instinct in their affinity for Zen Buddhism, which conceives of the man–nature relationship as very nearly the mirror image of the Christian view. Zen, however, is as deeply conditioned by Asian history as Christianity is by the experience of the West, and I am dubious of its viability among us.

Possibly we should ponder the greatest radical in Christian history since Christ: Saint Francis of Assisi. The prime miracle of Saint Francis is the fact that he did not end at the stake, as many of his left-wing followers did. He was so clearly heretical that a general of the Franciscan Order, Saint Bonaventura, a great and perceptive Christian, tried to suppress the early accounts of Franciscanism. The key to an understanding of Francis is his belief in the virtue of humility – not merely for the individual but for man as a species. Francis tried to depose man from his monarchy over creation and set up a democracy of all God's creatures. With him the ant is no longer simply a homily for the lazy, flames a sign of the thrust of the soul towards union with God; now they are Brother Ant and Sister Fire, praising the Creator in their own ways as Brother Man does in his.

Later commentators have said that Francis preached to the birds as a rebuke to men who would not listen. The records do not read so: he urged the little birds to praise God, and in spiritual ecstasy they flapped their wings and chirped rejoicing. Legends of saints, especially the Irish saints, had long told of their dealings with animals but always, I believe, to show their human dominance over creatures. With Francis it is different. The land around Gubbio in the Apennines was being ravaged by a fierce wolf. Saint Francis, says the legend, talked to the wolf and persuaded him of the error of his ways. The wolf repented, died in the odour of sanctity, and was buried in consecrated ground.

What Sir Steven Runciman calls 'the Franciscan doctrine of the animal soul' was quickly stamped out. Quite possibly it was in part inspired, consciously or unconsciously, by the belief in reincarnation held by the Cathar heretics who at that time teemed in Italy and southern France, and who presumably had got it originally from India. It is significant that at just the same moment, about 1200 AD, traces of met-empsychosis are found also in western Judaism, in the Provençal *Cabbala*. But Francis held neither to transmigration of souls nor to pantheism. His view of nature and of man rested on a unique sort of pan-psychism of all things animate and inanimate, designed for the glorification of their transcendent Creator, who, in the ultimate gesture of cosmic humility, assumed flesh, lay helpless in a manger, and hung dying on a scaffold.

I am not suggesting that many contemporary Britons who are concerned about our ecologic crisis will be either able or willing to counsel with wolves or exhort birds. However, the present increasing disruption of the global environment is the product of a dynamic technology and science which were originating in the Western medieval world against which Saint Francis was rebelling in so original a way. Their growth cannot be understood historically apart from distinctive attitudes towards nature which are deeply grounded in Christian dogma. The fact that most people do not think of these attitudes as Christian is irrelevant. No new set of basic values has been accepted in our society to displace those of Christianity. Hence we shall continue to have a worsening ecologic crisis until we reject the Christian axiom that nature has no reason for existence save to serve man.

The greatest spiritual revolutionary in Western history, Saint Francis, proposed what he thought as an alternative Christian view of nature and man's relation to it: he tried to substitute the idea of the quality of all creatures, including man, for the idea of man's limitless rule of creation. He failed. Both our present science and our present technology are so tinctured with orthodox Christian arrogance towards nature that no solution for our ecologic crisis can be expected from them alone. Since the roots of our trouble are so largely religious, the remedy must also be essentially religious, whether we call it that or not. We must rethink and refeel our nature and destiny. The profoundly religious, but heretical, sense of the primitive Franciscans for the spiritual autonomy of all parts of nature may point a direction. I propose Francis as a patron saint for ecologists.

Play for more than you can afford to lose, and you will learn the game.

Sir Winston Churchill

Hell upon Earth

Lord Ritchie-Calder

Civilizations are buried in the graveyards of their own mistakes but as each died of its greed, its carelessness, or its effeteness another took its place. That was because civilizations took their character from a locality or a region. Today, ours is a global civilization. It is not bounded by the Tigris and the Euphrates; it is the whole world. It is a closed community, a planet shrunk to a neighbourhood round which a man-made satellite can circle sixteen times a day. It is a community so interdependent that every mistake we make is exaggerated on a world-scale.

For the first time in history Man has the power of veto over the evolution of his own species. He can destroy it in a nuclear holocaust. Today in the stockpiles of the nuclear powers there is at least 100 tons of TNT-equivalent in nuclear bombs, for every man, woman and child on earth. We could wipe out the human race and all our fellow lodgers—the animals, the birds, the insects—and reduce our planet to a radioactive desert. That would be a melodramatic way for Man to expiate his follies.

On 16th July, 1945, the atom exploded as a cataclysmic bomb. I have often said that the safebreakers got at the lock of the nucleus before the locksmith knew how it worked and the proof of it is that in the last quarter-century hundreds of millions of pounds have been spent on studying the physics of fundamental particles, the components of the nucleus, and they still don't know how they interrelate. You will remember also that in the secret work which produced the bomb the biologists were never consulted. It was the physicists' bomb just bigger and better and taking no account of the genetic effects. This is amazing because the genetic effects of radiation had been clear since 1927 and H. J. Muller had been awarded the Nobel Prize for the evidence he had produced. Then we had the bomb testing, of fission and fusion bombs, and we were given assurances that the fall-out could be confined within the testing area. Well, we know what happened. There was the case of the *Lucky Dragon*, the unlucky Japanese fishing-boat well outside the predicted range. Then we had the story of radiostrontium. Strontium is an analogue of calcium. That means that in bone formation, for example, an atom of strontium can take the place of an atom of calcium. Therefore, radioactive strontium can do likewise. Radiostrontium did not exist in the world before 1945. It is a manmade element. Today every young person who grew up during the bomb testing has in his or her bones this radioactive element. I say 'every young person' and I mean everywhere in the world. It is medically insignificant although if we had not had the test ban to prevent the escalation of atmospheric testing it might have been serious. Anyway, it is the brand mark which the atomic age has set upon its own generation.

And why? Because those reponsible for the H-bomb testing miscalculated. They assumed that the upthrust of the H-bomb would punch a hole into the stratosphere where gaseous radioactivity would dissipate itself. One of these gases was radioactive krypton which quickly decayed into radioactive strontium, not a gas but a particulate. They had also been wrongly briefed on the nature of the troposphere, the climatic ceiling. They thought that this would keep the fallout from falling in but they did not realize that between the equatorial troposphere and the polar troposphere there is a sort of fanlight. The radiostrontium came back through that fanlight, was caught up by the climatic jet streams and swept all round the world to come back as radioactive rain, to be deposited on food crops and pastures, to get into our food animals, into milk, into babies, and into children and adolescents whose bones were then being formed. All that those responsible could say was, 'Sorry, chums!' Fortunately, it was an argument that was listened to in securing the test ban.

I was the chairman of a series of inquiries which were carried out at the University of Chicago, conscious of its responsibility that it was there that the first atomic reactor began operating in 1942. From these inquiries I wrote a book called *Living with the Atom*. We knew we could not, and we did not want to, stop progress of peaceful atomic energy but we were concerned to bring together authorities from many disciplines to foresee risks and forestall the consequences. One of the most difficult problems we had to deal with was the disposal of radioactive waste. Where were we going to put all the stuff? There are strict rules about the handling of radioactive effluence from nuclear installations. That is all right in dealing with what is called lower level activity. The problem lies in the high level – the really dangerous stuff. Some of it like heavily contaminated equipment, etc., can be buried in concrete, taken out to sea and dumped in the deep, natural trenches. I recall one occasion when Professor Roger Revelle heard a British account of where these dangerous packages were deposited. He rose, protesting, to his feet and said, 'Don't you realize that through that submarine canyon races a fifty mile an hour current. It could smash the concrete blocks.' On another occasion in our Chicago discussions, a Japanese marine biologist agreed that at certain depths in the sea there is no natural radiation. That is to say there are none of the cosmic rays which bombard the surface of the earth from outer space and provide the natural radiation background to which living things have adapted themselves. And at those depths there are no radioactive rocks, like the granite which, again, is part of our normal background. What is dangerous is when the background radiation is artificially increased to the point where it can double the rate of mutations. This would have serious genetic effects by altering hereditary traits. The Japanese scientist was asked whether it wouldn't be safe to put radioactive waste in such oceanic places. He said, 'yes'. This worried me and I didn't know why until I realized that in radiation-free waters any radiation introduced would affect any living plant or fish, or sea creature which had never been exposed to any radiation of any kind. We would be introducing an unpredictable evolutionary factor. My colleagues agreed. But it shows the danger of being scientifically simplistic.

19

There are other ways of locking up unwanted atoms – you can vitrify them, put them into glass beads. But the trouble is that the water can leach the atoms out. Another method is to send them to the salt mines – put them into the caves of extracted salt. But there are difficulties here too. A great deal of this waste is in nitric acid and if you mix that with salt you get aqua regia and in the heat of the atoms this produces very dangerous gases. You can pump them down disused oil wells but the trouble there would be that by seepage you would be liable to make a whole oil field radioactive and you might even have a radioactive geyser spouting, under heat-generated pressure, to the surface. By any method of burial there is always the possibility of the activity getting into a ground-water system. Or of the vaults being broken up by earthquakes. But there is one method which overcomes this. It is what is known as 'hydraulic fracture'. If you bore a tube down into a shale formation, below the ground water-level, you can, by liquid pressure, force apart the faces of the shale-rock. You can mix your high level waste products with liquid concrete and so similarly produce a horizontal fracture. When the cement sets, with the radioactive materials in it, it forms the ham in the sandwich. Even the upheavals of an earthquake will not release the atom.

Take another piece of stupidity which shows how much we are at the mercy of ignorant men pretending to be knowledgeable. During the International Geophysical Year, 1957–8, the Van Allen Belt was discovered. This is an area of magnetic phenomena. Immediately the 'bright boys' decided to carry out an experiment to explode a bomb in the Belt to see whether they could produce an artificial aurora. The colourful draperies, luminous skirts of the aurora borealis is caused by the drawing in of cosmic particles through the rare gases of the upper atmosphere – ionization it is called; it is like passing electrons through the vacuum tubes of our familiar strip lighting. It was called the Rainbow Bomb in anticipation of the colourful display it was expected to produce. Every eminent scientist in the field of cosmology, radio-astronomy or physics of the atmosphere, protested at this irresponsible tampering with a system which we did not understand. And typically of the casual attitude to this kind of thing the Prime Minister of the day, answering protests in the House of Commons, and calling upon him to intervene with the Americans, asked what all the fuss was about. After all they hadn't known that the Van Allen Belt had existed a year before. This was the cosmic equivalent of Chamberlain's remark about Czechoslovakia, at the time of Munich, about that distant country of which we knew so little.

They exploded the bomb. They got their pyrotechnics and we still do not know the cost we may have to pay for this artificial magnetic disturbance. One could, of course, blame our freakish summer on it but even that we wouldn't know for sure. In the same way we can look with misgivings on those tracks – the white tails of the jets. These are introducing into our climatic system new factors, the effects of which are immeasurable. You know that formations of rain clouds depend upon water vapour having a nucleus on which to form – that is how artificial precipitation is introduced – the so-called rain-making. So the jets, criss-crossing the weather system, playing noughts and crosses with it, can provide for those nuclei and produce a manmade change.

One more instance of the far-flung consequences of men's localized mistakes. No insecticides or pesticides have ever been allowed into the continent of Antarctica. Yet they have been found in the fauna along the northern coasts. This has come almost certainly from the Northern Hemisphere carried from the rivers of the farm-states into the currents sweeping south.

I do not need to remind this audience of the great achievements of *Homo sapiens* which become the disaster-ridden blunders of Unthinking Man, *Homo insapiens*, of poisoned rivers and dead lakes, polluted with the effluents of industries which give something called 'prosperity' at the expense of posterity. They treat rivers like sewers and lakes like cesspools. These natural systems – and they are living systems – have struggled hard. The benevolent micro-organisms which

21

cope with reasonable amounts of organic matter were destroyed by mineral detergents.

Always and everywhere we come back to the problem of population – more people to make more mistakes, more people to be the victims of the mistakes of others, more people to suffer Hell upon Earth.

Place the six days of creation in Genesis against the four billion years or so of the Earth's age. That is a ratio of 8,000 years to one second. All day Monday and up to Tuesday noon is the sheer formation of matter until there is a globe with oceans on it, and mountains. Then a cell begins to undergo mitosis, dividing in two, and life is aboard the planet by Tuesday noon. All the rest of Tuesday and Wednesday, Thursday and Friday, and well into Saturday, life expands and becomes more diverse, more stable, more beautiful. At four o' clock on the afternoon of Saturday, the last day of creation, the age of reptiles comes on-stage; at nine o'clock, it goes off stage. Just before the age of reptiles ends, there are redwoods – and just before redwoods, the pelican, a 90-million-year-old life form now threatened with extinction by DDT and man's urge to usurp the Earth. At three minutes before midnight, man appears. One quarter of a second before midnight, a bearded man, anti-establishment, talking of peace and brotherhood and Christianity is on the planet.

Then, one-fortieth of a second before midnight, enters the industrial revolution. You have heard it predicted that we can go on at this rate that has worked so splendidly for one fortieth of a second because 'technology knows all the answers'. I am urging that we worry just a little bit about how much we do know.

David R. Brower

Too Many People

Paul R. Ehrlich

from *The Population Bomb*

Everyone is beginning to realize that the undeveloped countries of the world face an inevitable population-food crisis. Each year food production in undeveloped countries falls a bit further behind burgeoning population growth, and people go to bed a little bit hungrier. While there are temporary or local reversals of this trend, it now seems inevitable that it will continue to its logical conclusion: mass starvation. The rich are going to get richer, but the more numerous poor are going to get poorer. Of these poor, a minimum of three and one-half million will starve to death this year, mostly children. But this is a mere handful compared to the numbers that will be starving in a decade or so. And it is now too late to take action to save many of those people.

In a book about population there is a temptation to stun the reader with an avalanche of statistics. I'll spare you most, but not all, of that. After all, no matter how you slice it, population is a numbers game. Perhaps the best way to impress you with numbers is to tell you about the 'doubling time' – the time necessary for the population to double in size.

It has been estimated that the human population of 6000 BC was about five million people, taking perhaps one million years to get there from two and a half million. The population did not reach 500 million until almost 8,000 years later – about AD 1650. This means it doubled roughly once every thousand years or so. It reached a billion (1,000 million) in 1850, doubling in some 200 years. It took only 80 years or so for the next doubling, as the population reached two billion around 1930. We have not completed the next doubling to four billion yet, but we now have well over three billion people. The doubling time at present seems to be about 37 years.[1] Quite a reduction in doubling times: 1,000,000 years, 1,000 years, 200 years, 80 years, 37 years. Perhaps the meaning of a doubling time of around 37 years is best brought home by a theoretical exercise. Let's examine what might happen on the absurd assumption that the population continued to double every 37 years into the indefinite future.

If growth continued at that rate for about 900 years, there would be some 60,000,000,000,000,000 people on the face of the earth. Sixty million billion people. This is about 100 persons for each square yard of the Earth's surface, land and sea. A British physicist, J. H. Fremlin,[2] guessed that such a multitude might be housed in a continous, 2,000-storey building covering our entire planet. The upper 1,000 storeys would contain only the apparatus for running this gigantic warren. Ducts, pipes, wires, lift shafts, etc., would occupy about half of the space in the bottom 1,000 storeys. This would leave three or four yards of floor space for each person. I will leave to your imagination the physical details of existence in this ant heap, except to point out that all would not be black. Probably each person would be limited in his travel. Perhaps he could take lifts through all 1,000 residential storeys but could travel only within a circle of a few hundred yards' radius on any floor. This would permit, however, each person to choose his friends from among some ten million people! And, as Fremlin points out, entertainment on the worldwide TV should be excellent, for at any time 'one could expect some ten million Shakespeares and rather more Beatles to be alive'.

Could growth of the human population of the Earth continue beyond that point? Not according to Fremlin. We would have reached a 'heat limit'. People themselves, as well as their activities, convert other forms of energy into heat which must be dissipated. In order to permit this excess heat to radiate directly from the top of the 'world building' directly into space, the atmosphere would have been pumped into flasks under the sea well before the limiting population size was reached. The precise limit would depend on the technology of the day. At a population size of one billion billion people, the temperature of the 'world roof' would be kept around the melting point of iron to radiate away the human heat generated.

But, you say, surely Science (with a capital 'S') will find a way for us to occupy the other planets of our solar system and eventually of other stars before we get all that crowded. Skip for a moment the virtual certainty that those planets are uninhabitable. Forget also the insurmountable logistic problems of moving billions of people off the Earth. Fremlin has made some interesting calculations on how much time we could buy by occupying the planets of the solar system. For instance, at any given time it would take only about fifty years to populate Venus, Mercury, Mars, the moon, and the moons of Jupiter and Saturn to the same population density as Earth.[3]

What if the fantastic problems of reaching and colonizing the other planets of the solar system, such as Jupiter and Uranus, can be solved? It would take only about 200 years to fill them 'Earth-full'. So we could perhaps gain 250 years of time for population growth in the solar system after we had reached an absolute limit on Earth. What then? We can't ship our surplus to the stars. Professor Garrett Hardin[4] of the University of California at Santa Barbara has dealt effectively with this fantasy. Using extremely optimistic assumptions, he has calculated that Americans, by cutting their standard of living down to 18 per cent of its present level, could in *one year* set aside enough capital to finance the exportation to the stars of *one day's* increase in the population of the world.

Interstellar transport for surplus people presents an amusing prospect. Since the ships would taken generations to reach most stars, the only people who could be transported would be those willing to exercise strict birth control. Population explosions on space ships would be disastrous. Thus we would have to export our responsibile people, leaving the irresponsible at home on Earth to breed.

Enough of fantasy. Hopefully, you are convinced that the population will have to stop growing sooner or later and that the extremely remote possibility of expanding into outer space offers no escape from the laws of population growth. If you still want to hope for the stars, just remember that, at the current growth rate, in a few thousand years everything in the visible universe would be converted into people, and the ball of people would be expanding with the speed of light![5] Unfortunately, even 900 years is much too far in the future for those of us concerned with the population explosion. As you shall see, the next *nine* years will probably tell the story.

Of course, population growth is not occurring uniformly over the face of the Earth. Indeed, countries are divided rather neatly into two groups: those with rapid growth rates and those with relatively slow growth rates. The first group, making up about two-thirds of the world population, coincides closely with what are known as the 'undeveloped countries' (UDCs). The UDCs are not industrialized, tend to have inefficient agriculture, very small gross national products, high illiteracy rates and related problems. That's what UDCs are technically, but a short definition of undeveloped is 'starving'. Most Latin American, African, and Asian countries fall into this category. The second group consists, in essence, of the 'developed countries' (DCs). DCs are modern, industrial nations, such as the United States, Canada, most European countries, Israel, Russia, Japan, and Australia. Most people in these countries are adequately nourished.

Doubling times in the UDCs range around 20 to 35 years. Examples of these times (from the 1968 figures released by the Population Reference Bureau) are Kenya, 24 years; Nigeria, 28; Turkey, 24; Indonesia, 31; Philippines, 20; Brazil, 22; Costa Rica, 20; and El Salvador, 19. Think of what it means for the population of a country to double in 25 years. In order to just to keep living standards at the present inadequate level, the food available for the people must be doubled. Every structure and road must be duplicated. The amount of power must be doubled. The capacity of the transport system must be doubled. The number of trained doctors, nurses, teachers, and administrators must be doubled. This would be a fantastically difficult job in the United States – a rich country with a fine agricultural system, immense industries, and rich natural resources. Think of what it means to a country with none of these.

Remember also that in virtually all UDCs, people have got the word about the better life it is possible to have. They have seen coloured pictures in magazines of the miracles of Western technology. They have seen cars and aeroplanes. They have seen American and European movies. Many have seen refrigerators, tractors, and even TV sets. Almost all have heard transistor radios. They *know* that a better life is possible. They have what we like to call 'rising expectations'. If twice as many people are to be happy, the miracle of doubling what they now have will not be enough. It will only maintain today's standard of living. There will have to be tripling or better. Needless to say, they are not going to be happy.

Doubling times for the populations of the DCs tend to be in the 50-to-200-year range. Examples of 1968 doubling times are the United States, 63 years; Austria, 175; Denmark, 88; Norway, 88; United Kingdom, 140; Poland, 88; Russia, 63; Italy, 117; Spain, 88; and Japan, 63. These are industrialized countries that have undergone the so-called demographic transition – a transition from high to low growth rate. As industrialization progressed, children became less important to parents as extra hands to work on the farm and as support in old age. At the same time they became a financial drag – expensive to raise and educate. Presumably these are the reasons for a slowing of population growth after industrialization. They boil down to a simple fact – people just want to have fewer children.

This is not to say, however, that population is not a problem for the DCs. First of all, most of them are over-populated. They are overpopulated by the simple criterion that they are not able to produce enough food to feed their populations. It is true that they have the money to buy food, but when food is no longer available for sale they will find the money rather indigestible. Then, too, they share with the UDCs a serious problem of population distribution. Their urban centres are getting more and more crowded relative to the countryside. This problem is not as severe as it is in the UDCs (if current trends should continue, which they cannot, Calcutta could have 66 million inhabitants in the year 2000). As you are well aware, however, urban concentrations are creating serious problems even in America. In the United States, one of the more rapidly growing DCs, we hear constantly of the headaches caused by growing population: not just garbage in our environment, but overcrowded highways, burgeoning slums, deteriorating school systems, rising crime rates, riots, and other related problems.

From the point of view of a demographer, the whole problem is quite simple. A population will continue to grow as long as the birth rate exceeds the death rate – if immigration and emigration are not occurring. It is, of course, the balance between birth rate and death rate that is critical. The birth rate is the number of births per thousand people per year in the population. The death rate is the number of deaths per thousand people per year.[6] Subtracting the death rate from the birth rate, and ignoring migration, gives the rate of increase. If the birth rate is 30 per thousand per year, and the death rate is 10 per thousand per year, then the rate of increase is 20 per thousand per year $(30-10=20)$. Expressed as a per cent (rate per hundred people), the rate of 20 per thousand becomes 2 per cent. If the rate of increase is 2 per cent, then the doubling time will be 35 years. Note that if you simply added 20 people per thousand per year to the population, it would take 50 years to add a second thousand people $(20 \times 50=1,000)$. But the doubling time is actually much less because populations grow at compound interest rates. Just as interest money itself earns interest, so people added to populations produce more people. It's growing at compound interest that makes populations double so much more rapidly than seems possible. Look at the relationship between the annual per cent increase (interest rate) and the doubling time of the population (time for your money to double):

Annual per cent increase	Doubling time
1.0	70
2.0	35
3.0	24
4.0	17

Those are all the calculations – I promise. If you are interested in more details on how demographic figuring is done, you may enjoy reading Thompson and Lewis's excellent book, *Population Problems*.[7]

There are some professional optimists around who like to greet every sign of dropping birth rates with wild pronouncements about the end of the population explosion. They are a little like a person who, after a low temperature of five below zero on 21st December, interprets a low of only three below zero on 22nd December as a cheery sign of approaching spring. First of all, birth rates, along with all demographic statistics, show short-term fluctuation caused by many factors. For instance, the birth rate depends rather heavily on the number of women at reproductive age. In the United States the current low birth rates soon will be replaced by higher rates as more post World War II 'baby boom' children move into their reproductive years. In Japan, 1966, the Year of the Fire Horse, was a year of very low birth rates. There is widespread belief that girls born in the Year of the Fire Horse make poor wives, and Japanese couples try to avoid giving birth in that year because they are afraid of having daughters.

But, I repeat, it is the relationship between birth rate and death rate that is most critical. Indonesia, Laos, and Haiti all had birth rates around 46 per thousand in 1966. Costa Rica's birth rate was 41 per thousand. Good for Costa Rica? Unfortunately, not very. Costa Rica's death rate was less than nine per thousand, while the other countries all had death rates above 20 per thousand. The population of Costa Rica in 1966 was doubling every 17 years, while the doubling times of Indonesia, Laos, and Haiti were all above 30 years. Ah, but, you say, it was good for Costa Rica – fewer people per thousand dying each year. Fine for a few years

29

perhaps, but what then? Some 50 per cent of the people in Costa Rica are under 15 years old. As they get older, they will need more and more food in a world with less and less. In 1983 they will have twice as many mouths to feed as they had in 1966, if the 1966 trend continues. Where will the food come from? Today the death rate in Costa Rica is low in part because they have a large number of physicians in proportion to their population. How do you suppose those physicians will keep the death rate down when there's not enough food to keep people alive?

One of the most ominous facts of the current situation is that roughly 40 per cent of the population of the undeveloped world is made up of people *under 15 years old*. As that mass of young people moves into its reproductive years during the next decade, we're going to see the greatest baby boom of all time. Those youngsters are the reason for all the ominous predictions for the year 2000. They are the gunpowder for the population explosion.

How did we get into this bind? It all happened a long time ago, and the story involves the process of natural selection, the development of culture, and man's swollen head. The essence of success in evolution is reproduction. Indeed, natural selection is simply defined as differential reproduction of genetic types. That is, if people with blue eyes have more children on the average than those with brown eyes, natural selection is occurring. More genes for blue eyes will be passed on to the next generation than will genes for brown eyes. Should this continue, the population will have progressively larger and larger proportions of blue-eyed people. This differential reproduction of genetic types is the driving force of evolution; it has been driving evolution for billions of years. Whatever types produced more offspring became the common types. Virtually all populations contain very many different genetic types (for reasons that do not concern us), and some are always outreproducing others. As I said, reproduction is the key to winning the evolutionary game. Any structure, physiological process, or pattern of behaviour that leads to greater reproductive success will tend to be perpetuated. The entire process by which man

30

developed involves thousands of millennia of our ancestors being more successful breeders than their relatives. Facet number one of our bind – the urge to reproduce has been fixed in us by billions of years of evolution.

Of course through all those years of evolution, our ancestors were fighting a continual battle to keep the birth rate ahead of the death rate. That they were successful is attested to by our very existence, for, if the death rate had overtaken the birth rate for any substantial period of time, the evolutionary line leading to man would have gone extinct. Among our apelike ancestors, a few million years ago, it was still very difficult for a mother to rear her children successfully. Most of the offspring died before they reached reproductive age. The death rate was near the birth rate. Then another factor entered the picture – cultural evolution was added to biological evolution.

Culture can be loosely defined as the body of non-genetic information which people pass from generation to generation. It is the accumulated knowledge that, in the old days, was passed on entirely by word of mouth, painting, and demonstration. Several thousand years ago the written word was added to the means of cultural transmission. Today culture is passed on in these ways, and also through television, computer tapes, motion pictures, records, blueprints, and other media. Culture is all the information man possesses except for that which is stored in the chemical language of his genes.

The large size of the human brain evolved in response to the development of cultural information. A big brain is an advantage when dealing with such information. Big-brained individuals were able to deal more successfully with the culture of their group. They were thus more successful reproductively than their smaller-brained relatives. They passed on their genes for big brains to their numerous offspring. They also added to the accumulating store of cultural information, increasing slightly the premium placed on brain size in the next generation. A self-reinforcing selective trend developed – a trend towards increased brain size.[8]

But there was, quite literally, a rub. Babies had bigger and bigger heads. There were limits to how large a woman's pelvis could conveniently become. To make a long story short, the strategy of evolution was not to make a woman bell-shaped and relatively immobile, but to accept the problem of having babies who were helpless for a long period while their brains grew after birth.[9] How could the mother defend and care for her infant during its unusually long period of helplessness? She couldn't, unless Papa hung around. The girls are still working on that problem, but an essential step was to get rid of the short, well-defined breeding season characteristic of most mammals. The year-round sexuality of the human female, the long period of infant dependence on the female, the evolution of the family group, all are at the roots of our present problem. They are essential ingredients in the vast social phenomenon that we call sex. Sex is not simply an act leading to the production of offspring. It is a varied and complex cultural phenomenon penetrating into all aspects of our lives – one involving our self-esteem, our choice of friends, cars, and leaders. It is tightly interwoven with our mythologies and history. Sex in man is necessary for the production of young, but it also evolved to ensure their successful rearing. Facet number two of our bind – our urge to reproduce is hopelessly entwined with most of our other urges.

Of course, in the early days the whole system did not prevent a very high mortality among the young, as well as among the older members of the group. Hunting and food-gathering is a risky business. Cavemen had to throw very impressive cave bears out of their caves before the men could move in. Witch-doctors and shamans had a less than perfect record at treating wounds and curing disease. Life was short, if not sweet. Man's total population size doubtless increased slowly but steadily as human populations expanded out of the African cradle of our species.

Then about 8,000 years ago a major change occurred – the agricultural revolution. People began to give up hunting food and settled down to grow it. Suddenly some of the risk was removed from life. The chances of dying of starvation diminished greatly in some human groups. Other threats as-

32

sociated with the nomadic life were also reduced, perhaps balanced by new threats of disease and large-scale warfare associated with the development of cities. But the overall result was a more secure existence than before, and the human population grew more rapidly. Around 1800, when the standard of living in what are today the DCs was dramatically increasing due to industrialization, population growth really began to accelerate. The development of medical science was the straw that broke the camel's back. While lowering death rates in the DCs was due in part to other factors, there is no question that 'instant death control', exported by the DCs, has been responsible for the drastic lowering of death rates in the UDCs. Medical science, with its efficient public health programmes, has been able to depress the death rate with astonishing rapidity and at the same time drastically increase the birth rate; healthier people have more babies.

The power of exported death control can best be seen by an examination of the classic case of Ceylon's assault on malaria after World War II. Between 1933 and 1942 the death rate due directly to malaria was *reported* as almost two per thousand. This rate, however, represented only a portion of the malaria deaths, as many were reported as being due to 'pyrexia'.[10] Indeed, in 1934–5 a malaria epidemic may have been directly responsible for fully half of the deaths on the island. In addition, malaria, which infected a large portion of the population, made people susceptible to many other diseases. It thus contributed to the death rate indirectly as well as directly.

The introduction of DDT in 1946 brought rapid control over the mosquitoes which carry malaria. As a result, the death rate on the island was halved in less than a decade. The death rate in Ceylon in 1945 was 22. It dropped 34 per cent between 1946 and 1947 and moved down to ten in 1954. Since the sharp postwar drop it has continued to decline and now stands at eight. Although part of the drop is doubtless due to the killing of other insects which carry disease and to other public health measures, most if it can be accounted for by the control of malaria.

Victory over malaria, yellow fever, smallpox, cholera, and other infectious diseases has been responsible for similar plunges in death rate throughout most of the UDCs. In the decade 1940–50 the death rate declined 46 per cent in Puerto Rico, 43 per cent in Formosa, and 23 per cent in Jamaica. In a sample of 18 undeveloped areas the average decline in death rate between 1945 and 1950 was 24 per cent.

It is of course, socially very acceptable to reduce the death rate. Billions of years in evolution have given us all a powerful will to live. Intervening in the birth rate goes against our evolutionary values. During all those centuries of our evolutionary past, the individuals who had the most children passed on their genetic endowment in greater quantities than those who reproduced less. Their genes dominate our heredity today. All our biological urges are for more reproduction, and they are all too often reinforced by our culture. In brief, death control goes with the grain, birth control against it.

In summary, the world's population will continue to grow as long as the birth rate exceeds the death rate; it's as simple as that. When it stops growing or starts to shrink, it will mean that either the birth rate has gone down or the death rate has gone up or a combination of the two. Basically, then, there are only two kinds of solutions to the population problem. One is a 'birth rate solution', in which we find ways to lower the birth rate. The other is a 'death rate solution', in which ways to raise the death rate – war, famine, pestilence – *find us*. The problem could have been avoided by *population control*, in which mankind consciously adjusted the birth rate so that a 'death rate solution' did not have to occur.

NOTES

1. Since this was written, 1968 figures have appeared, showing that the doubling time is now 35 years.
2. J. H. Fremlin, 'How Many People Can the World Support?' *New Scientist*, 29th October, 1964.
3. To understand this, simply consider what would happen if we held

the population constant at three billion people by exporting all the surplus people. If this were done for 37 years (the time it now takes for one doubling) we would have exported three billion people – enough to populate a twin planet of the Earth to the same density. In two doubling times (74 years) we would reach a total human population for the solar system of 12 billion people, enough to populate the Earth and three similar planets to the density found on Earth today. Since the areas of the planets and moons mentioned above are not three times that of the Earth, they can be populated to equal density in much less than two doubling times.

4. 'Interstellar Migration and the Population Problem.' *Heredity* 50: 60–70, 1959.

5. I. J. Cook, *New Scientist*, 8th September, 1966.

6. The birth rate is more precisely the total number of births in a country during a year, divided by the total population at the midpoint of the year, multiplied by 1,000. Suppose that there were 80 births in Lower Slobbovia during 1967, and that the population of Lower Slobbovia was 2,000 on 1st July, 1967. Then the birth rate would be:

$$\text{Birth rate} = \frac{80 \text{ (total births in L. Slobbovia in 1967)}}{2,000 \text{ (total population, 1st July, 1967)}} \times 1,000$$

$$= \cdot 04 \times 1,000 = 40$$

Similarly if there were 40 deaths in Lower Slobbovia during 1967, the death rate would be:

$$\text{Death rate} = \frac{40 \text{ (total deaths in L. Slobbovia in 1967)}}{2,000 \text{ (total population, 1st July, 1967)}} \times 1,000$$

$$= \cdot 02 \times 1,000 = 20$$

Then the Lower Slobbovian birth rate would be 40 per thousand, and the death rate would be 20 per thousand. For every 1,000 Lower Slobbovians alive on 1st July, 1967, 40 babies were born and 20 people died. Subtracting the death rate from the birth rate gives us the rate of natural increase of Lower Slobbovia for the year 1967. That is, 40 − 20 = 20; during 1967 the population grew at a rate of 20 people per thousand per year. Dividing that rate by ten expresses the increase as a per cent (the increase per hundred per year). The increase in 1967 in Lower Slobbovia was 2 per cent. Remember that this rate of increase ignores any movement of people into and out of Lower Slobbovia.

7. McGraw-Hill, 1965.

8. Human brain size increased from an apelike capacity of about 500 cubic centimetres (cc) in *Australopithecus* to about 1,500 cc in modern *Homo sapiens*. Among modern men small variations in brain size do not seem to be related to significant differences in the ability to use cultural information, and there is no particular reason to believe that our brain size will continue to increase. Further evolution may occur more readily in a direction of increased efficiency rather than increased size.

9. This is, of course, an oversimplified explanation. For more detail see Ehrlich and Holm, *The Process of Evolution*, McGraw-Hill, 1963.
10. These data and those that follow on the decline of death rates are from Kingsley Davis's 'The Amazing Decline of Mortality in Underdeveloped Areas', *The American Economic Review*, Vol. 46, pp. 305–318.

Perhaps when the time comes that there is no more silence and no more aloneness, there will also be no longer anyone who wants to be alone. If man is the limitlessly conditionable creature so many believe him to be, then inevitably the desire for a thing must disappear when it has become no longer attainable. Even now fewer and fewer are aware of any desire to escape from crowds, and most men and women who still make traditional excursions to beach or picnic grounds unpack their radios without delay and turn on a noise to which they do not listen. But it is not certain that this is not a morbid appetite rather than one which has become normal or that it, any more than any other morbid appetite, brings real satisfaction when it is gratified.

Joseph Wood Krutch

The Limits of Adaptability

René Dubos

Let me state why I believe that the health of the environment in which man functions is crucial for his well-being in the here and now and for the quality of life in the future.

The phrase 'health of the environment' is not a literary convention. It has a real biological meaning, because the surface of the earth is truly a living organism. Without the countless and immensely varied forms of life that the earth harbours, our planet would be just another fragment of the universe with a surface as drab as that of the moon and an atmosphere inhospitable to man. We human beings exist and enjoy life only by virtue of the conditions created and maintained on the surface of the earth by the microbes, plants, and animals that have converted its inanimate matter into a highly integrated living structure. Any profound disturbance in the ecological equilibrium is a threat to the maintenance of human life as we know it now. Admittedly, there are scientists who claim that it will soon be possible to alter man's genetic code so as to make it better suited to whatever conditions may arise in the future. But I do not take them seriously. Indeed I believe that any attempt to alter the fundamental being of man is a biological absurdity as well as an ethical monstrosity.

Man has a remarkable ability to develop some form of tolerance to conditions extremely different from those under which he evolved. This has led to the belief that, through social and technological innovations, he can endlessly modify his ways of life without risk. But the facts do not justify this euphoric attitude. Modern man can adapt biologically to the technological environment only in so far as mechanisms of adaptation are potentially present in his genetic code. For this reason, we can almost take it for granted that he cannot achieve successful biological adaptation to insults with which he has had no experience in his evolutionary past, such as the shrill noises of modern equipment, the exhausts of motor cars and factories, the countless new synthetic products that get into air, water, and food. The limits that must be imposed on social and technological innovations are determined not by scientific knowledge or practical know-how, but by the biological and mental nature of man which is essentially unchangeable.

Some recent experiences appear at first sight to provide evidence that the immense adaptability of man is much greater than I suggest. For example, people of all races have survived the horrors of modern warfare and concentration camps. The population continues to grow even amidst the appalling misery prevailing in some underprivileged urban areas. The other side of the coin, however, is that continuous exposure to biological stresses always results in biological and mental alterations that mean hardships for the future. For example, people born and raised in the industrial areas of northern Europe have survived and multiplied despite constant exposure to smogs made worse by the inclemency of the Atlantic climate. But the long-range consequence of this so-called adaptation is a very large incidence of chronic pulmonary diseases.

Social regimentation and standardization is compatible with the survival and multiplication of biological man, but not with the quality of human life. Step-by-step, people become tolerant of worse and worse environmental conditions without realizing that the expressions of this tolerance will emerge later in the form of debilitating ailments and what is even worse, in a form of life that will retain little of true humanness.

Experiments in animals and observations in man leave no doubt that environmental influences exert their most profound and lasting effects when they impinge on the organism during the early phases of its biological and mental development. In consequence, it can be anticipated that the deleterious effects of the present crisis will not reach their full expression until around the end of the present century, when today's children have become young adults. A very large percentage of these children will have been exposed from birth and throughout their formative years to conditions that will almost certainly elicit maladaptive responses in the long run – not only organic diseases but also, and perhaps most importantly, distortions of mental and emotional attributes.

We are naturally concerned with the unpleasant effects that the environmental crisis has for us in the here and now, but these are trivial when compared with the distant effects that it will have on the human beings who are being exposed to it throughout their development. Although I have emphasized – because of my professional specialization – the disease aspects of environmental insults, I do not believe that these are the most important. The mind is affected by environmental factors just as much as the body. Its expressions can be atrophied or distorted by the surroundings in which it develops, and by the hostile stimuli to which it has to respond.

The increase in the world population is one of the determinants of the ecological crisis and indeed may be at its root. But few persons realize that the dangers posed by overpopulation are more grave and more immediate in the highly industrialized than in the less industrialized countries. This is due in part to the fact that citizens in the industrialized countries use more of the world's natural resources. and destroy them more rapidly, thereby contributing massively to the pollution of their own surroundings and of the earth as a whole – let alone the pollution of the moon and of space.

The American Wilderness

Kenneth Brower

Wilderness, and the problem of preserving it, has been on the American mind for some time. 'A world from which solitude has been extirpated is a very poor ideal,' wrote John Stuart Mill. 'What is the use of a house if you haven't got a tolerable planet to put it on?' Thoreau wondered. 'It is the love of country that has lighted and that keeps glowing the holy fire of patriotism. And this love is excited, primarily, by the beauty of the country,' J. Horace McFarland said, in 1908. Joseph Wood Krutch agrees.

The desire to experience the reality of the great poem Thoreau wrote about, the great terrestrial poem before its best pages were ripped out and thrown away, is the desire, Krutch feels, that brought the best people to America's shores. Solitude, wildness, and beauty of earth are at their most solitary, wild, and beautiful in wilderness. Wilderness is a citadel for the forces that bore on us during the formative years of our national consciousness, the forces that brought the best to our shores. And wilderness is more, of course. If man destroys wilderness, Dr J. A. Rush writes, he will have repudiated more than an American tradition – he will have repudiated the tradition that put him on the planet, and will find himself terribly alone.

As Nancy Newhall observes, wilderness has answers to questions that man has not learned how to ask. Why is it, for example, that of all mammals in creation only the wolverine is free of arthritis? The wolverine requires a sizable wilderness to range about in, and that wilderness holds the answer. How many discoveries, like quinine, or the antibiotic virtues of abalone blood, or paper, even, remain undiscovered in wilderness? How much more do we need to learn about evolutionary processes there? What was it that enabled Eskimo shamen, their minds a product of the taiga, tundra, and sea ice, to travel on spirit journeys under the ocean and to talk with the fishes and the potent beings who lived on the bottom? How did the shamen develop the hypnotic power they employed in their seances? What can we learn from the shamen who survive about thought transference and ESP? The answers are in the arctic wilderness still left to us.

Wilderness is a bench mark, a touchstone. In wilderness we can see where we have come from, where we are going, how far we've gone. In wilderness is the only unsullied earth sample of the forces generally at work in the universe.

New perspectives come out of the wilderness. Jesus, Zoroaster, Moses, and Mohammed went to the wilderness and came back with messages. It was from the wilderness, and the people who knew wilderness, that the first concern about pollution and environmental decay came. Men and women who knew how water should taste, air should breathe, and grass should grow, were the first to detect when these things were happening wrong.

More important, perhaps, than its value as a place for research and a place to touch home – more than its value to mankind – is the value of wilderness to individual men, its value as balm, quiet, solitude; as a place to catch a breath, to connect consecutive thoughts, to sleep early, to wake to the light, dry, aromatic air of uncultivated places that Willa Cather wrote about. Recreation, in the real sense of the world, happens best in wilderness.

Wilderness is important as an idea. For Aldo Leopold, the most interesting part of a map was the blank places. They were spots he might explore some day, and he made imaginary use of them. Wilderness, Wallace Stegner wrote, developing the idea, is part of the Geography of Hope. It's a commodity we make use of even when we aren't in it; its existence makes New York City or Oakland more tolerable, because we know that there is something else. What comes out of the wilderness can become a possession of the entire race, John Collier writes. Scott died in the Antarctic wilderness but his journal survived to challenge mankind forever, Collier notes. *Green Mansions* came from the Patagonian desert (and W. H. Hudson). It's not hard to add to Collier's list. *Moby Dick* came from the contiguous wildernesses of the sea and Herman Melville's mind. Most of the best of American writers, even modern ones like Twain, Steinbeck, Hemingway, set their stories against the land. The American earth is the source of our great wealth in more than a commercial way.

All of the preceding defences of wilderness are sound, I think, but they come a little too easily to me. I am the son of an eloquent conservationist, and I grew up in the years that he was developing his eloquence. All the wilderness arguments were old when I was still very young. Children need to find their own causes. I became a ten-year-old expert on injustices against the American Indian and an historian of Western Indian wars.

But lately I have been rereading my father's arguments. I began casually, just to see what the old man had been up to. I was struck first by how well he wrote, after all, then by the number of references he made to us, his children. He wrote a lot of children and sons, of our children's children, of each generation's obligation to generations yet unborn, but just as often he wrote of us by name. I remember once thinking that this must be a rhetorical device, or perhaps a way of apologizing to us for all the times his work kept him away. I knew our father loved us, but I also knew how intensely he worked at conservation, and it was hard for me to imagine that he thought much about us when he was gone. Now, closer to being a father myself, hearing the distant patter of little feet, I think I understand better.

'Thomas Jefferson,' my father wrote, 'long ago, said that one generation could not bind another; each had the right to set its own course. Go out across this land and try to find someone to argue that he was wrong. You won't find a taker. It is the national consensus that we don't have this right.

'But deeds are not matching words. This generation is speedily using up, beyond recall, a very important right that belongs to future generations – the right to have wilderness in their civilization, even as we have it in ours; the right to find solitude somewhere; the right to see, and enjoy, and be inspired and renewed, somewhere, by those places where the

43

hand of God has not been obscured by the industry of man.

'Our decisions today will determine the fate of that right, so far as people of our time can pass opportunity along to our sons. Apathy here can mean that we pass them a dead torch. Or we can keep it aflame, knowing that this is a very special torch that man cannot light again.'

I can understand that sentiment, though with its flaming torch it sounds a bit like J. Horace McFarland. I prefer my father's introduction to his Manual of Ski Mountaineering, which took the form of a series of winter suggestions to my brother and me, suggestions he would have liked to give us, he wrote, but refrained because we were teenagers and would not have listened:

Finally I would have tried to explain to them what ski mountaineering had meant to me; about the peaks I had made first ascents of, for the most part on skis; of the high snow camps I had known and what it was like to be up on top in early winter morning and evening, when the world is painted with a very special light; of the kind of competence and even braveness, maybe, that one picks up from good friends and challenging peaks, up there when the storms hit and the snow pelts the fabric all through the night; of the kind of exhilaration we got when, after two winter struggles, the third put us on top of a fourteen-thousander and we were first to be there in winter and see how magnificently winter treats a high land we already knew well in summer but in a lesser beauty; of the long vibrant moments when we were back on our skis, skimming down the uncrevassed glacier on just the right depth of new powder, letting our skis go, finding that every turn worked, hearing the vigorous flapping of our ski pants even though the wind was singing in our ears and stinging our faces, sensing how rapidly the peaks climbed above us, those peaks that had dropped so reluctantly to our level in all the slow day's climb; of the care we had to take after night found us out and we sideslipped and side-stepped down into the tortuous little basins and then into

44

the hummocky forest floor that lay in darkness between us and camp; I would have described that hot cup of soup I cuddled in my hand in exhaustion, sipping slowly to absorb its warmth and its energy at a retainable rate; and I would speak of the morning after and, not its hangover, but its glow as I looked back up to the rocky palisade above the glacier and was just pleased as hell to have got there at last – pleased with the weather, the companions, and the luck – and also forgiveably pleased a little that I could do it.

In writing of my little brother, who saw his first moose when he was three, yet knew instantly and cried 'moose:' three years later when he saw his second, my father wrote, 'The image fixed well, as wild images do, on that perfectly sensitized but almost totally unexposed film of his mind.'

My own first memories are of the wilderness of the Sierra Nevada. I remember the people. There was Tommy Jefferson, a packer, a full-blooded Mono Indian – Tommy Jefferson and his full Indian face, strong back and short Indian legs, his boots and levis, sprinting in delight after a bronco mule that was throwing its load, jumping on the mule and biting its ear until the mule calmed itself. There was Tommy's boss Bruce Morgan, owner of Mt Whitney Pack Trains, with his two white riding mules and the .45 pistol in case one of his pack animals broke its leg. There was my father, the campfire speaker, the singer, the rock climber, the man with more alpine medals on his hat than anyone else.

But mostly I remember me in the mountains. I remember walking over Army Pass in the hailstorm, the lightning striking so close that a blue light shone ahead of us, the hailstones dancing on the rocks around us. I remember wild onions, and the long descent from the High Sierra down to the desert of the Owens Valley. I remember how in elementary school, every year about spring, I would begin to long for the mountains. The mountains were something I had, like a disguised prince his secret.

My own son should have the same memories, or the

chance to have them. For me, the atavistic joy in first intimations of fatherhood are mixing with the determination that there be wilderness left for my son to ramble in. My father's passion is creeping up on me.

I hope he stays in good shape, so the three of us can go together.

And as we lengthen and elaborate the chain of technology that intervenes between us and the natural world, we forget that we become steadily more vulnerable to even the slightest failure in that chain.

The time has long since passed when a citizen can function responsibly without a broad understanding of the living landscape of which he is inseparably a part.

Paul B. Sears

The Tragedy of the Commons

Garrett Hardin

from *Science*

At the end of a thoughtful article on the future of nuclear war, Wiesner and York[1] concluded that: 'Both sides in the arms race are ... confronted by the dilemma of steadily increasing military powers and steadily decreasing national security. *It is our considered professional judgement that this dilemma has no technical solution.* If the great powers continue to look for solutions in the area of science and technology only, the result will be to worsen the situation.'

I would like to focus your attention not on the subject of the article (national security in a nuclear world) but on the kind of conclusion they reached, namely that there is no technical solution to the problem. An implicit and almost universal assumption of discussions published in professional and semi-popular scientific journals is that the problem under discussion has a technical solution. A technical solution may be defined as one that requires a change only in the techniques of the natural sciences, demanding little or nothing in the way of change in human values or ideas of morality.

In our day (though not in earlier times) technical solutions are always welcome. Because of previous failures in prophecy, it takes courage to assert that a desired technical solution is not possible. Wiesner and York exhibited this courage; publishing in a science journal, they insisted that the solution to the problem was not to be found in the natural sciences. They cautiously qualified their statement with the phrase, 'It is our considered professional judgement ...' Whether they were right or not is not the concern of the present article. Rather, the concern here is with the important concept of a class of human problems which can be called 'no technical solution problems', and, more specifically, with the identification and discussion of one of these.

It is easy to show that the class is not a null class. Recall the game of noughts and crosses. Consider the problem, 'How can I win the game of noughts and crosses? It is well known that I cannot, if I assume (in keeping with the conventions of game theory) that my opponent understands the game perfectly. Put another way, there is no 'technical solution' to the problem. I can win only by giving a radical meaning to the word 'win'. I can hit my opponent over the head; or I can drug him; or I can falsify the records. Every way in which I 'win' involves, in some sense, an abandonment of the game, as we intuitively understand it. (I can also, of course, openly abandon the game – refuse to play it. This is what most adults do.)

The class of 'No technical solution problems' has members. My thesis is that the 'population problem', as conventionally conceived, is a member of this class. How it is conventionally conceived needs some comment. It is fair to say that most people who anguish over the population problem are trying to find a way to avoid the evils of overpopulation without relinquishing any of the privileges they now enjoy. They think that farming the seas or developing new strains of wheat will solve the problem – technologically. I try to show here that the solution they seek cannot be found. The population problem cannot be solved in a technical way, any more than can the problem of winning the game of noughts and crosses.

WHAT SHALL WE MAXIMIZE?

Population, as Malthus said, naturally tends to grow 'geometrically', or, as we would now say, exponentially. In a finite world this means that the *per capita* share of the world's goods must steadily decrease. Is ours a finite world?

A fair defence can be put forward for the view that the world is infinite; or that we do not know that it is not. But, in terms of the practical problems that we must face in the next few generations with the foreseeable technology, it is clear that we will greatly increase human misery if we do not, during the immediate future, assume that the world available to the terrestrial human population is finite. 'Space' is no escape.[2]

A finite world can support only a finite population; therefore, population growth must eventually equal zero. (The case of perpetual wide fluctuations above and below zero is a trivial variant that need not be discussed.) When this condition is met, what will be the situation of mankind? Specifically, can Bentham's goal of 'the greatest good for the greatest number' be realized?

No – for two reasons, each sufficient by itself. The first is a theoretical one. It is not mathematically possible to maximize for two (or more) variables at the same time. This was clearly stated by von Neumann and Morgenstern,[3] but the principle is implicit in the theory of partial differential equations, dating back at least to D'Alembert (1717–83).

The second reason springs directly from biological facts. To live, any organism must have a source of energy (for example, food). This energy is utilized for two purposes: mere maintenance and work. For man, maintenance of life requires about 1,600 kilo-calories a day ('maintenance calories'). Anything that he does over and above merely staying alive will be defined as work, and is supported by 'work calories' which he takes in. Work calories are used not only for what we call work in common speech; they are also required for all forms of enjoyment, from swimming and motor car racing to playing music and writing poetry. If our goal is to maximize population it is obvious what we must do: We must make the work calories per person approach as close to zero as possible, No gourmet meals, no vacations, no sports, no music, no literature, no art ... I think that everyone will grant, without argument or proof, that maximizing population does not maximize goods. Bentham's goal is impossible.

In reaching this conclusion I have made the usual assumption that it is the acquisition of energy that is the problem. The appearance of atomic energy has led some to question

49

this assumption. However, given an infinite source of energy, population growth still produces an inescapable problem. The problem of the acquisition of energy is replaced by the problem of its dissipation, as J. H. Fremlin has so wittily shown.[4] The arithmetic signs in the analysis are, as it were, reversed; but Bentham's goal is still unobtainable.

The optimum population is, then, less than the maximum. The difficulty of defining the optimum is enormous; so far as I know, no one has seriously tackled this problem. Reaching an acceptable and stable solution will surely require more than one generation of hard analytical work – and much persuasion.

We want the maximum good per person; but what is good? To one person it is wilderness, to another it is ski lodges for thousands. To one it is estuaries to nourish ducks for hunters to shoot; to another it is factory land. Comparing one good with another is, we usually say, impossible because goods are incommensurable. Incommensurables cannot be compared.

Theoretically this may be true; but in real life incommensurables *are* commensurable. Only a criterion of judgement and a system of weighting are needed. In nature the criterion is survival. Is it better for a species to be small and hideable, or large and powerful? Natural selection commensurates the incommensurables. The compromise achieved depends on a natural weighting of the values of the variables.

Man must imitate this process. There is no doubt that in fact he already does, but unconsciously. It is when the hidden decisions are made explicit that the arguments begin. The problem for the years ahead is to work out an acceptable theory of weighting. Synergistic effects, nonlinear variation, and difficulties in discounting the future make the intellectual problem difficult, but not (in principle) insoluble.

Has any cultural group solved this practical problem at the present time, even on an intuitive level? One simple fact proves that none has: there is no prosperous population in the world today that has, and has had for some time, a

50

growth rate of zero. Any people that has intuitively identified its optimum point will soon reach it, after which its growth rate becomes and remains zero.

Of course, a positive growth rate might be taken as evidence that a population is below its optimum. However, by any reasonable standards, the most rapidly growing populations on earth today are (in general) the most miserable. This association (which need not be invariable) casts doubt on the optimistic assumption that the positive growth rate of a population is evidence that it has yet to reach its optimum.

We can make little progress in working towards optimum population size until we explicitly exorcize the spirit of Adam Smith in the field of practical demography. In economic affairs, *The Wealth of Nations* (1776) popularized the 'invisible hand', the idea that an individual who 'intends only his own gain', is, as it were, 'led by an invisible hand to promote . . . the public interest'.[5] Adam Smith did not assert that this was invariably true, and perhaps neither did any of his followers. But he contributed to a dominant tendency of thought that has ever since interfered with positive action based on rational analysis, namely, the tendency to assume that decisions reached individually will, in fact, be the best decisions for an entire society. If this assumption is correct it justifies the continuance of our present policy of *laissez-faire* in reproduction. If it is correct we can assume that men will control their individual fecundity so as to produce the optimum population. If the assumption is not correct, we need to re-examine our individual freedoms to see which ones are defensible.

TRAGEDY OF FREEDOM IN A COMMONS

The rebuttal to the invisible hand in population control is to be found in a scenario first sketched in a little-known pamphlet[6] in 1833 by a mathematical amateur named William Forster Lloyd (1794–1852). We may well call it 'the tragedy of the commons', using the word 'tragedy' as the philosopher Whitehead used it:[7] 'The essence of dramatic tragedy is not unhappiness. It resides in the solemnity of the remorseless working of things.' He then goes on to say, 'This inevitableness of destiny can only be illustrated in terms of human life by incidents which in fact involve unhappiness. For it is only by them that the futility of escape can be made evident in the drama.'

The tragedy of the commons develops in this way. Picture a pasture open to all. It is to be expected that each herdsman will try to keep as many cattle as possible on the commons. Such an arrangement may work reasonably satisfactorily for centuries because tribal wars, poaching, and disease keep the numbers of both man and beast well below the carrying capacity of the land. Finally, however, comes the day of reckoning, that is, the day when the long-desired goal of social stability becomes a reality. At this point, the inherent logic of the commons remorselessly generates tragedy.

As a rational being, each herdsman seeks to maximize his gain. Explicitly or implicitly, more or less consciously, he asks, 'What is the utility *to me* of adding one more animal to my herd?' This utility has one negative and one positive component.

1. The positive component is a function of the increment of one animal. Since the herdsman receives all the proceeds from the sale of the additional animal, the positive utility is nearly $+1$.

2. The negative component is a function of the additional overgrazing created by one more animal. Since, however, the effects of overgrazing are shared by all the herdsmen, the negative utility for any particular decision-making herdsman is only a fraction of -1.

Adding together the component partial utilities, the rational herdsman concludes that the only sensible course for him to pursue is to add another animal to his herd. And another; and another ... But this is the conclusion reached by each and every rational herdsman sharing a commons. Therein is the tragedy. Each man is locked into a system that compels him to increase his herd without limit – in a world that is limited. Ruin is the destination towards which all men rush, each pursuing his own best interest in a society that believes in the freedom of the commons. Freedom in a commons brings ruin to all.

Some would say that this is a platitude. Would that it were! In a sense, it was learned thousands of years ago, but natural selection favours the forces of psychological denial.[8] The individual benefits as an individual from his ability to deny the truth even though society as a whole, of which he is a part, suffers. Education can counteract the natural tendency to do the wrong thing, but the inexorable succession of generations requires that the basis for this knowledge be constantly refreshed.

A simple incident that occurred a few years ago in Leominster, Massachusetts, US, shows how perishable the knowledge is. During the Christmas shopping season the parking meters downtown were covered with plastic bags that bore tags reading: 'Do not open until after Christmas. Free parking courtesy of the mayor and city council.' In other words, facing the prospect of an increased demand for already scarce space, the city fathers reinstituted the system of the commons. (Cynically, we suspect that they gained more votes than they lost by this retrogressive act.)

In an approximate way, the logic of the commons has been understood for a long time, perhaps since the discovery of agriculture or the invention of private property in real estate. But it is understood mostly only in special cases which are not sufficiently generalized. Even at this late date, cattlemen leasing national land on America's western ranges demonstrated no more than an ambivalent understanding, in constantly pressuring federal authorities to increase the head count to the point where over-grazing produces erosion and weed-dominance. Likewise, the oceans of the world continue to suffer from the survival of the philosophy of the commons. Maritime nations still respond automatically to the shibboleth of the 'freedom of the seas'. Professing to believe in the 'inexhaustible resources of the oceans', they bring species after species of fish and whales closer to extinction.[9]

The national parks present another instance of the working out of the tragedy of the commons. At present, they are open to all, without limit. The parks themselves are limited in extent – whereas population seems to grow without limit. The values that visitors seek in the parks are steadily eroded. Plainly, we must soon cease to treat the parks as commons or they will be of no value to anyone.

POLLUTION

In a reverse way, the tragedy of the commons reappears in problems of pollution. Here it is not a question of taking something out of the commons, but of putting something in – sewage, chemical, radioactive, and heat wastes into water; noxious and dangerous fumes into the air; and distracting and unpleasant advertising signs into the line of sight. The calculations of utility are much the same as before. The rational man finds that his share of the cost of the wastes he discharges into the commons is less than the cost of purifying his wastes before releasing them. Since this is true for everyone, we are locked into a system of 'fouling our own nest', so long as we behave only as independent, rational, free-enterprisers.

The tragedy of the commons as a food basket is averted by private property. But the air and waters surrounding us cannot readily be fenced, and so the tragedy of the commons as a cesspool must be prevented by different means, by coercive laws or taxing devices that make it cheaper for the polluter to treat his pollutants than to discharge them untreated. We have not progressed as far with the solution of this problem as we have with the first. Indeed, our particular concept of private property, which deters us from exhausting the positive resources of the earth, favours pollution. The owner of a factory on the bank of a stream – whose property extends to the middle of the stream – often has difficulty seeing why it is not his natural right to muddy the waters flowing past his door. The law, always behind the times, requires elaborate stitching and fitting to adapt it to this newly perceived aspect of the commons.

The pollution problem is a consequence of population. It did not much matter how a lonely nineteenth-century crofter in the Scottish Highlands disposed of his waste; in some very remote areas, it does not matter all that much even today. 'Flowing water purifies itself every ten miles,' my grandfather used to say, and the myth was near enough to the truth when he was a boy, for there were not too many people. But as population became denser, the natural chemical and biological re-cycling processes became overloaded, calling for a re-definition of property rights.

HOW TO LEGISLATE TEMPERANCE?

Analysis of the pollution problem as a function of population density uncovers a not generally recognized principle of morality, namely: the morality of an act is a function of the state of the system at the time it is *performed*.[10] Using the commons as a cesspool does not harm the general public under wild countryside conditions, because there is no public; the same behaviour in a metropolis is unbearable.

In passing, it is worth noting that the morality of an act cannot be determined from a photograph. One does not know whether a man killing an elephant or setting fire to the grassland is harming others until one knows the total system in which his act appears. 'One picture is worth a thousand words,' said an ancient Chinese; but it may take 10,000 words to validate it. It is as tempting to ecologists as it is to reformers in general to try to persuade others by way of the photographic short-cut. But the essence of an argument cannot be photographed: it must be presented rationally – in words.

That morality is system-sensitive escaped the attention of most codifiers of ethics in the past. 'Thou shalt not . . .' is the form of traditional ethical directives which make no allowance for particular circumstances. The laws of our society follow the pattern of ancient ethics, and therefore are poorly suited to governing a complex, crowded, changeable world. Our epicyclic solution is to augment statutory law with administrative law. Since it is practically impossible to spell out all the conditions under which it is safe to burn refuse in the back garden or to run a car without smog-control, by law we delegate the details to bureaus. The result is administrative law, which is rightly feared for an ancient reason – *Quis custodiet ipsos custodes?* – 'Who shall watch the watchers themselves?' John Adams said that we must have 'a government of laws and not men'.

Prohibition is easy to legislate (though not necessarily to enforce); but how do we legislate temperance? Experience indicates that it can be accomplished best through the mediation of administrative law. We limit possibilities unnecessarily if we suppose that the sentiment of *Quis custodiet* denies us the use of administrative law. We should rather retain the phrase as a perpetual reminder of fearful dangers we cannot avoid. The great challenge facing us now is to invent the corrective feedbacks that are needed to keep custodians honest. We must find ways to legitimate the needed authority of both the custodians and the corrective feedbacks.

FREEDOM TO BREED IS INTOLERABLE

The tragedy of the commons is involved in population problems in another way. In a world governed solely by the principle of 'dog eat dog' – if indeed there ever was such a world – how many children a family had would not be a matter of public concern. Parents who bred too exuberantly would leave fewer descendants, not more, because they would be unable to care adequately for their children. David Lack and others have found that such a negative feedback demonstrably controls the fecundity of birds.[11] But men are not birds, and have not acted like them for millenniums, at least.

If each human family were dependent only on its own resources; *if* the children of improvident parents starved to death; *if*, thus, overbreeding brought its own 'punishment' to the germ line – *then* there would be no public interest in controlling the breeding of families. But our society is deeply committed to the welfare state,[12] and hence is confronted with another aspect of the tragedy of the commons.

In a welfare state, how shall we deal with the family, the

religion, the race, or the class (or indeed any distinguishable and cohesive group) that adopts overbreeding as a policy to secure its own aggrandizement?[13] To couple the concept of freedom to breed with the belief that everyone born has an equal right to the commons is to lock the world in a tragic course of action.

Unfortunately this is just the course of action that is being pursued by the United Nations. In late 1967, some thirty nations agreed to the following:[14]

> The Universal Declaration of Human Rights describes the family as the natural and fundamental unit of society. It follows that any choice and decision with regard to the size of the family must irrevocably rest with the family itself, and cannot be made by anyone else.

It is painful to have to deny categorically the validity of this right; denying it, one feels as uncomfortable as a resident of Salem, Massachusetts, who denied the reality of witches in the seventeenth century. At the present time, in liberal quarters, something like a taboo acts to inhibit criticism of the United Nations. There is a feeling that the United Nations is 'our last and best hope', that we shouldn't find fault with it; we shouldn't play into the hands of the archconservatives. However, let us not forget what Robert Louis Stevenson said: 'The truth that is suppressed by friends is the readiest weapon of the enemy.' If we love the truth we must openly deny the validity of the Universal Declaration of Human Rights, even though it is promoted by the United Nations. We should also join with Kingsley Davis[15] in attempting to get Planned Parenthood-World Population to see the error of its ways in embracing the same tragic ideal.

CONSCIENCE IS SELF-ELIMINATING

It is a mistake to think that we can control the breeding of mankind in the long run by an appeal to conscience. Charles Galton Darwin made this point when he spoke on the centennial of the publication of his grandfather's great book. The argument is straightforward and Darwinian.

People vary. Confronted with appeals to limit breeding, some people will undoubtedly respond to the plea more than others. Those who have more children will produce a larger fraction of the next generation than those with more susceptible consciences. The difference will be accentuated, generation by generation.

In C. G. Darwin's words: 'It may well be that it would take hundreds of generations for the progenitive instinct to develop in this way, but if it should do so, nature would have taken her revenge, and the variety *Homo contracipiens* would become extinct and would be replaced by the variety *Homo progenitivus*.'[16]

The argument assumes that conscience or the desire for children (no matter which) is hereditary – but hereditary only in the most general formal sense. The result will be the same whether the attitude is transmitted through germ cells, or exosomatically, to use A. J. Lotka's term. (If one denies the latter possibility as well as the former, then what's the point of education?) The argument has here been stated in the context of the population problem, but it applies equally well to any instance in which society appeals to an individual exploiting a commons to restrain himself for the general good – by means of his conscience. To make such an appeal is to set up a selective system that works towards the elimination of conscience from the race.

PATHOGENIC EFFECTS OF CONSCIENCE

The long-term disadvantage of an appeal to conscience should be enough to condemn it; but it has serious short-term disadvantages as well. If we ask a man who is exploiting a commons to desist 'in the name of conscience', what are we saying to him? What does he hear? – not only at the moment but also in the wee small hours of the night when, half asleep, he remembers not merely the words we used but also the non-verbal communication cues we gave him unawares? Sooner or later, consciously or subconsciously, he

58

senses that he has received two communications, and that they are contradictory: (i) (intended communication) 'If you don't do as we ask, we will openly condemn you for not acting like a responsible citizen'; (ii) (the unintended communication) 'If you *do* behave as we ask, we will secretly condemn you for a simpleton who can be shamed into standing aside while the rest of us exploit the commons.'

Every man then is caught in what Bateson has called a 'double bind'. Bateson and his co-workers have made a plausible case for viewing the double bind as an important causative factor in the genesis of schizophrenia.[17] The double bind may not always be so damaging, but it always endangers the mental health of anyone to whom it is applied. 'A bad conscience,' said Nietzsche, 'is a kind of illness.'

To conjure up a conscience in others is tempting to anyone who wishes to extend his control beyond the legal limits. Leaders at the highest level succumb to this temptation. Has any prime minister in recent years failed to call on labour unions to moderate voluntarily their demands for higher wages, or to steel companies to honour voluntary guidelines on prices? I can recall none. The rhetoric used on such occasions is designed to produce feelings of guilt in non-cooperators.

For centuries it was assumed without proof that guilt was a valuable, perhaps even an indispensable, ingredient of the civilized life. Now, in this post-Freudian world, we doubt it.

Paul Goodman speaks from the modern point of view when he says: 'No good has ever come from feeling guilty, neither intelligence, policy, nor compassion. The guilty do not pay attention to the object but only to themselves, and not even to their own interests, which might make sense, but to their anxieties.'[18]

One does not have to be a professional psychiatrist to see the consequences of anxiety. We in the Western world are just emerging from a dreadful two-centuries-long Dark Ages of Eros that was sustained partly by prohibition laws, but perhaps more effectively by the anxiety-generating mechanisms of education. Alex Comfort has told the story well in *The Anxiety Makers*.[19] it is not a pretty one.

Since proof is difficult, we may even concede that the results of anxiety may sometimes, from certain points of view, be desirable. The larger question we should ask is whether, as a matter of policy, we should ever encourage the use of a technique the tendency (if not the intention) of which is psychologically pathogenic. We hear much talk these days of responsible parenthood; the coupled words are incorporated into the titles of some organizations devoted to birth control. Some people have proposed massive propaganda campaigns to instil responsibility into the nation's (or the world's) breeders. But what is the meaning of the word responsibility in this context? Is it not merely a synonym for the word conscience? When we use the word responsibility in the absence of substantial sanctions are we not trying to browbeat a free man in a commons into acting against his own interest? Responsibility is a verbal counterfeit for a substantial *quid pro quo*. It is an attempt to get something for nothing.

If the word responsibility is to be used at all, I suggest that it be in the sense Charles Frankel uses it.[20] 'Responsibility,' says this philosopher, 'is the product of definite social arrangements.' Notice that Frankel calls for social arrangements – not propaganda.

MUTUAL COERCION
MUTALLY AGREED UPON

The social arrangements that produce responsibility are arrangements that create coercion, of some sort. Consider bank-robbing. The man who takes money from a bank acts as if the bank were a commons. How do we prevent such action? Certainly not by trying to control his behaviour solely by a verbal appeal to his sense of responsibility. Rather than rely on propaganda we follow Frankel's lead and insist that a bank is not a commons; we seek the definite social arrangements that will keep it from becoming a commons. That we thereby infringe on the freedom of would-be robbers we neither deny nor regret.

The morality of bank-robbing is particularly easy to understand because we accept complete prohibition of this activity. We are willing to say 'Thou shalt not rob banks,' without providing for exceptions. But temperance also can be created by coercion. Taxing is a good coercive device. To keep downtown shoppers temperate in their use of parking space we introduce parking meters for short periods, and traffic fines for longer ones. We need not actually forbid a citizen to park as long as he wants to; we need merely make it increasingly expensive for him to do so. Not prohibition, but carefully biased options are what we offer him. A Madison Avenue man might call this persuasion; I prefer the greater candour of the word coercion.

Coercion is a dirty word to most liberals now, but it need not forever be so. As with the four-letter words, its dirtiness can be cleansed away by exposure to the light, by saying it over and over without apology or embarrassment. To many, the word coercion implies arbitrary decisions of distant and irresponsible bureaucrats; but this is not a necessary part of its meaning. The only kind of coercion I recommend is mutual coercion, mutually agreed upon by the majority of the people affected.

To say that we mutually agreed to coercion is not to say that we are required to enjoy it, or even to pretend we enjoy it. Who enjoys taxes? We all grumble about them. But we accept compulsory taxes because we recognize that voluntary taxes would favour the conscienceless. We institute and (grumblingly) support taxes and other coercive devices to escape the horror of the commons.

An alternative to the commons need not be perfectly just to be preferable. With real estate and other material goods, the alternative we have chosen is the institution of private property coupled with legal inheritance. Is this system perfectly just? As a genetically trained biologist I deny that it is. It seems to me that, if there are to be differences in individual inheritance, legal possessions should be perfectly correlated with biological inheritance – that those who are biologically more fit to be the custodians of property and power should · legally inherit more. But genetic

61

recombination continually makes a mockery of the doctrine of 'like father, like son' implicit in our laws of legal inheritance. An idiot can inherit millions, and a trust fund can keep his estate intact. We must admit that our legal system of private property plus inheritance is unjust – but we put up with it because we are not convinced, at the moment, that anyone has invented a better system. The alternative of the commons is too horrifying to contemplate. Injustice is preferable to total ruin.

It is one of the peculiarities of the warfare between reform and the *status quo* that it is thoughtlessly governed by a double standard. Whenever a reform measure is proposed it is often defeated when its opponents triumphantly discover a flaw in it. As Kingsley Davis has pointed out,[21] worshippers of the *status quo* sometimes imply that no reform is possible without unanimous agreement, an implication contrary to historical fact. As nearly as I can make out, automatic rejection of proposed reforms is based on one of two unconscious assumptions: (i) that the *status quo* is perfect; or (ii) that the choice we face is between reform and no action; if the proposed reform is imperfect, we presumably should take no action at all, while we wait for a perfect proposal.

But we can never do nothing. That which we have done for thousands of years is also action. It also produces evils. Once we are aware that the *status quo* is action, we can then compare its discoverable advantages and disadvantages with the predicted advantages and disadvantages of the proposed reform, discounting as best we can for our lack of experience. On the basis of such a comparison, we can make a rational decision which will not involve the unworkable assumption that only perfect systems are tolerable.

RECOGNITION OF NECESSITY

Perhaps the simplest summary of this analysis of man's population problems is this: the commons, if justifiable at all, is justifiable only under conditions of low-population density. As the human population has increased, the commons has had to be abandoned in one aspect after another.

First we abandoned the commons in food gathering, enclosing farm land and restricting pastures and hunting and fishing areas. These restrictions are still not complete throughout the world.

Somewhat later we saw that the commons as a place for waste disposal would also have to be abandoned. Restrictions on the disposal of domestic sewage are widely accepted in the Western world; we are still struggling to close the commons to pollution by motor cars, factories, insecticide sprayers, fertilizing operations, and atomic energy installations.

In a still more embryonic state is our recognition of the evils of the commons in matters of pleasure. There is almost no restriction on the propagation of sound waves in the public medium. The shopping public is assaulted with mindless music, without its consent. The governments of Britain, France and the Soviet Union are paying out enormous sums to create supersonic aircraft, each of which will disturb 50,000 people for every one person who is whisked through the air faster than sound. We are a long way from outlawing the commons in matters of pleasure. Is this because our Puritan inheritance makes us view pleasure as something of a sin, and pain (that is, the pollution of advertising) as the sign of virtue?

Every new enclosure of the commons involves the infringement of somebody's personal liberty. Infringements made in the distant past are accepted because no contemporary complains of a loss. It is the newly proposed infringements that we vigorously oppose; cries of 'rights' and 'freedom' fill the air. But what does 'freedom' mean? When men mutually agreed to pass laws against robbing, mankind became more free, not less so. Individuals locked into the logic of the commons are free only to bring on universal ruin; once they see the necessity of mutual coercion, they become free to pursue other goals. I believe it was Hegel who said, 'Freedom is the recognition of necessity.'

The most important aspect of necessity that we must now recognize, is the necessity of abandoning the commons in breeding. No technical solution can rescue us from the misery of overpopulation. Freedom to breed will bring ruin to all. At the moment, to avoid hard decisions many of us are tempted to propagandize for conscience and responsible parenthood. The temptation must be resisted, because an appeal to independently acting consciences selects for the disappearance of all conscience in the long run, and an increase in anxiety in the short.

The only way we can preserve and nurture other and more precious freedoms is by relinquishing the freedom to breed, and that very soon. 'Freedom is the recognition of necessity' and it is the role of education to reveal to all the necessity of abandoning the freedom to breed. Only so, can we put an end to this aspect of the tragedy of the commons.

NOTES

1. J. B. Wiesner and H. F. York, *Sci. Amer.*, 211 (No 4), 27 (1964). Offprint series in UK by W. H. Freeman.
2. G. Hardin, *J. Hered*, 50, 68 (1959); S. von Hoerner, *Science*, 137, 18 (1962).
3. J. von Neumann and O. Morgenstern, *Theory of Games and Economic Behaviour*, Wiley, 1947.
4. J. H. Fremlin, *New Sci.*, No 415 (1964), p. 285.
5. A Smith, *The Wealth of Nations*, Dent, Methuen, 1950, 1961.
6. W. F. Lloyd, *Two Lectures on the Checks to Population* (OUP, England, 1833), reprinted in part in *Population, Evolution, and Birth Control*, G. Hardin (ed), W. H. Freeman, 1964.
7. A. N. Whitehead, *Science and the Modern World*, Camb. UP.
8. G. Hardin (ed), *Population, Evolution, and Birth Control*, W. H. Freeman, 1964.
9. S. McVay, *Sci. Amer.*, 216 (No 8), 13 (1966). Offprint series by W. H. Freeman.
10. J. Fletcher, *Situation Ethics, Lib. of Philos. & Theol.*, SCMP.
11. D. Lack, *The Natural Regulation of Animal Numbers*, OUP.
12. H. Girvetz, *From Wealth to Welfare* (Stanford Univ. Press, Stanford, Calif., 1950).
13. G. Hardin, *Perspec. Biol. Med.*, 6, 366 (1963), W. H. Freeman, 1966.

14. U. Thant, *Int. Planned Parenthood News*, No 168 (Feb. 1968).
15. K. Davis, *Science*, *158*, 730 (1967).
16. S. Tax (ed), *Evolution after Darwin*, Univ. of Chicago Press.
17. G. Bateson, D. D. Jackson, J. Haley, J. Weakland, *Behav. Sci.*, 1, 251 (1956).
18. P. Goodman, *New York Rev. Books*, 10 (8), 22 (23rd May, 1968).
19. A. Comfort, *The Anxiety Makers* (Nelson, London, 1967).
20. C. Frankel, *The Case for Modern Man* (Harper, New York, 1955).
21. J. D. Roslansky, *Genetics and the Future of Man* (Appleton Century-Crofts, New York, 1966), p. 177.

You can go through contemporary life fudging and evading, indulging and slacking, never really hungry nor frightened nor passionately stirred, your highest moment a mere sentimental orgasm, and your first real contact with primary and elemental necessities the sweat of your deathbed.

H. G. Wells

The Obsolete Ocean

Wesley Marx

from *The Frail Ocean*

Recently I roamed through a dying forest. The blades of bulldozers and the teeth of power saws accomplish such destruction rather routinely today, though neither bulldozers nor humming power saws killed this particular forest. No towns or farms or log runs emerged to give meaning to its vanishing, for it lay deep within the sea. Huge seaweed plants called giant kelp once formed a lush foliage that sheltered life as profuse and vital as that of any land forest. Today the forest is no more. No leafy canopy sprawls over the sea surface to shaft the marine sun and shadow schools of fish. Instead the sun pours in, spotlighting an occasional survivor of this underwater devastation – a stray bass.

The disappearance of this sea forest is linked to a relatively new element in the ocean's make-up. Scientists now feel that the forest was subverted by the surprisingly subtle effects of a sewage outfall, jutting out from the coast of southern California.

It may be difficult to accept the fact that our progress can mean death to the ocean. Although the land has long been a sweating resource, the ocean has always been considered an impenetrable redoubt of nature, impervious to man's acquisitiveness and his carelessness alike. We celebrate its omnipotence in verse, in music, and in art. George Gordon, Lord Byron, who loved to body surf in the North Sea, wrote of the joys of the 'society where none intrudes' and wondered at its power:

> Roll on, thou deep and dark blue ocean – roll;
> Ten thousand fleets sweep over thee in vain;
> Man marks the earth with ruin – his control
> Stops with the shore.

The ocean stirred Melville, Conrad, Stevenson, and many of our most distinguished writers to their finest achievements. Even the simple beauty of an ocean marsh was enough to inspire Sidney Lanier:

Oh, what is abroad in the marsh and the terminal sea?
Somehow my soul seems suddenly free
From the weighing of fate and the sad discussion of sin.

And, over the years, it has been equally inspiring to musicians and artists. Claude Debussy's best-known work is a hymn to the sea. Winslow Homer, a fledgling artist in search of a subject, began painting the ocean off the New Jersey shore. Then he moved north, set up a portable painting booth on the surf-dashed cliffs of Maine, and donned oilskins to paint during savage storms. For the last twenty-seven years of his life Homer, the semi-recluse, painted the sea in all its moods. Today his work is admired in museums throughout the United States.

No other natural phenomenon on this planet – not even mountains five miles high, rivers spilling over cliffs, or redwood forests – evokes such reverence. Yet this same 'all-powerful' ocean now proves as slavishly subservient to natural laws as a moth caught by candlelight or a rose seed blown into the Atlantic. The ocean obeys. It heeds. It complies. It has its tolerances and its stresses. When these are surpassed, the ocean falters. Fish stocks can be depleted. The nurseries of marine life can be buried. Beaches can erode away. Seawater, the most common substance on this earth and the most life-nourishing – at once liquid soil and liquid atmosphere – can be hideously corrupted. It can host substances that in the stomachs of oysters or clams are refined into poisons that paralyse porpoise and man alike.

Or as it became appallingly clear on March 18th, 1967, an entire ocean region can suddenly find itself in direct jeopardy. The Atlantic Ocean off the southern tip of Great Britain sparkled deep blue, unsullied by running whitecaps or shadowing storm clouds. Guillemots, auks, redshanks. herons, and Penzance fishermen dipped into this blue world, drawing succour from its life-giving energy. At Land's End, hotel owners ordered new carpets to greet London's annual summer pilgrimage to the Cornish coast. Since the sapping of its tin mines and fertile lands, the magnet of ocean beaches alone keeps Cornwall from sinking into economic depression.

As the world discovered, the spilled cargo of one ship twenty miles away managed to shatter this serenity as no gale could do. The cargo of the reef-gashed *Torrey Canyon* was a liquid one, totalling thirty-six million gallons, ordinarily a raindrop in the vast solution of the ocean. But the ocean cannot absorb oil very efficiently. Within three days, slicks the colour of melted chocolate sprawled over one hundred square miles of ocean, a moving quagmire that ensnared seabirds by the thousands. The slicks, with their chirping cargo of flightless birds, rolled up on the golden beaches of Cornwall. Land's End smelled like an oil refinery. Like the oil-fouled birds, the oysters, clams, and teeming inhabitants of tidepools found themselves encased in a straightjacket of Kuwait crude. Three weeks later and some two hundred miles away, the pink granite coast of Brittany received the same greasy absolution from *la marée noire*. Silently, without the fanfare of howling winds and crashing waves, this oil-stricken ocean was coating the coastlines of two countries with havoc.

Great Britain, perhaps history's most famous maritime nation, swiftly mobilized its forces. RAF jets dropped napalm bombs on the slicks to fire them into oblivion. It was like a grand military campaign. (JENKINS TELLS OF PLAN TO USE THE VIETNAM HORROR BOMB, proclaimed an extra edition of the London *Daily Mirror*.) But the open ocean, heeding its own laws, dispersed the spilled oil into a slick solution that – the reporter on the scene for the *Economist* noted – is 'incombustible by anything short of the fires of hell'. From napalm bombs, the campaign accelerated to include a fleet of thirty warships armed with chemical detergents. Yet the detergent fleet could hardly cope with the extent of the slicks, and those that they did manage to emulsify drifted down into the ocean depths to asphyxiate schools of fish.

Great Britain retreated to its shores, and Tommies, along with children using garden spray cans, began deploying detergent on the beaches. Ironically, the detergent created a milky liquid more toxic to shellfish than Kuwait crude, and much of the muck had then to be shovelled up. Meanwhile, in makeshift hospitals, bird-lovers, their hands clawed red, cleaned terrified oil-smeared seabirds with talcum. The nation that started out to napalm the fireproof sea was hand-cleaning its beaches and its birds – and waiting for the next high tide. The British Prime Minister, who had called out the RAF, tried to cheer up Cornwall's worried hotel and shop owners, their livelihood suddenly threatened. 'I am not cancelling my holiday in that part of the world,' said Harold Wilson reassuringly. Some hotel-keepers cancelled their carpet orders; others rolled up their carpets, while one more inventive owner prohibited the wearing of shoes in his hotel. When oil from a Liberian tanker grounded in international waters and controlled by an American company smears your rugs, whom do you sue? Today marine bacteria, the only creatures that can stomach Kuwait crude, busily feast on the remains of the slicks.

Unlike a roaring tidal wave, this oil-tortured ocean overturned no ships, levelled no houses, and took no lives. Yet as no single wave could do, it endangered the coastal resources of two nations and compelled the British government to spend more than £1,400,000 to do no more than forestall its stealthy but inexorable invasion. There are now plans to make it easier to sue shipowners, to adapt a flight control system to crowded coastal navigation, and to empower nations to perform instant 'explosive surgery' on injured ships with potential oil slicks sloshing inside their hulls. Proposals are also under consideration to dynamite coastal reefs and similar navigational hazards.

Yet despite a clear day, calm waters, high tide, excellent charts, a warning flare from a lighthouse ship and a sterling 100A1 rating from Lloyd's Insurers, the *Torrey Canyon* still slammed into Seven Stones Reef to become a historic shipwreck. With the ocean being impressed into duty as a giant oil conduit, there will be more inevitable oil leaks and oil spills, whether off Cape Cod, in the Baltic or Mediterranean seas, or off Los Angeles Harbour, where the *Torrey Canyon* grounded once before – on a shoal of soft sand. There will also be a new style of oil spill – the offshore oil blowout that can coat 800 square miles of nearshore and smear 30 miles of beach, as happened in the Union Oil blowout off Santa Barbara, Ca., in 1969. We are becoming the demanding taskmaster of the ocean, yet the ocean is endowed with stresses and limits that cannot always tolerate our ambitions or our errors.

The stresses on the ocean are ceaselessly intensifying. As land resources shrink, the world's population and its expectations expand. Indeed, the functions of land on a congested planet that consists largely of water may narrow to one: providing living space for man. Already we contend with orange groves and cattle ranches for elbow room. The continuing depletion and/or usurpation of land resources raises the need for a new storehouse of energy to keep the Technological Revolution fuelled with food, water, pharmaceuticals, gas, and minerals. Barring cultivation of the universe, the ocean emerges as that vital storehouse.

Today the 'society where none intrudes' is being penetrated by submarines equipped with nuclear reactors and rockets, by oceanographers with silken dip-nets, by oil-drill islands built to hurricane specifications, and by scuba divers clad in pastel neopreme suits. 'A complete three-dimensional realm for the military, commercial, scientific and recreational operations of man,' exults Seabrook Hull, a new-style ocean admirer, in his book *The Bountiful Sea*. A 'sea of profit' gloats a Wall Street broker. Even the Boy Scouts offer a new merit badge for oceanography.

The technological penetration of the ocean is daring, inspiring, and, quite possibly, potentially disastrous. If the ocean is to be a jumbo resource, its exploitation must be carefully husbanded. The ocean can no longer take care of itself. It requires as much respect for its weakness as its strength. The concept of an all-powerful ocean is today obsolete.

The challenge of conserving as well as exploiting the

ocean weighs heavily on the United States. That country began as a maritime nation, something that seems inconceivable after a visit to the inevitable slum of any city – its waterfront. It will probably survive or end as one. Because of its technology, international politics, and geography, the United States is wedded to its marine destiny. Its eastern coast fronts on the Atlantic Ocean. Its southern coast sits atop the Gulf of Mexico and the Caribbean Sea. Its western coast confronts the North Pacific Ocean, the Bering and Chukchi seas, and the Arctic Ocean. Its fiftieth state lies in the Central Pacific, the territory of Guam and the UN trusteeship of Micronesia in the Western Pacific. The United States is part of a continent. It is also a big island surrounded by two oceans and a host of seas and gulfs; and in the middle of this big island lie the Great Lakes, a vast system of waterways, which helps to nourish the oceans through the mouth of the St Lawrence River. Yet we jeopardize this fantastic marine patrimony if we can spud submarine oil wells but cannot conserve sea forests.

The challenge of the ocean is international as well as national in scope. As marine technology generates more activities and ambitions, nations must learn how to preserve marine resources as well as their respective tempers. Nutrition experts promote the ocean as a food locker for future survival, but the high seas fishery competition seems little related to effective conservation or food distribution. The ocean promises to be the ultimate challenge to nations to coexist on a watery planet whirling through space. An indication of the ultimate seriousness of this challenge is that three estranged world powers, the United States, Mainland China, and Russia, now share a common border – the Pacific Ocean – perhaps the planet's richest resource.

A rather ominous question emerges. Byron claimed that 'Man marks the earth with ruin'. Many of our hills, valleys, and rivers – even the air we breathe – today testify grotesquely to the accuracy of his pessimism. Are we perhaps fated to mark the ocean with ruin, to plunder, pollute, and contend until we have a ghost ocean bereft of all but the voice of its waves?

To avoid such a fate will require comprehensive planning and policy making. Yet before rational planning can take place we must understand the ocean, its tolerances and stresses as well as its wealth. It would be comforting to find that man, spurred on by his intense and probing curiosity, was already busily divining and heeding these tolerances. Yet time and time again sanitary outfall engineers, fishermen, dredge operators, marine miners, oceanographers, and breakwater designers who think they understand the ocean must stand back and wonder. 'How did that happen?'

The only possible force that could be motivating the effort to preserve natural areas is the moral conviction that it is right – that we owe it to ourselves and to the good earth that supports us to curb our avarice to the extent of leaving a few spots untouched and unexploited. ... I think that when future philosophers scan back through the records of human history and human thought they may put their finger on this century as a time of outstanding advance in man's feeling of responsibility to the earth. Whether men can succeed in preserving an attractive and livable world is the problem that lies ahead.

A. Starker Leopold

Notes for a Little Play

Ted Hughes

from *Crow*

First – the sun coming closer, growing by the minute.
Next – clothes torn off.
Without a goodbye
Faces and eyes evaporate.
Brains evaporate
Hands arms legs feet head and neck
Chest and belly vanish
With all the rubbish of the earth.

And the flame fills all space.
The demolition is total
Except for two strange items remaining in the flames—
Two survivors moving in the flames blindly.

Mutations – at home in the nuclear glare.
Horrors – hairy and slobbery, glossy, and raw.
They sniff towards each other in the emptiness.
They fasten together. They seem to be eating each other.
But they are not eating each other.
They do not know what else to do.
They have begun to dance a strange dance.
And this is the marriage of these simple creatures –
Celebrated here, in the darkness of the sun,
Without guest or God.

The Economics of the Coming Spaceship Earth

Kenneth E. Boulding

from *Environmental Quality in a Growing Economy*

The closed earth of the future requires economic principles which are somewhat different from those of the open earth of the past. For the sake of picturesqueness, I am tempted to call the open economy the 'cowboy economy', the cowboy being symbolic of the illimitable plains and also associated with reckless, exploitative, romantic, and violent behaviour, which is characteristic of open societies. The closed economy of the future might similarly be called the 'spaceman' economy, in which the earth has become a single spaceship, without unlimited reservoirs of anything, either for extraction or for pollution, and in which, therefore, man must find his place in a cyclical ecological system which is capable of continuous reproduction of material form even though it cannot escape having inputs of energy. The difference between the two types of economy becomes most apparent in the attitude towards consumption. In the cowboy economy, consumption is regarded as a good thing and production likewise; and the success of the economy is measured by the amount of the throughput from the 'factors of production', a part of which, at any rate, is extracted from the reservoirs of raw materials and noneconomic objects, and another part of which is output into the reservoirs of pollution. If there are infinite reservoirs from which material can be obtained and into which effluvia can be deposited, then the throughput is at least a plausible measure of the success of the economy. The gross national product is a rough measure of this total throughput. It should be possible, however, to distinguish that part of the GNP which is derived from exhaustible and that which is derived from reproducible resources, as well as that part of consumption which represent effluvia and that which represents input into the productive system again. Nobody, as far as I know, has ever attempted to break down the GNP in this way, although it would be an interesting and extremely important exercise, which is unfortunately beyond the scope of this discussion.

By contrast, in the spaceman economy, throughput is by no means a desideratum, and is indeed to be regarded as something to be minimized rather than maximized. The essential measure of the success of the economy is not production and consumption at all, but the nature, extent, quality, and complexity of the total capital stock, including in this the state of the human bodies and minds included in this system. In the spaceman economy, what we are primarily concerned with is stock maintenance, and any technological change which results in the maintenance of a given total stock with a lessened throughput (that is, less production and consumption) is clearly a gain. This idea that both production and consumption are bad things rather than good things is very strange to economists, who have been obsessed with the income-flow concepts to the exclusion, almost, of capital-stock concepts.

There are actually some very tricky and unsolved problems involved in the questions as to whether human welfare or well-being is to be regarded as a stock or a flow. Something of both these elements seems actually to be involved in it, and as far as I know there have been practically no studies directed towards identifying these two dimensions of human satisfaction. Is it, for instance, eating that is a good thing, or is it being well fed? Does economic welfare involve having nice clothes, fine houses, good equipment, and so on, or is it to be measured by the depreciation and the wearing out of these things? I am inclined myself to regard the stock concept as most fundamental, that is, to think of being well fed as more important than eating, and to think even of so-called services as essentially involving the restoration of a depleting psychic capital. Thus I have argued that we go to a concert in order to restore a psychic condition which might be called 'just having gone to a concert', which, once established, tends to depreciate. When it depreciates beyond a certain point, we go to another concert in order to restore it. If it depreciates rapidly, we go to a lot of concerts; if it depreciates slowly, we go to few. On this view, similarly, we eat primarily to restore bodily homeostatis, that is, to maintain a condition of being well fed, and so on. On this view, there is nothing desirable in consumption at all. The less consumption we can maintain a given state with, the better off we are. If we had clothes that did not wear out, houses that did not depreciate, and even if we could maintain our bodily condition without eating, we would clearly be much better off.

It is this last consideration, perhaps, which makes one pause. Would we, for instance, really want an operation that would enable us to restore all our bodily tissues by intravenous feeding while we slept? Is there not, that is to say, a certain virtue in throughput itself, in activity itself, in production and consumption itself, in raising food and in eating it? It would certainly be rash to exclude this possibility. Further interesting problems are raised by the demand for variety. We certainly do not want a constant state to be maintained; we want fluctuations in the state. Otherwise there would be no demand for variety in food, for variety in scene, as in travel, for variety in social contact, and so on. The demand for variety can, of course, be costly, and sometimes it seems to be too costly to be tolerated or at least legitimated, as in the case of marital partners, where the maintenance of a homeostatic state in the family is usually regarded as much more desirable than the variety and excessive throughput of the libertine. There are problems here which the economics profession has neglected with astonishing singlemindedness. My own attempts to call attention to some of them, for instance, in two articles,[1] as far as I can judge, produced no response whatever; and economists continue to think and act as if production, consumption, throughput, and the GNP were the sufficient and adequate measure of economic success.

It may be said, of course, why worry about all this when the spaceman economy is still a good way off (at least beyond the lifetimes of any now living), so let us eat, drink, spend, extract and pollute, and be as merry as we can, and let posterity worry about the spaceship earth. It is always a little hard to find a convincing answer to the man who says, 'What has posterity ever done for me?' and the conservationist has always had to fall back on rather vague ethical principles postulating identity of the individual with some human community or society which extends not only back into the past but forward into the future. Unless the individual identifies with some community of this kind, conservation is obviously 'irrational'. Why should we not maximize the welfare of this generation at the cost of posterity? *Après nouse, le déluge* has been the motto of not insignificant numbers of human societies. The only answer to this, as far as I can see, is to point out that the welfare of the individual depends on the extent to which he can identify himself with others, and that the most satisfactory individual identity is that which identifies not only with a community in space but also with a community extending over time from the past into the future. If this kind of identity is recognized as desirable, then posterity has a voice, even if it does not have a vote; and in a sense, if its voice can influence votes, it has votes too. This whole problem is linked up with the much larger one of the determinants of the morale, legitimacy, and 'nerve' of a society, and there is a great deal of historical evidence to suggest that a society which loses its identity with posterity and which loses its positive image of the future loses also its capacity to deal with present problems, and soon falls apart.[2]

Even if we concede that posterity is relevant to our present problems, we still face the question of time-discounting and the closely related question of uncertainty-discounting. It is a well-known phenomenon that individuals discount the future, even in their own lives. The very existence of a positive rate of interest may be taken as at least strong supporting evidence of this hypothesis. If we discount our own future, it is certainly not unreasonable to discount posterity's future even more, even if we do give posterity a vote. If we discount this at 5 per cent per annum, posterity's vote or pound sterling halves every fourteen years as we look into the future, and after even a mere hundred years it is pretty small – only about 3½d on the pound. If we add another 5 per cent for uncertainty, even the vote of our grandchildren reduces almost to insignificance. We can argue, of course, that the ethical thing to do is not to discount the future at all, that time-discounting is mainly the result of myopia and perspective, and hence is an illusion which the moral man should not tolerate. It is a very popular illusion, however, and one that must certainly be taken into consideration in the formulation of policies. It explains, perhaps, why conservationist policies almost have to be sold under some other excuse which seems more urgent, and why, indeed, necessities which are visualized as urgent, such as defence, always seem to hold priority over those which involve the future.

All these considerations add some credence to the point of view which says that we should not worry about the spaceman economy at all, and that we should just go on increasing the GNP and indeed the gross world product, or GWP, in the expectation that the problems of the future can be left to the future, that when scarcities arise, whether this is of raw materials of or pollutable reservoirs, the needs of the then present will determine the solutions of the then present, and there is no use giving ourselves ulcers by worrying about problems that we really do not have to solve. There is even high ethical authority for this point of view in the New Testament, which advocates that we should take no thought for tomorrow and let the dead bury their dead. There has always been something rather refreshing in the view that we should live like the birds, and perhaps posterity is for the birds in more senses than one; so perhaps we should all call it a day and go out and pollute something cheerfully. As an old taker of thought for the morrow, however, I cannot quite accept this solution; and I would argue, furthermore, that tomorrow is not only very close, but in many respects it is already here. The shadow of the future spaceship, indeed, is already falling over our spendthrift merriment. Oddly enough, it seems to be in pollution rather than in exhaustion that the problem is first becoming salient. Los Angeles has run out of air, 5,000 miles of Britain's rivers are severely polluted, the oceans are filling up with lead and DDT, and the atmosphere may become man's major problem in another generation, at the rate at which we are filling it up with gunk. It is, of course, true that at least on a microscale, things have been worse at times in the past. The cities of today, with all their foul air and polluted waterways, are probably not as bad as the filthy cities of the pretechnical age. Nevertheless, that fouling of the nest which has been typical of man's activity in the past on a local scale now seems to be extending to the whole world society; and one certainly cannot view with equanimity the present rate of pollution of any of the natural reservoirs, whether the atmosphere, the lakes, or even the oceans.

NOTES

1. K. E. Boulding, 'The Consumption Concept in Economic Theory', *American Economic Review*, 35 (May 1945): 1–14; and 'Income or Welfare?', *Review of Economic Studies*, 17 (1949–50): 77–86.
2. Fred L. Polak, *The Image of the Future*, Vols. I and II, translated by Elise Boulding, New York: Sythoff, Leyden, and Oceana, 1961.

Economics and Ecosystems

John Breslaw

WASTES IN THE ECONOMY

If one regards the competitive British economy as a black box, then there are two processes which do not come within the economy's sphere of influence – inputs and outputs. The inputs are raw materials, or resources, used in the economy – air, water, metals, minerals, and wood. The outputs are the residuals – sewage, trash, carbon dioxide, and other gases released to the atmosphere, radioactive waste, and so on. We shall consider the residuals first.

The environment has a certain limited capability to absorb wastes without harmful effects. Once the ambient residuals rise above a certain level, however, they become unwanted inputs to other production processes or to final consumers. The size of this residual in fact is massive. In an economy which is closed,[1] the weight of residuals ejected into the environment is about equal to the weight of input materials, plus oxygen taken from the atmosphere. This result, while obvious upon reflection, leads to the surprising and even shocking corollary that the disposal of residuals is as large an operation, in sheer tonnage, as basic materials production. This incredible volume has to be disposed of. It is at this stage that the market process breaks down.

If the functioning of the economy gave rise to incentives, such as prices, which fully reflected the costs of disposing of residuals, such incentives would be very much in point. This would be especially true if the incentives fully reflected costs to the overall society associated with the discharge of the residuals to the environment. But it is clear that, whatever other normative properties the functioning of a market economy may have, it does not reflect these costs adequately.

Market economies are effective instruments for

organizing production and allocating resources, in so far as the utility functions are associated with two-party transactions. But in connexion with waste disposal, the utility functions involve third parties, and the automatic market exchange process fails.

Thus the need to see man's activities as part of an ecosystem becomes clear. The outputs from the black box go through other black boxes and become inputs again. If our black box is putting out too much and overloading the system, one can only expect trouble – and that is what one gets.

If we look at a particular production process, we find that there is a flow of goods or services that consumers or businesses get whether they want it or not. An upstream river may be polluted by an industry, and the downstream user cannot usually control the quality of the water he gets. If the polluted water wipes out a fishing industry, then there is some cost (the profit that used to be made by the fishing industry) that does not appear on the balance sheet of the upstream user. Similarly, there may be benefits involved – the upstream user may use the stream for cooling, and the hot water may support an oyster farm downstream.

The activities of an economic unit thus generate real effects that are external to it. These are called externalities. A society that relies completely on a decentralized decision-making system in which significant externalities occur, as they do in any society which contains significant concentrations of population and industrial activities, will find that certain resources are not used optimally.

The tool used by economists, and others, in determining a course of action in making social decisions is the technique of cost-benefit analysis. The basis is to list all the consequences arising from a course of action, such as building a new motorway, and to make estimates of the benefits or costs to the community of all these consequences. This is done in terms of money values and a balance is drawn up, which is compared with similar estimates of the consequences of alternative decisions, such as building a rapid transit network or doing nothing. The sensible decision is to go ahead with those projects where the benefits come out best, relative to the costs. The art of cost-benefit analysis lies in using the scanty information available to assign money values to these costs and benefits. Differences in house prices are a way of getting at noise valuation. Time is obviously worth money: how much can be estimated by looking at what people do when they have a choice between a faster and more expensive way of going from A to B and a slower but cheaper way?

Going back to our slaughtered fish, if the cost of reducing pollution by 50 per cent were less than the profit that could be realized from fishing at this level of pollution, then it makes sense to spend that amount. In fact, the level of pollution should be reduced until the marginal cost of reducing pollution (the cost of reducing pollution by a very small amount) is just equal to the marginal revenue from fishing (the extra revenue that is received as a result of that amount less pollution). The question is, where there is no market, how does one get to this state of affairs?

Method One is to internalize the problem so that a single economic unit will take account of all of the costs and benefits associated with the external effects. To do this, the size of the economic unit has to be increased. A good example of this is where one has several fisheries for one limited species of fish, e.g. whales. If the fisheries operate separately, each concern takes as many as it can, regardless of the effect on the total catch. If the fisheries were to act in unison, then the maximum catch compatible with a stable population of whales would be taken, and no more – the externalities would have been internalized. Unfortunately, waste products are often so widely propagated in nature and affect so many diverse interests that the merger route is not feasible.

Method Two is the one mostly used at the moment: the use of regulations set up by government and enforceable by law. There are many examples of these: minimum net-hole size in fishing, parking regulations on busy streets, limited number of flights at airports during the night, zoning regulations as applied to land use, and certain water quality laws for industrial and municipal river users. Ideally, these regulations would take into account the different nature of the environmental difficulty, varying both over place and time, e.g. high and low flows in streams, windy days for smoke control, etc. There are two main objections to such regulations. In the first place, they are often difficult to enforce, especially if there are high monetary returns involved and the likelihood of being caught is small – flushing oil tanks in the English Channel. The other objection is more sophisticated: in a competitive market the imposition of regulations does not normally lead to the best use of resources. It is better to do this by means of pricing, since this method makes it possible to balance incremental costs and gains in a relatively precise manner. Also, regulations do not provide the funds for the construction and operation of measures of regional scope, should these prove economical.

Method Three involves the legal system and the law of nuisance. Thus when there is an oil spill on your shore and you and your property get covered in goo, then in such an obvious and easy case one would expect prompt damages.

Method Four involves the paying of some monetary rent in order to get the practice of pollution stopped. One way is to pay a producer to stop polluting. Although such payments would be received favourably by the industries involved, the sheer size of the total payments necessary as a means of preventing pollution would put an impossible strain on any budget, and such a solution is only feasible for 'special case' industrial operations. Moreover, if a steel works is discharging its waste into a river, without charge, it is producing steel that is artificially cheap. Paying the works to stop pollution does nothing to get the steel price back to its rightful value (i.e. when all costs are met) in the short run. In the long run, this remains true only if the assumption of a competitive market is weakened.

Another way to implement Method Four would be to charge a polluter for the pollution that he causes. Examples of such charges or taxes would be a tax on sewage effluents which is related to the quality and quantity of the discharge; or a surcharge on the price of fuels with a high sulphur content which is meant to take account of the broader cost to society external to the fuel-using enterprise. This procedure is one usually favoured by economists, since it uses economic incentives to allocate the resources (the waste assimilative capacity of the environment) similar to those generated where market mechanisms can balance costs and returns. The revenue from these charges can be used to finance other anti-pollution facilities.

The use of charges for the wasted assimilative capacity of the environment implies that you have to pay in order to put things out of the black box. Before the environment's waste assimilative capacity was overloaded, it was not used to its full capacity. A resource which is not fully utilized has a zero price; once it is utilized it receives a positive price – which is why charges now have to be imposed. From an ecological point of view this is very good, since now that one has to pay to get rid of a product, it means that this product has a value attached to it, albeit negative. The effect is to restructure industrial processes to take this into account. A society that allows waste discharges to neglect the offsite costs of waste disposal will not only devote too few resources to the treatment of waste, but will also produce too much waste in view of the damage it causes. Or more simply, if you charge for waste disposal, industries will produce less waste, and the wastes produced will often find use in some other process – recycling. A paper-producing company using the sulphite method will find it advantageous to change to the sulphate method through increased effluent charges. In England, many firms have found profitable uses for waste products when forced to stop polluting. In a few instances, mostly in already depressed areas, plants may be capable of continuing operation only because they are able to shift all or most of that portion of production costs associated with waste disposal to other economic units. When this situation is coupled with one in which the plant is a major part of the employment base of a community, society may have an interest in assisting the plant to stay in business, while at the same time controlling the external costs it is imposing. However, these would be special cases which are used to help the adjustment to the new position of equilibrium rather than change the position of the new equilibrium.

Just such an operation has been used in the Ruhr Valley in Germany, starting in 1913. The political power of the Ruhrverband lies in the governing board made up of owners of business and other facilities in the Ruhrverband area, communities in the area, and representatives of the waterworks and other water facilities. It has built over one-hundred waste-treatment plants, oxidation lakes, and waterworks facilities. Capital came from the bond market, and operating expenses from a series of charges contingent on the amount and quality of the effluent discharged by the industries and municipalities in the region. This scheme is so successful that, though the Ruhr River flows through one of the most heavily industrialized regions of Germany, one can find ducks living on it.

NON-RENEWABLE RESOURCES

The inputs to our black box consist of renewable resources, such as food and water, and nonrenewable ones such as minerals and land. In considering free resources, it was stated that in a decentralized competitive market economy such resources are not used optimally. In fact, they are overutilized – rivers are overutilized as disposal units, hence pollution; roads are utilized above their intended capacity with resultant traffic snarl-ups. The same holds true for non-renewable resources: they are not used optimally.

Given a fixed technology, at any time in the past we would have run into a critical condition with respect to our supplies of minerals and metals. It is only changing technology, which makes for the profitable extraction of pretechnical change unprofitable deposits, that has enabled us to manage without really bad shortages. Hence the present rate of extraction is only justifiable in the belief of future technical progress. Yet this is just the assumption that is now undergoing examination. In the past, man's technical progress was a function of man's incentive and ingenuity; now, however, he has to take into account another factor – the ability of the environment to accept his ravages.

As any child will comment, on observing the empty beer cans and discarded packets lying on the roadside and around 'beauty spots', this is wrong. It is wrong because we do not put sufficient value on the natural resource – the countryside – to keep it clean. It is wrong for the same reason a second time: we do not put sufficient value on the natural resources – aluminium, plastic, paper or whatever – so that when we have used them for their original purposes, they are disposed of, as rapidly as possible. The conclusion is clear: both our renewable and non-renewable resources are not being used optimally.

Take a specific example – oil. What are the factors that determine its price? As usual, demand is a decreasing function of price, and supply an increasing function. The point of intersection dictates the price and quantity sold. When the optimal use of oil is considered, there are two points of view that have to be taken into account. One is the value of oil to future generations, and the other is the social cost of the use of the oil.

In considering future generations, optimal behaviour will take place in a competitive economy (with private ownership) if the private rate of return is the same as the social rate of return. In non-economic terms, all this means is that the rate at which the future is discounted by individuals is the same as the rate at which it is discounted by society. There is dispute on this point – that is, whether the two rates are equal or not. However, even if they are, because the individual companies seek to maximize their private benefit, like in the fisheries example, the total exploration of the resources is likely to not be optimal.

At this stage government comes into the picture. On the conservation side, a scientifically determined MER – maximum efficient rate (of oil flow) – is determined for a particular site. The main effect of this is to stop large fluctuations in the price of oil. Since half the total revenue of oil companies goes into the discovery and development of new deposits, this produces a high overhead cost. In the US, for example, the aim is to produce as large a growth in the GNP as possible, subject to constraints (inflation, full employment, balance of payments, etc.). Hence the tradition of allowing industries to write off the cost of capital equipment against tax, since new capital stimulates the economy (investment) and makes for more efficient production. The oil industry felt that the same principle should apply to its capital costs – the rent it pays on oil deposits. Hence the oil depletion allowance, which allows the costs of rents to be partially offset against profits. The effect of this is to move the supply curve to the right – which results in more oil being sold at a lower price. Thus it encourages oil companies to extract more oil and find new deposits. This is great from a military point of view, but disastrous when the effect of such exploitation of the environment is considered: oil spills at sea, the probable permanent scarring of the tundra in Alaska, and smog in our cities. Yet this is exactly what is meant by social costs, the externalities which do not get considered in the market price.

If the oil depletion allowances were removed or sharply reduced,[2] the oil producing industry could not continue to function at its accustomed level of operation and maintain its accustomed price structure. Similar considerations apply to minerals (mineral depletion allowance). Yet this is only the first step. Another method that would produce the same desired results would be to make the extractor pay for the quantity of mineral or metal that he mines, just as he should pay for the right to discard his waste. This solves a whole lot of problems – by making the original substance more expensive, the demand is reduced, be it for power-using dishwashers, oil-eating motor cars, or resource-demanding economies. Moreover, these products, being more expensive, will not be discarded, but recycled, thus solving in part a pollution problem, as well as a litter problem (if they can be separated). By recycling, there will be less demand for the minerals or metals from the mining companies, since there is this new source of these materials.

To a certain extent, this view of things is recognized. In England, one of the proposals considered for solving the problem of scrapped cars around the countryside was to charge an extra twenty-five pounds on the price of each new car. This would be refundable when the vehicle was brought in for scrapping – a bit like returnable bottles. In the US, the use of natural gas as boiler fuel was recognized as an inferior use of an exhaustible resource. 'One apparent method of preventing waste of gas is to limit the uses to which it may be put, uses for which another more abundant fuel may serve equally well' (Supreme Court, 1961). This same result could have been achieved by charging the gas producer for the quantity of gas that he took (as well as rent to the owner of the gas deposit for the right to extract gas from his property). The price that should be charged, like the prices charged for sewage disposal, vary from location to location and depend upon the characteristics of the environment. The price should be high enough to make recycling, if physically possible, both a feasible and desirable process. If the use of the resources causes some social cost – like air pollution – then this should be reflected in the price. So too should the relative scarcity of the resource, compared to substitutable alternatives, be a consideration.

If the socio-economic system fails to change quickly enough to meet changing conditions, then it is incumbent on the people to facilitate such change.

THE FUTURE

A prerequisite to any lasting solution to environmental pollution is a zero growth rate – the birth rate equalling the death rate. However, a stable population produces a difficult economic problem in an economy like that of the United Kingdom. To remain healthy (to stay the same size or grow), the economy needs a growing market, since only in a growing market can the capital goods sector remain efficient, given present technology. At first sight, then, the achievement of a stable population is linked to a recession. One might make the assumption that a growing market could still be achieved by allowing *per capita* consumption to increase at the same rate as the growth of the GNP. However, with

91

restrictions on extraction industries, this will probably not provide a total solution. The slack is more likely to be made up by producing a different type of service – education at regular periods throughout one's life, the move from cities to smaller communities and the investment involved in such a move, the rebuilding (or destruction) of old cities compatible with their new uses. Put another way, the economic slack that will have to be taken up to avoid a depression gives us the opportunity to plan for the future, without worrying about providing for an expanding population.

The essential cause of environmental pollution is overpopulation, combined with an excessive population growth rate; other anti-pollution measures can be used temporarily, but so long as the central problem is not solved, one can expect no lasting success.

BIBLIOGRAPHY

Day, Alan. 'Value on the Quality of Life', *Observer*, 1969.

Ehrlich, Paul. *The Population Bomb*. Ballantine, 1971.

Fair, Gordon. 'Pollution Abatement in the Ruhr District', in *Comparisons in Resource Management*, ed. H. Jarrett, 1961.

Hulstrunk, A. 'Air Pollution', Associated Press, NY, 1969.

Jarrett, H., ed., *Environmental Quality in a Growing Economy*. Resources for the Future. OUP.

Kneese, A. *Economics and the Quality of the Environment*. Resources for the Future, 1968.

Kneese, A., and Bower. *Managing Water Quality, Economics, Technology, Institutions*. Johns Hopkins Press, 1968.

Lichtblau, J. *The Oil Depletion Issue*.

NOTES

1. A closed economy is one with no imports or exports, and within which there is no net accumulation of stocks (plants, equipment, inventories, consumer durables, or residential buildings).

2. This departs from the original assumption of a perfect competitive market, and from the point of view of strict economic theory there is some objection to the charge procedure described – it violates the principle of marginal cost pricing. However, methods that are

less than theoretically ideal may be optimal in practice, since an important element in determining the best method for actual use is the cost of making marginal refinements. A comparatively crude method that is generally correct in principle will often realize the major share of the gains that could be achieved by more complex and conceptually more satisfying techniques.

... we shall have to overthrow the myth of the machine and replace it with a new myth of life, a myth based upon a richer understanding of all organic processes, a sharper insight into man's positive 'role in changing the face of the earth' – I deliberately use the words of the great geographer, Carl Sauer – and above all a deeply religious faith in man's own capacity to transform and perfect his own self and his own institutions in cooperative relation with all the forces of nature, and above all, with his fellow men. To put all our hope in the improvement of machines is the characteristic inversion and perversion of values of the present age; and that is the reason that our machines threaten us with extinction, since they are now in the hands of deplorably unimproved men.

Lewis Mumford

Education and Ecology

Garrett De Bell

Education, particularly higher education, is critically important to solving our ecological crisis. At present, universities do much of the specialized research which develops the technology that is raping the earth and threatening our survival. They do this job devastatingly well. Yet the knowledge and wisdom to apply technology wisely is neglected. The whole direction and purpose and thrust of our culture is towards greater production, greater exploitation. In many, if not in most of our universities, there is little criticism of the basic assumptions and value judgements that underline our current priorities. The university is quite capable of developing an automated machine to harvest almost any crop, but it is unable to evaluate the long-term social costs of such a development. Do farm workers want to be forced out of work and into the cities? Is it desirable to replace people with machines whenever it is feasible? Does this use of machines increase the crop, or just the profit? Some of these machines use gamma radiation to determine if the crop is ripe. Is this a safe and desirable practice? Special strains of crops are developed by plant-breeding programmes to meet the needs of the machine system – strains with synchronous ripening, uniform size, tough skins, and long storage life. Does this selection have a detrimental effect on food value? Use of machines makes us more dependent on high technology and the energy needed to make and run the machines. Should we continue to replace labour by energy-using machines when petroleum reserves are sufficient for only a few more generations and energy use pollutes the environment? These are the kind of questions that go unasked.

The universities are characterized by increasingly narrow specialization in all fields. For instance, ecology as a field emphasizing interrelationships – the study of the total impact of man and other animals on the balance of nature. Yet only a few professional ecologists are willing to brave the disapproval of their narrowly professional colleagues by pursuing the broad spectrum that ecology implies. Some of their names are household words – the late Rachel Carson, Paul Ehrlich, Kenneth Watt, Barry Commoner, Lamont Cole, and Garrett Hardin. The rest do very specialized studies that appear in very specialized journals.

The biological and social sciences are trying to emulate the elegant work of a few nuclear physicists and molecular biologists and are learning more and more about increasingly trivial subjects.

Very little research is aimed at developing alternatives to our present disastrous pattern of existence with excessive production – waste; conspicuous consumption; manipulative advertising; growth for its own sake; poverty in the midst of plenty; and destruction of the air, water, soil, and organisms that are the basis of the life-support system. One reason that we don't get the right answers is that we aren't asking the right questions.

Probably most important is that we are not providing the kind of education that will allow the electorate to evaluate the choices that are, or will be, available to them.

Our system is, in a word, geared to diplomas, not education. What is to be done? A statement of Paul Goodman's is appropriate:

Today, because of the proved incompetence of our adult institutions and the hypocrisy of most professionals, university students have a right to a large say in what goes on ... Professors will, of course, teach what they please. My advice to students is that given by Prince Kropotkin, in 'A Letter to the Young': 'Ask what kind of world do you want to live in? What are you good at and want to work at to build that world? What do you need to know? Demand that your teachers teach you that.' Serious teachers would be delighted by this approach.

It will be a challenging task to make our education system

both uplifting and truly relevant to our environment. There is a chance to revitalize the system around the central theme of survival and ecology as suggested in John Fischer's article on page 99. In their calls for a relevant education, students have shown tremendous enthusiasm for study that relates to solving the social and ecological problems that are threatening our existence. They would respond very favourably to efforts by faculty and administration to devote more of the universities' teaching and research to important environmental problems on all levels, especially where they could get directly involved, as through work-study programmes. Real inquiry may rescue the university from the sterile degree-and-diploma game it has become.

SUGGESTIONS FOR ACTION

Examine the course content, curriculum, and research of your university or college to see if there is a reasonable balance between pure and applied research; between teaching and research that perpetuates present trends and that which questions trends and suggests alternatives.

How can you make your field relevant to serving our environment? Take surveys of graduate students to see how many are pursuing relevant theses and how many would like to. If the numbers differ significantly, ask questions about the reasons they have not chosen relevant topics. Check into faculty salaries, fellowships, and grants in different fields and subfields to see where the main priorities are. Are these priorities good? Set up an experimental college with faculty controlled by students to get some open discussion and fresh ideas. Hire graduate students, uncredentialed people with experience in the real world, politicians, or anyone else you feel could get out of the over-specialized, study-problems-to-death academic syndrome. Appointments could be made by the student senate, if it is representative of the general student body. Provision might be able to ensure that small interest groups were able to have an influence. The purpose of the experimental college would be to counter the university's resistance to change. There are a great number of vested interests in the faculty and administration that resist any change that might alter their power. Students don't have the same vested interests and are more willing to experiment.

A world from which solitude is extirpated is a very poor ideal . . . Nor is there much satisfaction in contemplating the world with nothing left to the spontaneous activity of nature.

John Stuart Mill

Survival U: Prospectus for a Really Relevant University

John Fischer

from *Harper's*

For the first time in history, the future of the human race is now in serious question. This fact is hard to believe, or even think about – yet it is the message which a growing number of scientists are trying, almost frantically, to get across to us. Listen, for example, to Professor Richard A. Falk of Princeton and of the Centre for Advanced Study in the Behavioural Sciences:

> The planet and mankind are in grave danger of irreversible catastrophe ... Man may be sceptical about following the flight of the dodo into extinction, but the evidence points increasingly to just such a pursuit ... There are four interconnected threats to the planet – wars of mass destruction, over-population, pollution, and the depletion of resources. They have a cumulative effect. A problem in one area renders it more difficult to solve the problems in any other area ... The basis of all four problems is the inadequacy of the sovereign states to manage the affairs of mankind in the twentieth century.

Similar warnings could be quoted from a long list of other social scientists, biologists, and physicists, among them such distinguished thinkers as René Dubos, Buckminster Fuller, Loren Eiseley, George Wald, and Barry Commoner. They are not hopeless. Most of them believe that we still have a chance to bring our weapons, our population growth, and the destruction of our environment under control before it is too late. But the time is short, and so far there is no evidence that enough people are taking them seriously.

99

That would be the prime aim of the experimental university I'm suggesting here: To look seriously at the interlinking threats to human existence, and to learn what we can do to fight them off.

Let's call it Survival U. It will not be a multiversity, offering courses in every conceivable field. Its motto – emblazoned on a life-jacket rampant – will be: 'What must we do to be saved?' If a course does not help to answer that question, it will not be taught here. Students interested in musicology, junk sculpture, the Theatre of the Absurd, and the literary *dicta* of Leslie Fiedler can go somewhere else.

Neither will our professors be detached, dispassionate scholars. To get hired, each will have to demonstrate an emotional commitment to our cause. Moreover, he will be expected to be a moralist; for this generation of students, like no other in my lifetime, is hungering and thirsting after righteousness. What it wants is a moral system it can believe in – and that is what our university will try to provide. In every class it will preach the primordial ethic of survival.

The biology department, for example, will point out that it is sinful for anybody to have more than two children. It has long since become glaringly evident that unless the earth's cancerous growth of population can be halted, all other problems – poverty, war, racial strife, uninhabitable cities, and the rest – are beyond solution. So the department naturally will teach all known methods of birth control, and much of its research will be aimed at perfecting cheaper and better ones.

Its second lesson in biological morality will be: 'Nobody has a right to poison the environment we live in.' This maxim will be illustrated by a list of public enemies. At the top will stand the politicians, scientists, and military men – of whatever country – who make and deploy atomic weapons; for if these are ever used, even in so-called defensive systems like the ABM, the atmosphere will be so contaminated with strontium 90 and other radioactive isotopes that human survival seems most unlikely. Also on the list will be anybody who makes or tests chemical and biological weapons – or who even attempts to get rid of obsolete nerve gas, as the US recently did, by dumping the stuff in the sea.

Only slightly less wicked, our biology professors indicate, is the farmer who drenches his land with DDT. Such insecticides remain virulent indefinitely, and as they wash into the streams and oceans they poison fish, water fowl, and eventually the people who eat them. Worse yet – as John Hay noted in his recently published *In Defense of Nature* – 'The original small, diluted concentrations of these chemicals tend to build up in a food chain so as to end in a concentration that may be thousands of times as strong.' It is rapidly spreading throughout the globe. DDT already has been found in the tissues of Eskimos and of Antarctic penguins, so it seems probable that similar deposits are gradually building up in your body and mine. The minimum fatal dosage is still unknown.

Before he finishes this course, a student may begin to feel tinges of conscience himself. Is his motorcycle exhaust adding carbon monoxide to the smog we breathe? Is his sewage polluting the nearest river? If so, he will be reminded of two proverbs. From Jesus: 'Let him who is without sin among you cast the first stone.' From Pogo: 'We have met the enemy and he is us.'

In like fashion, our engineering students will learn not only how to build dams and highways, but where *not* to build them. Unless they understand that it is immoral to flood Welsh valleys or destroy first class farmland with airports, they will never pass the final exam. Indeed, our engineering graduates will be trained to ask a key question about every contract offered them: 'What will be its effect on human life?' That obviously will lead to other questions which every engineer ought to comprehend as thoroughly as his slide rule. Is this new motorway really necessary? Would it be wiser to use the money for mass transit – or to decongest traffic by building a new city somewhere else?

Our engineering faculty will also specialize in training men for a new growth industry: refuse disposal. In England

and Wales local authorities now collect more than fourteen million tons of house and trade refuse every year at a total annual cost of more than £60 million. On average, each dwelling produces nearly a ton of rubbish a year, and within twenty years this will probably double. The technology of refuse collection and disposal lags far behind the technology producing the things we throw away (including, yearly, some 6,000 million practically indestructible plastic bottles cast out by British housewives). Any industry with an alarming growth rate such as this deserves the specialist attentions of engineers.

Survival U's Department of Earth Sciences will study how fast mankind is using up the world's supply of raw materials. Already we are running short of silver, mercury, tin, and cobalt – all in growing demand by the high-technology industries. Even the commonest metals may soon be in short supply. Industrially advanced countries are consuming anything up to one ton of iron and eighteen pounds of copper every year, for each inhabitant. Poorer countries, struggling to industrialize, hope to raise their consumption of these two key materials to something like that level. If they should succeed – and if the globe's population doubles in the next forty years, as it will at present growth rates – then the world will have to produce, somehow, *twelve times* as much iron and copper every year as it does now. The same thing, of course, goes for other raw materials: timber, oil, natural gas, and water, to note only a few.

Survival U, therefore, will prepare its students to consume less. This does not necessarily mean an immediate drop in living standards – perhaps only a change in the yardstick by which we measure them. Conceivably Britons might be happier with fewer cars, neon signs, beer cans, supersonic jets, and similar metallic fluff. But happy or not, our students had better learn how to live The Simpler Life, because that is what most of them are likely to have before they reach middle age.

To help them understand how very precious resources really are, our mathematics department will teach a new kind of bookkeeping: social accounting. It will train people to analyse budgets – both government and corporate – with an eye not merely to immediate £ s d costs, but to the long-range costs to society.

The University's main goal will be to discover why our institutions have done so badly in their efforts (as Dr Charles F. Falk has put it) 'to manage the affairs of mankind in the twentieth century'. This will be a compulsory course for all first-year students, taught by professors who are capable of looking critically at every political artifact, from the Magna Carta to the local county council. They will start by pointing out that we are living in a state of near-anarchy, because we have no government capable of dealing effect-ively with public problems.

Instead we have nearly 2,000 separate local authorities. Their authority is so limited, and their jurisdictions so con-fused and overlapping, that many of them are virtually impotent. When Whitehall is called to help out – as it in-creasingly has been in recent decades – it often has proved ham-handed and entangled in its own archaic bureaucracy. The end result is that nobody in authority has been able to take care of the country's mounting needs. Our air and water get dirtier, housing gets scarcer, airports jam up, road traffic clots, railways fall apart, prices rise, slums spread.

The advanced students of government at Survival U will try to find out whether these institutions can be renewed and rebuilt. They will take a hard look at proposals for regional government. Looking beyond our borders, our students will be encouraged to ask even harder questions. Are nation-states actually feasible, now that they have power to destroy each other in a single afternoon? Can we agree on some-thing else to take their place, before the balance of terror becomes unstable? What price would most people be willing to pay for a more durable kind of human organization – more taxes, giving up national flags, perhaps the sacrifice of some of our hard-won liberties?

All these courses (and everything else taught at Survival U) are really branches of a single science. Human ecology is one of the youngest disciplines, and probably the most important. It is the study of the relationship between man and his environment, both natural and technological. It teaches us to understand the consequences of our actions – how sulphur-laden fuel oil burned in England produces an acid rain that damages the forests of Scandinavia, why a well-meant farm subsidy can force millions of Negro tenants in the US off the land and lead to race riots. A graduate who comprehends ecology will know how to look at 'what is going on in the world', and he will be equipped to do something about it. Whether he ends up as a city planner, a politician, an enlightened engineer, a teacher, or a reporter, he will have had a relevant education. All of its parts will hang together in a coherent whole.

And if we can get enough such graduates, man and his environment may survive a while longer, against all the odds.

Evolution demonstrates the value of learning from mistakes; so perhaps we can evolve a subservient technology – one that follows man instead of leading him.

David R. Brower

Where Does Responsibility Lie?

Sir Frank Fraser Darling

the final 1969 *Reith Lecture*

The euphoria of landing on the moon has been less hallucinatory than that of the flight of the first man in space. Ten years of this extraordinary way of getting around have almost got rid of the notion that if we wear out, eat up and generally defile our very unusual planet we shall be able to blast off to some other virgin globe. The Earth is our home; it was made ready for the rapid evolution of exploiting man by many millions of years of organic activity. Man had no place in an earlier world.

There may be other planets we can live on, reached in travel time longer than our normal life span, but the chances of our reaching a new world precisely at a time when man could make good use of it are remote. If advanced or even primitive cultures were present, should we employ forthwith the weapon of war to make room for ourselves, or should we exercise our usual unctuous hypocrisy of washing our hands in imaginary soap and water?

We can set aside this kind of day-dreaming and make up our minds that our concern is here on Earth in so far as persistence, nutrition and social wellbeing are our aims. Some economists and organic chemists have forecast the possibilities of extreme densities of human beings on our Earth which is over two-thirds covered by ocean, and assume that a social adjustment in our mentality will evolve as rapidly as our numbers increase. This seems to me unlikely and as an ecologist living on a known Earth now well surveyed from the air, and even minutely by satellites, I am bound to continue thinking in terms of solar energy and photosynthesis by chlorophyll. And I see these not only in terms of possible food production, but in the power of the forest wildernesses to be storage banks and regulators of our vital atmosphere, and our rising to continual awareness of the nobility of wilderness. Mere food plants would not act as such a store, because our bodies would recirculate the products so quickly. Energy flow and recycling is of the essence of organic existence, but there are different rates of flow.

In plain terms, we cannot give up our world to the production of human beings, yet the biggest problems facing the world today are the continuing rise in human population, the continuing rise and diversity of pollution, and finally, the increasing difficulty of preserving examples of the world's natural ecosystems with their species of plants and animals. In so far as the world of man is prepared to concede this last to be a problem at all, its gestures are patronizing and conciliatory rather than actions of prudence in conserving as wilderness those portions of our planet which the ecologists of all men are now making articulate. 'Speak to the earth and it shall teach thee', is the task and reward of the ecologist, but as he learns these truths of the wilderness silently contributing to man's own existence, his knowledge also becomes his sorrow and burden as he sees the wilderness recede.

Increasing population for years ahead is an inevitability; pollution need not increase, and were we ready to accept the idea that technology should use its own inventiveness resolutely to clean up after itself, we could have a healthier and more beautiful world within a reasonable time. There is an ethic of responsibility for the environment which is a growing body of philosophy, but it is not generally understood and it is followed only expediently. I admit to using petrol containing lead, and I fly fifty thousand miles a year. Yet I am supposed to be in the spearhead of thought and action attempting to contain the pollution, and wondering how we can contain the population. I live in my era; I could do no good by following the ultimate misapplication of logic by walking out naked to live by my beliefs, for I should be naked also of many of the skills of the savage in collecting his food and trying to live from a depleted wilderness. Nevertheless, it still does behove me to continue in the field of discovery and probe intellectually into an emergent ethic.

I believe that thought on the problem of population has been too pragmatic, though understandably so. And intellectual change of attitude might take a long time to filter through society, but such change must carry a conviction from within and *a priori*, quite distinct from hope of benefits to be derived.

For many years I have been interested in the pattern of sexual convention in human beings and the phenomenon of reproduction. Though sexual intercourse is still necessary for reproduction, reproduction is not necessarily the desired end of love-making. Religion has often wished to imply that whether desired or not, reproduction should be accepted as a consequence not to be hindered. Even among the many who do not feel that way, and with the great advances in the techniques of contraception, there is insufficient acceptance of the idea that sexuality is something existing in its own right, not to be confused with and clouded by unwanted reproduction. The necessity in our present world problem is to accept sexuality in this way, untrammelled by doubt. The extreme right wing of religion would imply that man should be able to rise above the animal function of sexuality except in the service of reproduction. The extreme left of behaviourism on the other hand would say, of course sexuality is animal and so are we, and therefore we should be free to exercise it as animals.

The animal quality is the common factor in these two views, but I think they are both mistaken. Why not look upon human sexuality as something that is potentially uniquely human? Presumably, the feathers of a bird first developed as a form of insulation against heat and cold. Feathers as a means of flight were an entirely different development, but they still continued to serve the function of insulation. A third entirely different function has developed in the patterns and colourings of feathers which have become means of recognition and of conveying signals as in display and in the almost unison of action in a flying flock. The other functions remain, nevertheless. There is nothing teleological about this, of course, just natural selection upon existing natural equipment. I think human sexuality should be looked upon in this way, that as an adjunct to reproduction was its first function, it is not necessarily its final one.

The phenomenon of human love has been observed for a long time in our history, certainly ever since we had means of conveying our thoughts through the instruments of speech and then writing. The great love stories of the world have a warm place in our hearts, even in periods and cultures where love by equal choice has been uncommon. We do not doubt the existence of love. At its highest, human love is exclusive and absolute, as expressed by Lancelot in his love for Guinevere. He could not go through the act of love with any other woman, even when such an act would have liberated him from captivity to continue his mission to rescue Guinevere, who was about to be burnt. And you will remember the story of the paternity of Galahad, when Elaine had no power over Lancelot until magic was employed to deceive him into thinking Elaine was Guinevere.

Nowadays we profess to believe in falling in love as the basis of marriage. Love as part of the expression of sexuality is the added human function which the act holds above and beyond the reproductive function which should be exercised so rarely. Within the idea, by which I mean the relationship of love between two people which leads to that exclusive state, sexuality should not be restrained but let free for its influence on spiritual development between the sexes. Modern contraceptive technique and the emancipation of woman in our age make possible this emancipation for man and woman together, of reproduction set in its right perspective. I consider the fears sometimes expressed of the dangers of such freedom becoming available to the adolescent as being quite prurient. Leave them alone, with the example of parents in love.

If our culture learned the potential quality of human sexuality as part of its very being, it would be more helpful in the world at large where population control is even more urgent than it is here. It is time that church and behaviourism dropped the 'animal' connotation and thought more of the uniquely human potential of developed sexuality not bound up with reproduction. The sexual act between lovers is of the very essence of unselfishness. The rare intention to conceive would then be approached as a sacrament of joy, rather than the possibility of conception being feared as the cloud of so many lives.

I have heard it said that the constant sexual desire of humanity is one of the crosses we bear. I would rather consider it the other way round as one of our greatest potential gifts. Over thirty years ago the anthropologist J. D. Unwin wrote of the drive of peoples in which there was apparent greater restriction of sexual freedom. The Epicurean and the Stoic would agree with that, and so would I, if restriction comes from within and is not imposed from without, because the spiritual force of human sexuality is within love and compassion and the naturally exclusive ideal. Within these restrictions there can be no over-indulgence because the individual appetite takes care of that. The human being ennobled by the sexual selflessness of love is ready to be the servant of his world. Promiscuity is dissipation of creative force.

An ethic of sexuality joined with an ethic of the wholeness of life, giving us a reverence for lowlier forms, and reacting on population growth or limitation, should influence the attitudes of the West towards our exploitation of land and animal life. We are degrading animals in our day by the methods of reproduction and rearing we are now employing. De-beaked hens, cooped-up calves fed on antibiotics, and our growing denial of the personal association to our domesticated animals, which is their right if we domesticate them, constitutes degradation not only of the animals but of ourselves. On these systems individual keepers of animals are not thinking in terms of starving millions but of profits easiest gotten; our acceptance from our positions of remoteness encourages these practices and so does governmental acquiescence, because governments really are fearful about what starving millions might do. When I read in a scientific journal of a bull in its brutish decency ultimately declining to serve the canvas cow and the rubber tube, and having to

109

be chased round a paddock with a stick to make it do so, I say that civilization is failing. Artificial insemination of cattle can be a force for good, but bulls should not be brought to a state of revulsion, to give us our 'pintaday' and all that. All governments should boldly face their responsibility to work out population and nutritional policies, not play the opposite game of subsidizing irresponsibly reproductive families. Is vote-catching to be the incurable weakness of democracy?

There is the third ethic of the land, our responsibility for the environment of the human species now and in the future. Such qualified pessimism as I have voiced in these lectures allows no relaxation in our care for the face of the planet in a problematic future. Care of the wilderness is part of that environmental conservation in which we now include the human being. The exclusion of man from the hierarchy of nature, so common in the past and even in our own time, is to put him in the position of a bourgeois *rentier*, living off an economy but having no responsibility for it. To make him an integrated functional member of the plant and animal world about us is no denigration of his high estate, no assumption of a mealy-mouthed egalitarian folksiness. Rather does man accept his position in nature as the species granted the privilege of fulfilling the aristocratic ideal of *noblesse oblige*, of being the servant of his people.

This is our responsibility towards the Earth and its denizens. We shall doubtless make honest mistakes in our exercise of service, but that is where research itself is no luxury, only one part of the fulfilment of our obligation. I have expressed my doubts whether we shall have a long posterity if we continue as we are doing, living off the capital of the world's ecosystems that evolved long before we were consciously men, throwing our poisonous refuse into air and water arrogantly as well as in ignorance. In the fulfilment of our humanity we should act as if posterity stretched into infinitude, and by thus acting we shall make this more possible. We know that the evolution of our species probably rests now in the psychological and, as I believe, in the spiritual sphere, and we have so far to go. When the apo-

110

cryphal Middle-West farmer contributing by his practices to the eventual dust-bowl said, 'Posterity never did nothin' fer me', he was indeed turning his back on the evolutionary potential of his species, selling his birthright for a mess of pottage. We have seen in recent years a deep questioning of the attitude that natural riches are there for the exploitation of man. A less anthropocentric philosophy of restraint, of identification with, rather than exclusion from, nature is developing its own ethic of love.

If we accept the philosophy of respect for life with its view that organisms exist in their own right as fellow members with us in the world community of living things, we must be guided constantly by the discipline of ecological observation, otherwise we are in danger of being rather silly. Man as an omnivore becoming philosophically a hyper-vegetarian does not reach his own ideals when he swallows lowly and invisible organisms on his lettuce, and the Jain bent double peering at the ground before each step lest he should kill anything, would needs eyes of an order not granted to us to see the still smaller creatures in his way. There is no room in our philosophy of responsibility for preciousness. We tread and eat and live as man, prepared to kill if the necessity or inevitability is there, but not for fun.

The American ecologist Aldo Leopold was in my opinion the clearest exponent of an emergent ethic of the land. He said, 'That land is a community is the basic concept of ecology, but that land is to be loved and respected is an extension of ethics ... We abuse land because we regard it as commodity belonging to us. When we see land as a community to which we belong, we may begin to use it with love and respect.'

The form and style of the land is part of our environment as surely as the community of living things. Landscape is near and touching to some of us, a constant and urgent concern as of someone we love. To others it does not seem to have this quality. You remember the Yorkshireman's comment on seeing the Lake District in an earlier day – 'There's nowt 'ere but scenery.' Yet even if not of conscious concern

111

to enough people, landscape is of importance. The reciprocation of conscious concern is of the very nature of love, which is essential to all human relationship.

Perpetuation of a derelict landscape as a background to children's lives is like rearing them to some extent in lovelessness, even if a rusting motorcar body does provide a lot of fun. Sometimes when I see examples of presumed art made up from the scrap-iron dump and hear music not unlike the sound of a tin can being kicked down some sunless alley, I feel that perhaps this is what must happen to the sensitive child reared in the industrial miasma. They have to express themselves and this is how they express the upwelling of art, having no sense of season, flower, or flow; there are only staccato skylines and cacophony and an outraged Earth.

By definition landscape architecture carries the connotation of artifact. If man enters into landscape at all he is influencing and reshaping it. If he merely exploits a landscape he is almost certainly degrading it and making it less beautiful. If he lives with it as a husbandman calling it home, he will almost unconsciously produce many of the rural landscapes and small towns of Europe which we find pleasing and which we know to be biologically productive. Sometimes landscapes have been engineered, but rarely of more than a few hundred acres in extent. Most of these we find pleasant, but they were made for the favoured few. We have now reached a point in time when we can deduce the history of land, and in so far as the land use has been deleterious we have sufficient ecological knowledge to architect the landscape on a regional plan for biological productivity and the content of man. Human tastes vary, but all in all the most general consensus of beautiful landscape would be found to be that which is in ecological repose or near to it.

Ian McHarg, a Scotsman who found freedom to work and develop his thought in America, has become an outstanding voice in this field, a highly individual one trying always to justify his ecological planning of landscape by return to basic principles of interrelationships and interdependencies within the site. The placement of buildings and their design, in following ecological principles, can so often be justified aesthetically. Whether we are conscious of it or not as subsequent observers, most of us find this kind of landscape architecture to be satisfying. The odd and the idiosyncratic rarely give content, and the bull-at-a-gatepost method of carving a landscape usually ends up in real trouble. McHarg's new book, *Design with Nature*, is at once a testament of belief backed by well-chosen case histories, and a thing of beauty in itself.

I have said little of the wilderness as a place where such men as can should spend their forty days alone or with a companion. This is a time for re-creation of the spirit for which too few men find opportunity. Whether it is forest, mountain or desert is immaterial as long as the wilderness is not a man-degraded one of recent time. I do not wish to dwell on this aspect because the fulfilment of it is the priviledge of the few and I have an uneasy feeling deep down that we should not burden the wilderness with this egocentric human purpose. The wilderness does not exist *for* our re-creation or delectation. This is something we gain from its great function of being, with the oceans part of the guardianship of the world in which we have come so recently to be a denizen.

The true natural wilderness from which we have carved our precarious plenty cannot be re-created in our time, possibly never. But that which we have taken from the wilderness we can treat with gratitude and responsibility. The full awareness of what man has done in creating dereliction and squalor has only come in our time. There has also come the knowledge of how to cope with it. The great earth-moving machines of our technological era can make some return by fashioning pleasances from these depressing landscapes.

Some of the pit heaps in the North of England, of Durham and Northumberland, are becoming wooded hills. They will not be true wilderness but places that the folk of the villages can reach in an afternoon or evening. The dark landscapes of industrial Wales, Glamorgan and the Rhondda, may disappear if a recommendation of local

113

bodies is implemented. The designers have planned 'a radically changed physical environment, with extensive forests clothing the mountains, and substantial areas of new development and rehabilitation'. The designers have consulted with the Forestry Commission, the Agricultural Land Service, the Derelict Land Unit, the National Coal Board, and the Nature Conservancy. Once again, in a country in which land is getting scarcer, there is a realization of the need for multiple use. It would seem that the land ethic has taken root in this place of so much suffering in the past. Those who create dereliction in our day in the brickfields and iron ore deposits in the Midlands should see what poorer folk are doing or trying to do, till eventually we could expect plain shame to be enough to efface previous dereliction and prevent new areas. The birds and wild flowers are the natural opportunists ready to people and enrich the new acceptable environments. Such, I repeat, is the therapy of the green leaf.

The British are but one nation concerned among so many. As part of a world movement of conservation and rehabilitation, linked with a positive population policy, we could have a changed industrial scene within a generation – and we have not more than that in which to do it. There can be no greater moral obligation in the environmental field than to ease out the living space and replace dereliction by beauty. Most people will never know true wilderness although its existence will not be a matter of indifference to them. The near landscape is valuable and lovable because of its nearness, not something to be disregarded and shrugged off; it is where children are reared and what they take away in their minds to their long future. What ground could be more hallowed?

PART TWO:

ENVIRONMENT — SOME THREATS AND ALTERNATIVES

... The need is not really for more brains, the need is now for a gentler, a more tolerant people than those who won for us against the ice, the tiger, and the bear. The hand that hefted the axe, out of some old blind allegiance to the past, fondles the machine gun as lovingly. It is a habit man will have to break to survive, but the roots go very deep.

Loren Eiseley

We have got into the doubling habit. We think that we must double our production of energy every ten years, for example, to satisfy our needs for convenience. If we assume that we are on a highway doubling our speed every ten seconds, we have an idea of what doubling does. If you go from one to two miles per hour and from two to four and from four to eight, it doesn't matter; you hardly notice it. When you go from eight to sixteen, you don't notice that too much either. But you are now at the maximum speed man can sustain with his own energy. Another doubling and you reach the top speed of a horse. Double that and you get the maximum speed attainable by natural energy on the planet, the cheetah's speed of about 64 mph. Now, double again – and you have been doubling now for only about a minute – and you are up to 128 mph, which is figuratively about the speed at which we are racing through our resources. If you are going 128 mph on the highway, you should have your hands – both hands – firmly on the wheel. You should be looking ahead quite intently. You should be feeling a little tense, and you should be hearing sirens. I think that is what we are hearing.

David R. Brower

Mankind's Inalienable Rights

Paul R. Ehrlich

from *The Population Bomb*

1. The right to limit our families.
2. The right to eat.
3. The right to eat meat.
4. The right to drink pure water.
5. The right to live uncrowded.
6. The right to avoid regimentation.
7. The right to hunt and fish.
8. The right to view natural beauty.
9. The right to breathe clean air.
10. The right to silence.
11. The right to avoid pesticide poisoning.
12. The right to be free of thermonuclear war.
13. The right to educate our children.
14. The right to have grandchildren.
15. The right to have great-grandchildren.

The Rape of our Environment

Edward J. Mishan

from *The Spectator*

There may have been a time when the Englishman's home was his castle. If so, it was before the middle of the twentieth century. About that time he began to discover that he could be bombarded with noise from aircraft overhead, from passing traffic, and from his neighbour's motorized garden machinery, without any practical means of redress.

Of course, it happens innocently enough. Machines that are employed to produce services for some, simultaneously produce 'disservices' for others. The recipients of the services acknowledge their value by a willingness to pay for these services. Symmetrical reasoning would require that the recipients of the disservices should receive payment for absorbing these disservices. Things have not worked out this way, however. It is true that such nice calculations would not matter much in a society with only rudimentary technology and an abundance of land relative to its population: but this is not the condition of Britain today. With the postwar growth of technology and population these disservices or 'spillover effects' – the noise, smell, smoke pollution or other noxious by-products of the operation of industry or their products – have become too conspicuous to be ignored any longer by civilized countries.

They range from the strangulation by traffic of cities, resorts and once-quiet hamlets to the extermination of wildlife by the indiscriminate use of pesticides; from ubiquitous jets to the spreading plague of beach transistors; from the destruction by mass tourism of the world's dwindling resources of natural beauty to the neighbour's petrol lawnmower. Indeed, together these spillover effects represent the most outstanding example of postwar growth yet recorded.

What, then, can be done to check this accelerating trend and, perhaps, to reverse it? I suggest that we might explore two alternative, though related, approaches to the problem: (1) the enactment of 'amenity rights', and (2) the extension to environmental areas of the concept of separate facilities.

The competitive market has long been regarded by economists as an inexpensive mechanism for allocating goods and services with tolerable efficiency. It may seem to have failed badly when the production of goods began to be accompanied by the production of 'bads' or noxious spillover effects. But the failure is not to be attributed so much to the mechanism of the market as to the legal framework within which it operates. In particular, we must remind ourselves that what constitutes a cost to commercial enterprise depends upon the law. If the law recognized slavery the costs of labour would be no greater than the costs involved in capturing a man and maintaining him thereafter at subsistence level.

How, then, can the law be altered so as to remove existing inequities and, at the same time, to recognize the simple economic fact that privacy and quiet and clean air are scarce goods – far scarcer than they were before the war – and sure to become scarcer in the foreseeable future? Clearly, if the world were so fashioned that clean air and quiet took on a physically identifiable form, and one that allowed it to be transferred as between people, we should be able to observe whether a man's share of the stuff had been appropriated or damaged, and we should be able to institute proceedings accordingly. The fact that the universe has not been very accommodating in this respect does not in the least detract from the principle of justice involved or from the principle of economy regarding the treatment of scarce goods. One has but to imagine a country in which men were invested by law with property rights in privacy, quiet and clean air – simple things, but for many indispensable to the enjoyment of life – to recognize that the extent of the compensatory payments that would perforce accompany the operation of industries, motorized traffic and airlines would constrain many of them to close down or to operate at levels far below those which would prevail in the absence of such a law, at least until industry and transport discovered economical ways of controlling their own noxious by-products.

The consequence of recognizing such rights in one form or another, let us call them amenity rights, would be far-reaching. Such innovations as the invisible electronic bugging devices currently popular in the US among people eager to 'peep in' on other people's conversations could be legally prohibited in recognition of such rights. The case against their use would rest simply on the fact that the users of such devices would be unable to compensate the victims, including all the potential victims, for living in a state of unease or anxiety. So humble an invention as the petrol-powered lawn-mower, and other petrol-driven garden implements, would come also into conflict with such rights. The din produced by any one man is invariably heard by dozens of families – who, of course, may be enthusiastic gardeners also; if they are all satisfied with the current situation or could come to agreement with one another, well and good. But once amenity rights were legally enacted, at least no man could be forced against his will to absorb these noxious by-products of the activity of others.

Admittedly, there are difficulties whenever actual compensation payments have to be made, say, to thousands of families disturbed by aircraft noise. Yet once the principle of amenity rights is recognized in law, a rough estimate of the magnitude of compensation payments necessary to maintain the welfare of the number of families affected would be entered as a matter of course into the social cost calculus. And unless these compensatory payments could also be somehow covered by the proceeds of the air service, there would be no *prima facie* case for maintaining the air service. If, on the other hand, compensatory payments could be made (and their payment costs the company less than any technical device that would effectively eliminate the noise) some method of compensation must be devised.

It is true that the courts, from time to time, have enunciated the doctrine that in the ordinary pursuit of industry a reasonable amount of inconvenience must be borne with. The recognition of amenity rights, however, does no more than impose an economic interpretation on the word 'reasonable', and therefore also on the word 'unreasonable', by transferring the cost of the inconvenience on to the shoulders of those who cause it. If by actually compensating the victims – or by paying to eliminate the disamenity by the cheapest technical method available – an existing service cannot be continued (because the market is unwilling to pay the increased cost) then the inconvenience that is currently being borne with is to be deemed unreasonable. And since those who cause the inconvenience are now compelled to shoulder the increased costs, there should be no trouble in convincing them that the inconvenience is unreasonable nor, therefore, in withdrawing the service in question.

A law recognizing this principle would have drastic effects on industry and commerce, which for too long have neglected the damage inflicted on society at large in producing their wares. For many decades now firms have, without giving it a thought, polluted the air we breathe, poisoned lakes and rivers with their effluence, and produced gadgets that have destroyed the quiet of millions of families, gadgets that range from motorized lawn-mowers and motorcycles to transistors and private planes. What is being proposed therefore may be regarded as *an alteration of the legal framework within which private firms operate in order to direct their enterprise towards ends that accord more closely with the interests of society*. More specifically, it would provide industry with the incentive necessary to undertake prolonged research into methods of removing the potential amenity-destroying features of so many of today's existing products and services.

The social advantage of enacting legislation embodying amenity rights is further reinforced by a consideration of the regressive nature of many of these external diseconomies. The rich have legal protection of their property and have less need, at present, of protection from the disamenity created by others. The richer a man is, the wider his choice of neighbourhood. If the area he happened to choose appears to be sinking in the scale of amenity, he can move, if at some inconvenience, to a quieter area. He can select a suitable town house, secluded perhaps, or made soundproof throughout, and spend his leisure in the country or abroad at times of his own choosing. *Per contra*, the poorer the family the less opportunity there is for moving from its present locality. To all intents it is stuck in the area and must put up with whatever disamenity is inflicted upon it.

And, generalizing from the experience of the last ten years or so, one may depend upon it that it will be the neighbourhoods of the working and lower middle classes that will suffer most from the increased construction of fly-overs and fly-unders and road-widening schemes intended to speed up the accumulating road traffic that all but poisons the air. Thus the recognition of amenity rights has favourable distributive effects also. It would promote not only a rise in the standards of environment generally: it would raise them most for the lower-income groups that have suffered more than any other group from unchecked 'development' and the growth of motorized traffic since the war.

There is an alternative to reaching mutually satisfying arrangements *within* a given area. It is that of providing *separate* areas for groups having conflicting interests. Even if it then transpired, which I doubt, that people who place a high value on clean air, quiet, and a pleasant environment are in a minority in this country, the principle of amenity rights still warrants the creation of separate areas.

Any government at all concerned with the welfare of its citizens could not excuse itself from making a start and planning for large residential areas through which no motorized traffic is permitted to pass and over which no aircraft is permitted to fly, or from prohibiting motor-boats on the lakes in certain districts, and traffic in general from such lake districts. Municipalities should be able to make a start by providing stretches of beach free from transistor noise (while, of course, freely allowing it along other parts of the beach), by keeping motor traffic away from certain shopping areas, from narrow roads, from cathedral precincts and other places of beauty or historic interest that can be enjoyed only in a quiet traffic-free setting.

Decent residential areas could be set aside for those 'backward-looking' people who would be glad to abolish the use of all engines outside the home and for eccentrics who would prefer to dwell in areas admitting only horses and horse-drawn vehicles as means of transport. It they are prepared to pay for it – and there is no reason why any such arrangement should cost more to operate, rather than less, compared with existing modern arrangements – there is no advantage to the rest of the country in depriving them of their wants. In between there should be a wide variety, some areas having no more than large pedestrian precincts, or traffic-free shopping islands, to distinguish them, others permitting only public transport or electrically-powered transport on their roads, others yet prohibiting all types of motorized vehicles, or prohibiting them between certain hours, and many of them refusing airline compensation in order to remain free from aerial disturbance.

With almost all the convenient and desirable areas close to the metropolis and many other desirable towns and villages already shaped for a motorized society, heavy capital costs may have to be incurred in 'reconverting' suitable places to amenity areas. In conformity with the principles laid down, however, if the value to potential inhabitants of any such amenity area – estimated as the minimum sum required to compensate them in foregoing their legal rights to amenity – exceeds the capital costs of converting the area, social welfare and equity is advanced in creating such an area.

Business economists have ever been glib in equating economic growth with an expansion of the range of choices facing the individual; they have failed to observe that as the carpet of 'increased choice' is being unrolled before us by the foot, it is simultaneously being rolled up behind us by the yard. In all that contributes in trivial ways to his ultimate satisfaction, the things at which modern business excels – new models of cars and transistors, prepared foodstuffs and plastic *objets d'art*, electric boot brushes and an increasing range of push-button gadgets – man has ample choice. In all that directly destroys his enjoyment of life, he has none.

In sum, then, an extension of choice in respect of environment is the one really significant contribution to social welfare that is immediately feasible. As suggested, however, it is not likely to be brought about by market forces working within the given legal framework. Legal recognition of amenity rights, on the other hand, would touch off government, and private, initiative in creating a wide diversity of residential environment offering to all men those vital choices that have too long been denied them.

Energy

Garrett De Bell

All power pollutes.

Each of the major forms of power generation does its own kind of harm to the environment. Fossil fuels – coal and oil – produce smoke and sulphur dioxide at worst; even under ideal conditions they convert oxygen to carbon dioxide. Hydroelectric power requires dams that cover up land, spoil wild rivers, increase water loss by evaporation, and eventually produce valleys full of silt. Nuclear power stations produce thermal and radioactive pollution and introduce the probability of disaster.

We are often told that it is essential to increase the amount of energy we use in order to meet demand. This 'demand', we are told, must be met in order to increase or maintain our 'standard of living'. What these statements mean is that if population continues to increase, and if *per capita* power continues to increase as in the past, the power generation facilities must be increased indefinitely.

Such statements ignore the environmental consequences of building more and more power generation facilities. They ignore the destruction of wild rivers by dams, the air pollution by power stations: the visual outrage of more and more giant pylons striding across the countryside (there are now more than 50,000 pylons in England and Wales), the increasing danger of disease and disaster from nuclear power facilities.

These effects can no longer be ignored, but must be directly confronted. *The perpetually accelerating expansion of power output is not necessary.*

It is assumed by the power suppliers that the demand for power is real because people continue to purchase it. However, we are all bombarded with massive amounts of advertising encouraging us to buy appliances, gadgets, new cars, and so on. There is no comparable public service advertising

127

pointing up the harmful effects of over-purchase of 'convenience' appliances that increase use of power. The electricity, gas and coal boards aggressively advertise to encourage increasing use of power. For instance, we are all implored to buy more and yet more luxury electrical appliances for our homes. The unbeautifying results of building more power stations is, of course, not mentioned – and already, in England and Wales, there are well over 200 stations supplying well over 160,000 million kWh's a year.

But perhaps it is unrealistic to expect the power suppliers and the appliance and car builders to call a halt, to flatly say, 'This is where we stop. The limits have been reached, even exceeded.' The limits can, and must, be set by the consumer. It is the consumer, ultimately, who must decide for himself what appliances he needs and which he can forego. The producers of power and power-using appliances will feel the pinch but they will, ultimately, cease to produce that which will not *sell*.

We *can* control our population and thus decrease our *per capita* use of power. Population may be stabilized, and use of power reduced to what is necessary for a high quality of life. But population control will take time. We can begin now by ceasing to use power for trivial purposes.

We must decide which uses improve the quality of people's lives sufficiently to justify the inevitable pollution that results from power generation and use.

The term 'standard of living' as used in Britain today generally means abundant luxuries, such as the following, for the affluent: electric blenders, power saws and mowers, luxury cars, electric clothes dryers and kitchen refuse grinders, electric blankets, and hair dryers.

Are these necessary for a high quality of life? We must realize that a decision made to purchase one of these 'conveniences' is also a decision to accept the environmental deterioration that results from the production, use, and disposal of the 'convenience'. Hand-operated blenders and saws, clotheslines, blankets, bicycles, and feet produce much less pollution than the powered equivalents.

We can make the ecologically sensible decision to reject

the concept of increasing perpetually the 'standard of living' regardless of the human or ecological consequences. We can replace the outmoded industrial imperative – the 'standard of living' concept – by the more human 'quality of life' concept.

Many of us feel that the quality of our lives would be higher with far less use of energy in this country. We would be happy to do with fewer cars, substituting a transportation system that can make us mobile without dependence on the expensive, polluting, and dangerous car. We would be happy to see the last of neon signs, noisy power mowers, infernally noisy motorcycles. The quality of our lives is improved by each power station not constructed near our homes or in areas of outstanding beauty. Quality of life is a positive ethic. Peace and quiet and fresh air are positive values; noisy smoking machines are negative ones.

If you wanted to design a transportation system to waste the earth's energy reserves and pollute the air as much as possible, you couldn't do much better than our present system dominated by the car. Only by following the advice of the popular science journals, placing in every garage a helicopter (using three times as much petrol per passenger mile as a car) could you manage to do greater environmental damage.

Compared to a bus, the car uses from four to five times as much fuel per passenger mile. Compared to a train, it uses ten times as much. Walking and bicycling, of course, require no fuel at all.

Switching from cars to a system of rapid transit, with more bicycling and walking in cities, would reduce fossil fuel consumption for transportation by a factor of almost 10. Added benefits would be fewer deaths and injuries by cars, which have much higher injury rates than any form of public transportation; the liberation of much of the cities' space presently dedicated to the car; and less air pollution.

The term 'standard of living' usually seems to apply only to people in the affluent nations and usually just to the present generation. It is important to think of all people in the world, and of future generations. The question must be asked whether it is fair to the rest of the world for the affluent societies to use up such a disproportionate share of the world's energy resources.

Not only does the burning of fossil fuels produce local pollution, but it also increases the carbon dioxide-to-oxygen ratio in the atmosphere. This occurs because each molecule of oxygen consumed in burning fuels results in the production of a carbon dioxide molecule (CH_2O plus O_2 yields CO_2 plus H_2O). This has the doubly adverse effect of taking oxygen out of the atmosphere, and putting carbon dioxide in, in equal amounts. The latter effect is of most concern to us because the CO_2 percentage in the atmosphere is minute compared to the huge reservoir of oxygen. While the atmosphere contains 20 per cent oxygen, it has only 0.02 per cent CO_2. Thus, fuel combustion reducing the O_2 concentration by only 1 per cent would simultaneously increase the CO_2 concentration *tenfold*.

Each year the burning of fossil fuels produces an amount of carbon dioxide equal to about 0.5 per cent of the existing carbon dioxide reservoir in the atmosphere. Of this production, half stays in the atmosphere, resulting in a 0.25 per cent increase in atmosphere CO_2 per year. Of the other half, some becomes bound up with calcium or magnesium to become limestone, some becomes dissolved in the sea, and some is stored as the bodies of plants that fall to the deep, oxygen-poor sediments of the ocean and do not decompose.

If no CO_2 were being disposed of by the physical and biological processes in the ocean, then the CO_2 concentration of the atmosphere would increase by twice the present rate, because all of the CO_2 produced each year would remain in the atmosphere.

Burning all the recoverable reserves of fossil fuels would produce three times as much carbon dioxide as is now present in the atmosphere. If the present rate of increase in fuel use continues, and the rate of CO_2 dispersal continues unchanged, there will be an increase of about 170 per cent in the CO_2 level in the next 150 years (which is the minimum estimate of the amount of time our fossil fuels will last). If the fuels last longer, say up to the 'optimistic' 400 years that some predict, we will have that much more CO_2 increase, with the attendant smog and oil spills.

Scientists are becoming worried about increasing CO_2 levels because of the greenhouse effect, with its possible repercussions on the world climate. Most of the sun's energy striking the earth's surface is in the form of visible and ultraviolet rays from the sun. Energy leaves the earth as heat radiation or infrared rays. Carbon dioxide absorbs infrared rays more strongly than visible or ultraviolet rays. Energy coming towards the earth's surface thus readily passes through atmospheric carbon dioxide, but some escaping heat energy is absorbed and trapped in the atmosphere by carbon dioxide, much as heat is trapped in a greenhouse. This effect of carbon dioxide on the earth's climate has, in fact, been called the 'greenhouse effect'. Scientists differ in their opinions as to the eventual result this will have on our climate. Some believe that the earth's average temperature will increase, resulting in the melting of polar ice caps with an accompanying increase of sea levels and inundation of coastal cities. Others feel that there will be a temporary warming and partial melting of polar ice, but then greater evaporation from the open Arctic seas will cause a vast increase in snowfall, with an ensuing ice age.

Many people believe that green plants can produce a surplus of oxygen to compensate for that converted to CO_2 in burning fuels. This is not true. A plant produces only enough oxygen for its own use during its life plus enough extra for the oxidation of the plant after death to its original buildings blocks (CO_2 plus H_2O). Whether this oxidation occurs by fire, by bacterial decay, or by respiration of an animal eating the plant, has no effect on the ultimate outcome. When the plant is totally consumed by any of these three means, all of the oxygen it produced over its life is also consumed. The only way a plant leaves an oxygen surplus is if it fails to decompose, a relatively rare occurrence.

The important point is that fossil fuel combustion results in a change in the ratio of carbon dioxide to oxygen in the atmosphere, whereas use of oxygen by animals does not. This point is not generally understood, so two examples are discussed below.

First, since 70 per cent of the world's oxygen is produced in the ocean, it has been forecast that death of the plankton in the ocean would cause asphyxiation of the animals of the earth. This is not the case because oxygen and carbon dioxide cycle in what is called the carbon cycle. A plant, be it a redwood tree or an algal cell, produces just enough oxygen to be used in consuming its carcass after death. The ocean plankton now produce 70 per cent of the oxygen, but animals in the ocean use it up in the process of eating the plants. Very little of it is left over. The small amount that is left over is produced by plankton that have dropped to the oxygen-poor deep sediments and are essentially forming new fossil fuel.

If the plankton in the ocean were all to die tomorrow, all the animals in the ocean would starve. The effect of this on the world's oxygen supply would be very small. The effect on the world's food supply, however, would be catastrophic. A large number of nations rely significantly on the ocean for food, particularly for high-quality protein. Japan, for example, is very heavily dependent on fisheries to feed itself.

'Eco-catastrophe!' by Paul Ehrlich (see page 205), stresses the danger of poisoning plankton, and puts the emphasis where it belongs, on the effect on animal life.

Second, fears about reducing the world's oxygen supply have been expressed in reference to the cutting down of large forest areas, particularly in the tropics, where the soil will become hardened into bricklike laterite and no plant growth of any sort will be possible in the future. It will be a disaster if the Amazon rain forest is turned into laterite because the animals and people dependent on it could not exist. But this would have no effect on the world's oxygen balance. If the Amazon Basin were simply bricklike laterite, the area would produce no oxygen and consume no oxygen. At present the Amazon Basin is not producing surplus organic material. The same amount of organic material is present in the form of animal bodies, trees, stumps, and humus from year to year; therefore no net production of oxygen exists. The oxygen produced in the forest each year, which obviously is a large amount, is used up by the animals and microorganisms living in the forest in the consumption of the plant material produced over the preceding year.

In summary, I suggest that one goal of the environmental movement should be the reduction of total energy use in the highly developed countries by as much as 25 per cent over the next decade. By doing this, we will have made a start towards preventing possibly disastrous climatic changes due to CO_2 buildup and the greenhouse effect. We will so reduce the need for oil that we can leave Alaska as wilderness and its oil in the ground. We will be able to stop offshore drilling with its ever-present probability of oil slick disasters, and won't need new supertankers which can spill more oil than the *Torrey Canyon* dumped on the beaches of Britain and France. We will be able to do without the risks of disease and accident from nuclear power plants. And perhaps most important, we can liberate the people from the car, whose exhausts turn the air over our cities oily brown and which is turning our landscape into a sea of concrete.

Many of the steps needed to reduce energy consumption are clear. We can press for:

1. A substantial proportion of motor vehicle and petrol tax money to go to public transport, not more roads for cars.
2. More bicycle and footpaths.
3. Better rail services.
4. A premium on conserving resources. Give householders power for essential needs at cost, with heavy rate increases for extra energy for luxuries.

Man, Pesticides and Wildlife

Kenneth Mellanby

from *Pesticides and Pollution*

The disappearance of all pesticides would profoundly affect British agriculture, but substantial crops of various kinds could still be produced. In many parts of the world, including North America, and the tropics, the situation is different. There it is common for pests and disease to render a crop a total loss; we are almost always able to salvage something. It is not surprising, therefore, that we have escaped some of the worst side-effects of the use, and abuse, of dangerous pesticides.

The importance of weedkillers to wildlife is that they may profoundly change the habitat. MCPA and similar substances used on arable crops have minimal effects, provided care is taken to avoid damage from spray drift. As these herbicides have only replaced hand-weeding, their use is generally accepted. The real danger of herbicides is that they are so efficient. It has become so much easier to clean up patches of rough ground and scrub, which may now be important wildlife sanctuaries. With labour costs too high to continue hand-cutting of roadside verges, cheaper measures are being introduced. Here weedkillers may not always be the worst solution, but much more study is needed. The use of Paraquat to improve rough grazing is a typical case of a relatively harmless susbstance which can be used to do great damage. Here, as in so many other situations, we have to decide just what we want to preserve. In the past this has been left to chance. We even have one government department paying a subsidy to a farmer to spray and cultivate an area which another department is trying to preserve in its original state. Without efficient herbicides the risk of damage is very much less, so some sort of control is needed even of substances which are not, technically, poisons, if wildlife preservation is to succeed.

Insecticides are the substances which have caused most concern in Britain, and throughout the world. These are all, by definition, poisonous to insects, and they are, to a lesser or greater degree, poisonous to other animals also. In the past there have been unpleasant incidents clearly implicating the more toxic organo-phosphorous insecticides, but the substances in this group now in common use are much less poisonous to vertebrates and probably do them little harm. They are easily decomposed, and do not yield long persisting toxic residues. The search for more selective organo-phosphorus compounds continues, with some success, as does also the discovery of insecticides with some persistence (perhaps for a season) but which do not cause environmental pollution which lasts for years.

There is one thing which may delay the discovery of really selective insecticides. Such subtances, effective against a single pest and otherwise harmless, may be discovered. They will, by their very desirable qualities, have a very limited market, while a 'broad spectrum' insecticide useful against many pests (and lethal to many animals which are not pests) will sell in far greater quantities. Most of our insecticide research has been done by industry. It may cost a million pounds to develop a new compound to the stage when it is marketed; a great deal must be sold to recover this cost. It is likely that in future very much greater sums of government money will have to be spent on pesticide research if more selective, and less profitable, substances are to be made available.

It is the persistent organo-chlorines that are the villains of the piece. There are well authenticated reports of serious incidents affecting vast numbers of birds in America and other parts of the world, where DDT, dieldrin, and several other substances have been implicated. Not only have many individual birds been killed, but also various species have been eliminated from large areas and some are in serious danger of extinction. In Britain we have, on the whole, been more fortunate. Until we stopped using dieldrin-dressed seed in spring, great numbers of birds were poisoned and died, but since 1961 this cause of death has been very greatly reduced. We have good evidence to show that several predatory birds have been seriously affected.

The main worry caused by the persistent organo-chlorine insecticides is that they have polluted not only all of Britain, but the whole of the world. It is difficult if not impossible to find a field in England which does not contain a detectable amount of pesticide, or a bird or mammal without residues in its tissues. There is no doubt that many have greatly exaggerated the danger of this pollution. Most of the residues are so low that their discovery is a credit to the chemist rather than a menace to wildlife. Nevertheless, residues at a toxic level *are* found, commonly in raptorial birds, not infrequently in other species. The general level of contamination is high enough to warrant concern, particularly as concentration of a persistent chemical is always possible. For radiation, a lower level of general pollution for the population is accepted than is tolerated for the few individuals who are at risk from their employment in the industry. For pesticides, we should similarly be concerned about any general increase in pollution even if this does not necessarily damage particular individuals. Ecologists in particular are concerned about this general pollution. They point out that effects in the field cannot be fully foretold by a study of toxicological data. This is of course true, but ecology is still such an inexact science that none of us can be dogmatic, and the need for more research is constantly being revealed.

Some writers have suggested that low levels of pollution, particularly with pesticides, may endanger the health of the individual by causing cancer and the health of the species by affecting its genetical make-up. It is true that some pesticides are related, chemically, to known carcinogens, but there is no evidence that any widely used pesticide, applied in the proper way, ever causes cancer. Nevertheless, this risk must always be borne in mind. The dangers of long-term exposure to apparently harmless radiation levels proved far greater than had been expected by the experts, and on an analogy with this we will not know until too late whether exposure to a few parts per million for twenty years of DDT or other apparently harmless chemical has had some damaging effect.

The best way to reduce possible environmental damage from pesticides is to reduce their use to a minimum. In this connexion, great importance is placed on the use of 'Biological Control'. This term covers a great many processes. To some it means primarily the use of beneficial insects, predators and parasites which keep pest numbers down and so reduce or prevent damage. It also covers the use of insect diseases, or various techniques to induce sterility or upset sexual behaviour and cultural methods which make crops unattractive. Emphasis is also put on 'integrated control'; this means different things to different scientists, but in general implies a combination of chemical and biological methods, with, if possible, the minimum use of toxic pesticides.

Biological control has had its spectacular successes: these have so often been described that I need only mention the subject briefly. The citrus scale insect, introduced from Australia to California, was ruining the industry. An Australian ladybird beetle, which fed on the scale insect, was transported to California and gave complete control. This was effective until insecticide sprays (for other pests, not controlled by the ladybird) killed so many ladybirds that the scale again achieved pest numbers. The prickly pear, introduced to Australia from America, was a troublesome weed in pasture. A caterpillar from America wiped it out almost completely. These two instances are typical examples. A pest, or a weed, is introduced into a new habitat without bringing the insects which keep it in check in its home territory. The pest gets out of hand, the balance is restored by a suitable introduction. The great advantage of this method is that control may continue, without any help from man, or cost to the farmer, almost indefinitely once the useful insect is established.

Britain does not appear a promising place to produce such dramatic results. First we have few really devastating insect pests, and secondly our pests, such as they are, are mostly indigenous. They are not more serious because they are already subject to considerable biological control; as we have seen already, excessive use of insecticides can make a pest (red spider mite, cabbage root fly) more serious, by removing the beneficial insects which were controlling it. Biological control is most likely to succeed in a perennial crop, such as apples, or where an annual crop is grown year after year in the same situation. Many of our worst pests in annual crops grown in rotations are bad targets for parasites and predators, but work on this subject should be intensified. Insects introduced from other countries may control our pests even better than do indigenous parasites and predators, and may reduce the need for much chemical control, even if the chance of this eliminating insecticides in all British farms is remote.

The safest method of pest control is to grow plants which are not attacked or which can tolerate attacks without suffering economic damage. Our plant breeders have had some success. We have varieties of sugar beet which are not attractive to aphids, we have strains which are tolerant of virus disease. Much more research on this subject, which could make it quite unnecessary to use chemical pesticides for the crops concerned, is obviously needed.

Farmers and gardeners know that they can avoid or reduce insect attack and damage by planting crops at the right time. Broad beans planted early develop their crop before the aphids do any damage. Oats sown in February are too big to be attractive to the frit fly when these insects are egg-laying in May. Early sown winter wheat is strong enough to survive the wheat-bulb fly larva's attack when it emerges from its eggs in March. All these cultural methods are important and reduce the need for insecticides.

Private gardens pose particularly important problems today. They are increasingly valuable refuges for wildlife. Many birds are found there in greater numbers than in any other habitats. A great deal of damage is done by the over-enthusiastic amateur gardener if he is too liberal in his application of pesticides. The Ministry of Agriculture produces a shilling booklet called *Chemicals for the Gardener*; I find it a rather frightening compilation. Though excellent advice on the avoidance of dangerous practices is given, the reader finds himself advised to apply an enormous range of substances. He should use 2, 4-D or MCPA on his lawns, simazine and similar long-lasting weedkillers on the path, dalapon to kill couch grass, Paraquat instead of weeding the beds. Fruit trees may be sprayed with DNOC, tar oil, BHC, DDT, malathion, and a host of other chemicals. Practically every other crop should receive one or more of these same insecticides. The question is, is this all necessary? The farmer has to control pests if he is to make a living.

Most of our shops insist that fruit is unblemished and uniform, even if few questions are asked about its flavour. But does a little damage matter to the amateur, unless he wants to exhibit at his local flower show? No doubt if he sprays and sprays he will have 'clean' crops, and a higher level of pesticide in his, and his neighbours', tissues. He may find his wild birds are dying, and that eggs are left cold in the nests. Sometimes he will find that if he forgets to spray again he will have even more serious damage, for his garden will be devoid of predators. An unsprayed garden usually gives reasonable crops. A few apples may contain grubs but these can be cut out – some people think the rest of the flesh is all the sweeter! A garden, with diversity of trees, shrubs, grass and crops is unlike a huge area of agricultural monoculture. There are many beneficial insects. Biological control goes on all the time, not a hundred per cent successful, but sufficient to satisfy most householders who suffer more often from a glut than a shortage. They will find their friends appreciate their produce all the more, even if it bears a few marks of insects' jaws, if they know that it is free from pesticide residues. And there are now even some commercial shops which have discerning customers willing to pay more for slightly scabby apples with a good flavour and no organo-chlorine content. If our gardens could be kept free from at least the more dangerous pesticides, the effect on the wildlife of Britain might be enormous.

Crops pests only need to be reduced below levels where

they cause economic damage. Today medical entomologists would mostly prefer not to use insecticides, which give only temporary relief, and would rely on changes of the habitat to make it unsuitable for pests and disease vectors to breed. This can be an admirable solution, but it can also bring conflict with wildlife interests. Conservationists are very worried by the disappearance of 'wet-lands', marshes, and swamps famous for bird life. Some areas have been lost to agriculture, some have been drained to control disease. In some cases it seems preferable, for the benefit of bird life, actually to use insecticides and leave the habitat otherwise unchanged.

Unchecked pollution is a real danger, an even greater danger than it would be if all the other pressures on the countryside did not also exist. Unless we control pollution, particularly the insidious effects of persistent poisonous substances, the losses may be irreversible. But pollution control by itself is valueless. Our need is for a more positive approach on the part of the whole nation, not just a few enthusiasts, often thought of as cranks, to the problem of wildlife conservation in our crowded island.

British Farming: Revolution or Suicide?

Michael Allaby

The British countryside is in trouble and farming is heading for a major crisis. Town dwellers are largely unaware of this, just as they are largely unaware of the nature of the changes that have taken place in farming over the last twenty-five years. There is a popular romantic image of country life and country people that is difficult to dislodge, partly because there are places still that correspond to the ideal – although they are likely to be rather crowded – and partly because the ideal is so obviously *right*, it is what the countryside ought to be, all fresh eggs and butter and homemade wholemeal bread, eaten amid green meadows and buttercups, with oak and hawthorn and a crystal clear brook babbling in the background.

The truth is very different. British farm land is a factory floor and it is highly productive. In 1968–9 it yielded 3,106,000 tons of wheat, 5,018,000 tons of barley, 893,000 tons of beef, 2,648,000,000 gallons of milk and 1,045,000,000 eggs (not counting those kept back for hatching). In 1946 the average yield of wheat was 19·1 cwts per acre: in 1968–9 it was 28·2 cwts. The barley yield rose from an average 17·8 cwts per acre in 1946 to 27·4 cwts in 1968–9. All other produce has shown a similar increase.

The increases in production have been achieved by what is sometimes called the Agricultural Revolution: in fact, the intensification and industrialization of farming. Men have been replaced by machines and chemicals. Individual farms and whole wide areas of the countryside have specialized. Every last square yard has been put under the plough. It has been found more profitable to bring concentrated food to animals than to allow them to graze grass, and so poultry, cattle, and pigs have moved indoors to semi-industrial units where the energy they once used to find their food and to maintain a constant body temperature is conserved and converted into body tissue. The land they once grazed has been given over to the production of their foodstuffs although, even so, it is necessary to import large quantities of vegetable protein from developing countries for conversion into animal protein.

The changes in farming are visible for those sufficiently familiar with the countryside to see them. The absence of men is striking and the abandoned, derelict cottages bear witness to the rate at which workers have been leaving. Over large parts of the country hedges and trees have been removed. This is less noticeable in the west, where there were smaller fields and more hedges to begin with, than in the east. Estimates of the rate of hedgerow removal vary, but an agreed compromise figure is 5,000 miles a year. At harvest time the combine harvesters move three or four abreast across the East Anglian plain amid a landscape more reminiscent of the North American prairie than the countryside of Constable. The intensive livestock units, the broiler houses, and barley beef lots, are squat and ugly and frequently smelly.

Perhaps we should accept the social price. As industries become more highly mechanized, men are bound to be displaced. The general level of urban unemployment is not high and it is not difficult for farm workers to retrain for other occupations. Perhaps we must allow rural communities to wither. Perhaps, too, we must accept the aesthetic price. The landscape of Constable was entirely manmade and the planting of hedges during the period of the enclosures caused as much misgiving, and a good deal more direct hardship, than their removal today.

Unfortunately, there are other prices we cannot accept. Agriculture has come to be regarded as an industry. Government policies are designed by economists, more used to dealing with factory production than farming, and themselves brought up and educated in an urban environment. Yet there are radical differences between farm and factory and grave dangers in treating the land as a shop floor.

144

The production of manufactured goods is a linear process. It begins with the mining of minerals and is concerned with a series of processes by which they are converted into an end product. The separation of these processes increases overall efficiency: it would make no sense to have the miner smelt the ore he extracts. The raw materials of industry are inert and non-renewable. There is no theoretical limit to the acceleration of the process beyond the ultimate availability of the resource. Agriculture, on the other hand, is cyclical. It deals with living materials and its basic resources are renewable. This means they must be allowed to replenish themselves within the production programme: what is taken from the land must be returned to it. Specialization and the separation of enterprises makes less sense here and it is not unthinkable to ask the stockman to help with the cereal harvest. If we treat agriculture as linear, if we take more than we return, again there is no theoretical limit to the increased production we may achieve in the short term, but in the long-term we may destroy the land and lose the ability to produce food at all. History is full of examples.

Since factory industry is based on the exploitation of non-renewable resources, it has no choice but to live on its capital. Agriculture should live on interest: we should aim for optimum, rather than maximum, production. There is reason to believe that we are now using up this credit balance. Farming is living on its capital.

An ecologist might describe farming as the art of cheating an ecosystem. A stable ecosystem will contain a wide variety of species. If any one should increase in numbers beyond a certain point, controls within the system will restore the balance. Parasites, disease organisms, pests and predators, as well as hunger, all serve as controls. When the farmer clears a piece of land in order to grow one species alone he creates an imbalance which nature will strive to correct. The art lies in minimizing the impact on the environment by retaining as much diversity as possible. Small fields, surrounded by hedges, with different crops in each and a regular crop rotation, and with small stands of trees nearby, represent a far more stable situation than a vast area devoted to one crop year after year, or a large livestock unit. Farmers know this, of course, so how has it happened? Why, for example, have the hedges gone?

A traditional stockfarmer who grazes his animals out of doors may have 150 acres divided into fifteen fields of ten acres each. This means he will have about $4\frac{1}{2}$ miles of hedgerow, of which $2\frac{1}{4}$ miles mark the boundaries of his farm. The cheapest method of maintaining them, mechanical clipping, costs 6s per chain (22 yards) per year. If he wishes to have his hedges laid in the traditional way, this will cost him £6 per chain every ten years, or 10s a a chain per year. He may be tempted to remove some of his internal hedges, say half a mile of them, but leave the boundary hedges intact. The hedges that he removes he will replace with a wire fence. It will cost him £4 a chain to remove the hedges – £160 – and the wire fence will cost 6s a yard to erect – £264. He will save the £12 a year it cost him to clip the hedges, but the fence will cost £10 a year to maintain. He will be out of pocket. However, he may decide to grow arable crops. His ten-acre fields will hamper his machines and so he may remove internal hedges without replacing them. This will make for an immediate saving, his machines will be used more efficiently and for every mile of hedgerow he removes he will free an acre of land that could earn him £44 a year. He may expect an annual return of 23 per cent on the capital he invested in removing the hedge. The next step may be his discovery that the return on his arable crops is so much greater than that on his stock that he sells his animals. Now he needs no hedges to retain or shelter them and he may see no reason to keep any hedges at all. The increased acreage and the saving in maintenance will cover the cost of removal within a few years. Moreover, if their removal can be shown to improve his farming system, he may be eligible for a 25 per cent grant, while if any hedges need to be replaced by fences he may receive a further grant.

This is what has happened and it explains the disappearance of hedges. It makes economic sense, but there are side effects.

The removal of hedges reduces the diversity of species to a striking degree. Ecologically, a hedgerow is very similar to woodland edge, which is the richest natural habitat. An acre of woodland may contain two pairs of blackbirds; an acre of hedge may contain forty pairs.

Hedges and trees play a crucial role in the water economy and their removal may affect drainage. They provide shelter for the soil and crops, as well as for animals. Wind speed is reduced to zero on the lea side of a hedge for a distance equal to twice the hedge height; for a distance equal to twelve times the height of the hedge wind speed is halved. In this sheltered area moisture is conserved in the upper layers of the soil and the soil temperature is higher. This may be a mixed blessing to the farmer since some crops will ripen unevenly, but it can increase yields. Grass yields may increase by 20 per cent.

The removal of windbreaks may lead to erosion on light or sandy soils. In parts of East Anglia and the east Midlands topsoil is lost whenever the wind speed rises above 33 knots. From the 16th to the 20th March, 1968, the wind speed over the fens rose to 20 knots gusting to 40. Dykes were filled to the brim and snow ploughs were called out to clear roads. This was unusually severe, but each year a little more topsoil is lost.

Wind and the removal of windbreaks is not the only cause of erosion, however. In part it is due to a general deterioration in soil structure.

As livestock has left the land, and as human populations have moved to the towns, there has been a progressive reduction in the amount of organic material returned to the soil. For a long time it has been thought that the nutrients removed from the soil by cropping can be returned in the form of fertilizers: soluble plant nutrients that feed the plant directly, by-passing the natural mechanisms in the soil that make nutrients available. Now it is known that this is only partly true. The application of concentrated doses of substances involved in biological cycles alters the balances within micropopulations which reduces the soil's ability to liberate the substances that are being applied. At the same time, the alterations within the micropopulation change the soil structure and reduce the soil's capacity for holding air and water. Thus fertilizers have an addictive effect: the amounts used must increase in order to maintain yields. This loss of structure has been accompanied by the use of ever-heavier machines, which compress the soil, and by the removal of hedges and trees, which further affects drainage. There are areas in which water drains horizontally, rather than vertically, because of a hard, impenetrable layer of compacted soil below the surface. The land suffers from successive droughts and floods.

Farmers have been aware of the deterioration of the soil for some time. Yields have begun to decline, suggesting that the increase in yields may have reached a peak. The crops appear to be less healthy: pest outbreaks, weeds, and disease are increasing. The National Farmers' Union set up an inquiry in 1969 to examine the problem. As a result of its report the then Minister of Agriculture, Mr Cledwyn Hughes, set up an official inquiry into soil fertility and soil structure. Evidence, including samples of soil, was collected from all parts of the country. It is expected to show that the decline in the organic content of soils over wide areas of Britain has reached very serious proportions. At one time it was believed that soil should contain an ideal 8 per cent of organic matter. This figure has been lowered over the years, first to 5 and then to 3 per cent. It seems that in some soils the organic content is now below 3 per cent.

Such information is published and discussed in technical terms that may not impress the town dweller. The experts may forget to tell him that what they are debating is, in fact, the fertility of the land, its ability to produce food.

While the soil suffers from a severe loss of fertility, the organic matter that might restore it produces sewage disposal problems in our towns and effluent disposal problems in the intensive livestock units. A cow or a pig produces far more waste than a human being and a livestock unit may produce as much effluent as a small town. The disposal of this effluent is a growing problem, since there is usually little or no land available to which it can be returned. By a strange irony it is not economically feasible to return it to the farms, on the other side of the country, whence it came in the form of feedingstuffs. It is likely that a number of farmers will be put out of business because they cannot afford to instal the plant necessary to treat their wastes to a standard acceptable for discharge into rivers or sewers.

The ever-present threat of disease among large numbers of animals kept in close proximity to one another has led to the widespread prophylactic use of antibiotics. This in turn has led to the appearance of bacterial strains that are immune to drugs. The Government's Swann Committee, set up to examine this problem, has recommended a ban on most of the antibiotics used in this way because of the implied threat to human health. If these recommendations were to be implemented it is debatable whether intensive livestock husbandry could continue in its present form.

From all sides the evidence is accumulating that the intensification of British farming has gone too far. We are living on our capital, mining the soil.

Technically, the remedies are not difficult. The situation has not yet passed a point of no return. Soil structure might be improved by an increase in the total area sown to grass, for grass produces a close network of roots that build up structure faster than does any other plant. The increase in the area sown to barley has been largely at the expense of grass. Between 1960 and 1967 there was a reduction in permanent and temporary grassland of over one million acres. At the same time, an increase in the area of grassland would encourage a return to a more mixed system of farming. Animals would begin to emerge from their sheds, and their wastes would be returned to help improve structure still further. There are ways of returning the organic part of urban waste to the land: these might be encouraged.

A grant for the maintenance, and perhaps for the planting, of hedges would provide shelter for the returning stock and reduce wind erosion.

The overall effect would be to check further intensification and there would be an end to the attempt to grow more each year than was grown the year before.

There is a price to be paid for everything. The price for saving our soils will be more expensive food. Whether this is paid for by the consumer in the form of higher prices, or by the taxpayer in the form of increased subsidies and guarantees, is immaterial, provided farmers can be paid for producing less. It will be difficult to explain the need for this to the population that lives in towns and accepts the economic arguments in favour of permanent growth. They may see this as feather-bedding. They may reject it and choose the alternative, which is to squeeze the farmer tighter and tighter.

There is a price to be paid for that, too.

Wasteland Britain

John Barr

Muck=money. This equation, originated and seldom questioned in the nineteenth century, has created some ugly arithmetic for us today: totting up the acres of Britain that are blighted or sterilized by the mess of past industrial activities. Statistics supplied by local authorities to the Department of the Environment show that more than 100,000 acres of England and Wales – an area larger than the whole of Rutland – are now buried under smouldering coal spoil mountains as high as 300 feet or hogsback waste ridges half a mile long – or gouged by conical marlholes 300 feet deep or lifeless manmade hillocks 100 feet down on the floors of clay pits, by heaps and holes and miscellaneous industrial junk of every imaginable description.

These are the *officially estimated* spoilands. In fact, the Government's annual reports of dereliction regrettably tell at most only half a very sad story. While the Government's definition of industrial dereliction *appears* adequate – 'Land so damaged by industrial or other development that it is incapable of beneficial use without treatment' – appended to this definition is a cluster of exceptions, the most omnibus of which is 'land in active use for any purpose'. This monumental exception means that land such as that already – and often for decades past – blanketed in spoil tips, but which is still being used for tipping, escapes the definition. This means that land already damaged by extractive industries but which is subject to planning permission for further development escapes the definition. This means that the avalanche of coal sludge that buried 144 children and adults in the Welsh mining village of Aberfan in 1966 was not considered 'derelict' – it was, indeed, 'land in active use for any purpose'.

The upshot of these exceptions is that in reality the total area of industrial wastelands in England and Wales is probably nearer 250,000 than 100,000 acres (and add to that 15,000 or so ruined acres in Scotland). More distressing still is the fact that while the inadequate Government statistics are concerned with our legacy of, largely, nineteenth-century despoliation (*disused* spoil heaps, *worked out* mineral excavations, *abandoned* industrial premises, land *already* damaged by subsidence) in fact Britain's derelict acres steadily increased in the 1960s, are increasing still in the 1970s. The Civic Trust's estimate of an annual increase of some 3,500 acres is probably accurate. The reason is quite simply that reclamation is not keeping pace with the new acres – more than 6,000 a year – being ravaged 'in the national interest' by the extractive industries (particularly deep-mined coal, sand and gravel, china clay, gypsum, and brick clay) which all too frequently hurl their wastes about the landscape with no more regard than a child with a just-smashed toy.

Though the legislative machinery for land reclamation now exists (see USE YOUR LAWS, pp 273–7) progress is lamentably slow. Between 1960 and September 1968 the (then) Ministry of Housing and Local Government approved only 152 reclamation schemes on derelict land in England, covering in all only 2,565 acres; a measly £640,000 was paid out in government grants during that eight-year period. In 1967 only 1,868 acres of dereliction in England and Wales were redeemed and in 1968 only 2,695 acres. Of 102 English counties and county boroughs with derelect land capable of being renewed, no fewer than 41 authorities failed that year to deal with *any* acreage. In 1969, the total increased to 3,157 acres, mainly as a result of the work of the derelict land unit set up at the Welsh Office after the Aberfan tragedy. Even so, at the present rate it will take about 25 years simply to clear the backlog of dereliction which the government considers capable of treatment – much less deal with the new dereliction increasingly scarring the countryside.

The reasons for this pathetic record of land reclamation are partly economic, but more a matter of attitudes. Beauty *does* cost money: on average it costs £1,100 an acre (including acquisition costs) to reclaim dereliction. Yet it is apathy at all levels which really prevents action. Despite periodic lip service, Whitehall has never got very excited about dereliction. And only a handful of local authorities – Lancashire, Staffordshire, Durham, and the West Riding in particular – have truly grasped the problem and made substantial progress. Dereliction, unlike housing or schools, is not a vote-swinging issue, and the great majority of local councils simply shut their eyes to their eyesores. Disinterest is also all too common among the very people who live amidst the ugliness of industrial wastelands: they are resigned to it, and they are unprepared to pay an extra penny rate to have their black badlands painted green with trees and grass.

At the same time, only a handful of industries – among them the Opencast Executive of the National Coal Board and the ironstone producers – care enough to clean up the messes they make. Most industries are too profit-obsessed to care; some, such as the brick industry, often make a double profit – first from the clay in the earth, then from *charging* others to fill their holes for them.

The only solution for this situation of apathy and inactivity, which has so far prevented a real attack on dereliction, is a Clean Land Act under which a central land reclamation agency would be established. The agency would need a minimum of £35 million over ten years to clear the hard core of existing dereliction – no great sum when one remembers that this nation spends nearly that much *each year* on pet accessories (dog beds, catnip mice, budgie toys) to improve the environment of our 13 million dogs, cats, and caged birds. These funds could be made up by the central government money now spent on reclamation grants, supplemented by a small levy per ton or cubic yard on mineral extractors, a system which has worked admirably in the ironstone industry for twenty years, all ironstone lands being restored and returned to farming shortly after excavation ends. Additionally, the Clean Land Act must *require* all industries presently creating new dereliction to restore their working areas as a natural part of the extractive process.

153

Without a concerted national clean-up of dereliction, the positive opportunities which industrial wastelands offer – as playing-fields, agricultural land, or simply as blessed green open space for urban dwellers to escape to – will not be seized. In an over-populated nation with only one acre of land per head of population and the prospect of at least another twelve million Britons by the year 2000, dereliction is a scandalous misuse of land. Rural Britain can even now scarcely support the pressures upon it: to permit some 250,000 acres to lie ugly and disused is shameful. If not all those acres can be returned to the stock of rural land (and many of them can) they can at least absorb many of the demands for housing and industrial estates, airports and roads which otherwise will invade yet more tracts of this not green enough, not pleasant enough land.

Coastline in Peril

Anthony Smith

In the old days they tended to resent the sea. It was all very well as a defensive moat, but it represented a forbidding environment. It was dangerous, cold, and something to be left well alone, save by mariners, fishermen, and others who had to suffer it, at their peril. The actual coastal frontier with the sea was also something to be left well alone. It was, in the main, poor agricultural land, only good for dumping rubbish on and good for burying people in. Houses were then built without a single window facing the sea, because the sea was cold and windy and a mere view was worth far less than warmth. In short, the great encircling sea, together with the beaches that it stormed so savagely, were best shunned, much like pestilence, much like any natural thing too harsh and unrewarding for humanity.

Suddenly that very unpleasantness became a source of wonder and attraction. The tradition that medicine must be nasty to be effective is old, and suddenly its old ruling became applied to the sea. Medical men recommended immersion in sea-water. They extolled the virtues of maritime air. They proclaimed the seaside to be a panacea for practically every ill – and Britons flocked. Of course only the top people did any flocking, as everyone else had their noses too deep in the business of grinding a living, but when the very top people took their turn at the seaside the future of the cult was assured. With royal patronage seaside resorts sprang up much as the inland spas had done, and noble buildings were built along the front to house the ailing nobility.

It is necessary not to forget, either now or indeed on any inclement coastal day, that the seaside habit grew out of its unpleasantness, and all its original virtues were discovered in the biting quality of its water, in the chilliness of its wind, and in the bracing enthusiasm of its very air. Therefore, from the desecration point of view, the sea and its coast were not yet sacrosanct as their unpleasantness was part of their excellence. There was no public pressure to stop the polluters, the destroyers, the industrialists from making use of the seaside in any way they thought fit. Besides, there was so much of it to spare, with plenty of room both for the Brightons and the Bognors and for the despoliation, wherever there was need of that.

Then came the railways. Quite suddenly travel for everyone became possible. The seas then were no warmer, the air no less keen, but the habit of going to the sea for a refreshing change had amassed a venerable history, if only for the wealthy. The less wealthy now followed suit. They bought day excursion tickets. They sat in open smoky trucks. They travelled to the nearest resort. They laid down the new traditions that the coast was a place for merry-making, for letting your hair down, for seeing things that only butlers saw. The masochistic dip in health-giving brine became a paddle, a giggle, and something to write home about as soon as there were postcards to write on.

Once again there were no pressures. There was plenty of room for the Southends, Margates, Blackpools, and Ramsgates, and these spots did not even have to rub shoulders with the elegant ballrooms and terraces along the way. There was still room also for industry to do its worst, to pour slag on to the waves, to take pebbles, sand, and anything it wanted from wherever it wanted whatsoever raw materials. Industry was the great god. Its smoke, its waste, its effluent were proud signs of hard work and good money. Its railways, boosted by incredible investment, trampled everywhere, and frequently went along the very shore-line owing to a desirable lack of contours in that area. In those days, say 100 years ago, there was still plenty of everything, plenty of space and open country, sand dune and wilderness. The poets of the day somehow travelled from the home counties to the Lake District, there to extol nature, without worrying about any of the intermediate awfulness being perpetrated – both to nature and to man – in the name of industry and endeavour.

It is impossible to get angry with those destroyers of the

environment. They were indeed subduing the earth, as Genesis instructed them to, but they were committing crimes in every other direction. It is difficult to be concerned about the niceties of life, such as fresh air and green fields, when its very fundamentals were insecure, such as food, a living wage, shelter, and warmth. If the destruction of a hillside, a potential beauty spot for the future, gave employment at once to many, although wealth to a few, its destruction was important owing to the greater needs on every side. At least the hill died in keeping men alive.

The last century ended with railways everywhere, with pollution rampant, with prosperity beginning to get the upper hand, with resorts of every kind, and with a prevailing delight in everything the seaside had to offer, whether hot sun on hot sand or the pleasure of knowing that there were miles and miles of freedom on every side. The beach, whether wide and flat, or steep and rocky, had been despised for so long that no one had cared what anyone else did with it, whether they carted its sand away or merely enjoyed the freedom it entailed. It was a piece of no-man's-land for everyone, and everyone had suddenly realized their inheritance of this national birthright.

With the arrival of the twentieth century it is possible, and only too easy, to get angry. It was known by then that the coast was a most precious piece of land. It was known that the building of houses should not be done in an indiscriminate manner. It was also known that a large and expanding population on a small island was creating fearful pressures on the land as a whole and its more desirable sections in particular. The National Trust, for example, had been created in 1895 in response to this alarm. It would defend places of historic interest and natural beauty, and it would be defending them not against any foreign invader but against its own citizens.

On looking back at this current century, and with the coast in mind, everything that should have been done seems to have been done an age after it ought to have been done. How was it possible that they could have built, and allowed to be built, those ribbons of seaside bungalows along the south coast? How, in that great building boom, could they have permitted so much that eventually one-third of the coastline of England and Wales was built upon? They knew it was a precious zone. They knew that a mile of seaview dwellings for the few could ruin that section for the majority, and yet Peacehaven was possible in an age, not so very long ago, when ribbon development along the coast was just as rapid as along our inland roads.

The caravan industry boomed before the Second World War. After that war it exploded, but only in 1960 did the caravan regulations get any bite to them. The result is that certain customs and various sites have become entrenched as prevailing practices. Of course people must have cheap holidays, but the colossal caravan encampments, without a tree, without most of the conveniences of life, are plainly a mistake. I think one of the reasons they look so ugly is not so much the way their awful pastel shades clash with the landscape but because one knows they are a poor compromise to the demand for cheap holidays. There is no need for them to look the way they almost always do, one site in East Lothian was given a Civic Trust award for its excellence.

At some ancient moment in history it was decided that all the land out to the three-mile limit was owned by the Crown. Therefore all the bit that we treasure as our own common ground between high tide and low is nothing of the sort. In fact the situation is even more remarkable. It was the practise, even deep into this century, for the Crown to let go of its ownership of this inter-tidal zone to various applicants, and the Crown now owns only 70 per cent of the foreshore of England and Wales. The rest is under the control of local boroughs and councils or, worst of all, in private hands. Fortunately most individual owners do not forbid the public, but they could. The local authorities certainly do not forbid the public, but they can do virtually what they like with their very own beach. Southport, for example, has turned part of it into an airport (when the tide is right) and much of the rest into a car park.

The Crown land is open to all, save where bits have been

leased to the three armed services, but it is very easy for the Crown Commissioners to prevent any particular kind of beach activity. In theory, according to their old rules, people are only allowed on the foreshore for the purposes of fishing or of navigation. In theory, therefore, people are not allowed to build sand-castles, remove shells or even bathe. The Crown's current policy is to turn a blind eye to these traditional activities, but it can immediately forbid any new infringement, perhaps some new sport, some new human antic as yet without the prestige of tradition. It is a shock to discover that, for example, a proposed horse ride around the British coast and between the tides could be totally forbidden both by the Crown and all the other owners.

'But you can't do that,' said the Army spokesman when we informed him that ten of us aimed to travel round Britain by the conventional means of a boat and a lorry. And he was right. The Ministry of Defence owns a slice of England and Wales the size of Cheshire, and much of that land is on the coast. Special rules of security are applied. Of the 145 coastal miles it owns in England and Wales many are in the loveliest parts, such as Dorset and Pembrokeshire. Of course the MOD has to possess land, and has to bomb it and storm it, but what kind of bullying organization has the power to make them see also the public's point of view, to make them open up their beaches at weekends, to encourage them to do their bombing during the ten months of the year when the holiday pressures are not so great? We must get used in this country to such double usage, to picnics on a silent firing range, to walks through the plantations of the Forestry Commission. Bird reserves should not be kept shut to people at those times when the birds have gone. Britain is too small to permit more single usage than is absolutely necessary.

On pollution we still treat the sea abominably. Coal mines in Durham still pour their pit waste straight into the sea. Most seaside communities still pour untreated sewage equally directly, and often the pipes are not long enough to reach the low tide sea. Industry is always cavalier with its waste products, given half a chance, because it will always be cheaper to tip the stuff over the side. The Atomic Energy Authority pours more radioactive waste into the sea than any other European country, and possibly more than all other European countries put together. The marine world still throws all its rubbish into the water on the mistaken assumption that none of it will float and the sea will be able to cope with it.

It does deal with it to some extent. It distributes, it dilutes, and the rest is thrown up on to the beaches. Some of these are now no more than elongated rubbish tips, with oil from tankers, bottles and cans from every land, local sewage, and anything else we have thrown away in the casual hope that it will not come floating back. Or, no better, in the hope that it will float back to someone else.

The British people spend 70 per cent of their holidays at the seaside. The custom is continuing despite a growing affection for the heat of the Mediterranean. The coastal fringe of Britain is therefore both a national asset and a national requirement, with over twenty million holidays a year being spent beside the sea. How extraordinary, therefore, that we are so slapdash about it. We pollute it, and yet how many beach cleaners have we ever seen? We love it, and yet form no pressure groups to make it all into some national park, much as we did to Snowdonia. We have no real policy about it and yet, with expanding leisure and increasing cars, we are in danger of destroying more and more of it.

A Britain without the excellence of its coastline is unthinkable. A British holiday without a trip to the wide open beaches is equally out of the question – for most people. And yet, when the ten of us got back from circumnavigating the entire coastline in the summer of 1970, having left no beach unseen, we were totally unconfident about the future. Dunes are becoming concrete. The built-up section is still expanding. We are still behaving in a manner that will bring resentment from our descendants, just as we now resent the lack of care in the first decades of this current century. The coast ought to be a kind of hallowed ground; but, as yet, it is nothing of the sort.

The Green Environment

Nan Fairbrother

During millions of years plants and animals have evolved together in the same conditions. We are complementary forms of life exquisitely adapted to the same environment, and where one thrives so does the other.

Equally the conditions which destroy vegetation are also potentially destructive to our co-evolved animal state and if foliage, for instance, is destroyed by the air of our cities then what about us who breathe the same air? If grass sickens and dies from pollution, what are the same poisons doing to us?

———

It is probably possible to show that the green environment is good for our health, perhaps physically, almost certainly psychologically. For green, so experimenters tell us, is an emotionally soothing colour, and the Quakers who ran the early enlightened mental hospitals found that for patients to walk about among green plants was an excellent relief of stress.

———

Subconsciously perhaps, but none the less convincingly, we feel that conditions which are all right for vegetation are also all right for us. It is like the canaries once used in the mines to give warning of gas, since they sickened before the miners. In modern cities we have begun to create conditions for working and living which are scarcely more natural than mines (to some people scarcely more tolerable) and for human creatures uneasy in an environment they were not evolved for, vegetation can be a profound reassurance. If trees and flowers are all right here – then so am I.

'To me it's very simple. Man is an animal, and his race memory is as an animal in trees' – Peter Shepheard. 1970.

―――――――

The God-wottery type of poems about lovesome gardens are enough to put us off Paradise, but none the less we see what the versifier meant. For although we're no nearer in a garden than anywhere else to God's extremely inscrutable heart, we're certainly nearer to man's. Very close in fact to the fundamental niceness of human beings. For no one grows flowers from nastiness – neither from a nasty nature nor from ill-will to their fellows. Gardens are friendly places always – 'innocent and virtuous' old writers called them – and the side of human nature expressed in making our gardens grow is entirely benign. It is why flowers and trees in the manmade landscape are always reassuring! Someone planted them for our pleasure and wishes us well; no horror-city in science fiction would ever have trees in its streets or window boxes on its buildings. And even in the worst of Hitler's war the wild flowers on the bomb-sites were a glad reassurance of better things than man's inhumanity to man.

―――――――

When architects draw buildings they almost invariably add trees. No matter whether the site is a sterile desert without so much as a half-dead bush, they still frame their buildings in tall and graceful trees decoratively placed to enhance its good qualities (and screen its bad).

And they are right. Modern architecture needs vegetation as no period of building ever has before; and that architects surround their creations with non-existent trees is their clear if unconscious recognition of this imperative need.

―――――――

Trees with modern buildings are like a decorative pattern in an otherwise plain room. Trees with decorated styles of building are one pattern added to another, which when the architecture is good produces a wonderful double richness. But that the result is always reasonably good whatever the quality of the architecture is because the trees at least are of superlatively good design.

'A tree, complicated but not confused.' The ideal decoration in fact. Uvedale Price. 1810.

A tree is a superb work of art which far surpasses anything we can create. It is an all-purpose, highly-decorative, all-style, self-creating structure – treasure which anyone can have anywhere simply for the planting. We have only to give it root-room and it does the rest for us.

———————

Our buildings now are not permanent long-term structures which we know will be there in a century's time; fifty years is already considered a reasonable life-span for a new building, and many seem likely to die much younger. Such ephemera can never create a mature setting; trees, for instance, planted on their terms will be swept away half-grown, and the impermanent environment will always be raw and flimsy. Well-grown trees and established sites are already far harder to come by than our modern instant architecture, yet we still casually tear up mature landscapes and cut down full-grown trees to make way for structures which, compared with what we destroy, are mere temporary huts.

An attractive setting should be cherished as a long-term inherited treasure. A tree takes far longer to replace than a building. Shouldn't a society which proclaims that time is money therefore consider the tree more valuable?

———————

What we need as nomads is contact with a settled background – mature, well-rooted, reassuring, its long-term

163

self independent of our human comings and goings; an established environment where our transient state can take temporary root in permanence.

Talking to transients – from the *Organization Man* by William H. Whyte. 'The minor note that recurs most frequently is trees – "You know the birds don't sing here yet," one transient explained to me, waving disgustedly at the little saplings outside the picture window. "The trees are so small. When I was a child I remember so well the great big trees outside the house. There were squirrels and birds around all the time. I think that's what I miss most of all." '

Development by established sites as the permanent but adaptable units of planning could provide the permanent big-tree setting both for our transient buildings and even more their transient occupants.

————

They are murderous villains who write specifications beginning with 'clear the site', for they are signing an indiscriminate death warrant for every tree and shrub in the area. And such blind destruction is folly even on purely mercenary grounds of profitable amenity, and already wise developers are learning to cherish trees as precious assets on any site, rooted treasure whose presence may decide the plan of the layout.

————

A built environment without vegetation presupposes a confidently humanized quality in building which we seldom now seem to achieve in our townscapes. Perhaps indeed it is no longer achievable with the inhuman scale and function of modern city structures. Could the eighteenth century have composed a harmonious scene of tower-blocks and walkers, motorways and houses? Even their original squares now need trees to veil the alien alterations we have made to them. It was the late eighteenth and nineteenth century developers who planted the squares with trees as we know them, and who also began the process of destruction and botching which we have continued so enthusiastically since. The trees are now imperative; they are the chief (sometimes the only) beauty of many of the squares.

But do we treasure this heritage which has taken a century and more to grow? Not at all. With a few heartening exceptions we carelessly and callously destroy them. We excavate round them and slice through their roots with bulldozers, we light fires beneath their branches and pile destructive spoil round their trunks, we hollow out car-parks beneath them and cut them off from the vital water-table. And worst of all in the long run, we plant no young trees to replace them. A search through dozens of squares and gardens beautiful with full-grown planes may produce not a single young tree growing on to take their place when they die.

For every old tree we enjoy we should plant ten new ones in gratitude to our ancestors and goodwill to our descendants. If the generations who follow us don't want them they can cut them down – there is nothing simpler, alas, than to fell in five minutes a tree which took fifty years to grow, but no way except by planting now to have trees for the twenty-first century.

We're Using Up the World

Suzanne Harris

We're using up the world,
Can't you see?
Saying that it's all
For you and me.
We're using up the world,
One more time,
And taking away
What's yours and mine.

1. I've seen the mighty redwoods
   Standing a hundred feet high,
   Then along came the loggingmen
   And chopped them all down
   And left a big hole in the sky.

2. Factories by the thousand
   Are turning the rivers black,
   And the working man says:
   'It's hard to make a living
   But easy to turn your back.'

3. Smoke and dust and oil and soot
   Fill every breath we breathe,
   So now it costs us our very life
   To have what once was free.

167

4. We can always blame the government
   Or men in foreign lands,
   But we're the ones
   Who've covered the green
   With rusty old cars and tin cans.

5. If you drive across my country
   You'll get your just reward,
   For the signs and rhymes
   Unite to tell you
   America's going by the board.

(*Chorus*)

6. There are influential ladies
   Who choose to wear their wealth,
   So the leopard and the tiger
   Are fast disappearing
   As the ladies admire themselves.

7. Some folks go on safari
   Just to watch the animals fall.
   They don't need the meat,
   They've got plenty to eat,
   They just want another trophy for the wall.

(*Chorus*)

8. We can always sing this song again,
   Or tell a story told before,
   But we cannot make earthly things
   Live and breathe once more.

The Technological Exponential

Sir Frank Fraser Darling

part of the third 1969 *Reith Lecture*

I was talking last time of the impacts of man on his environment, coming historically – and prehistorically as well – into the present day. The ecological consequences of technology since the Industrial Revolution are still the burden of what I want to say now, but it is difficult to avoid some reflection on what technology is doing to the nature of man himself. Man, as distinct from woman the family craft-worker, likes steady work rather less and brings his inventive mind to easing craft processes. I am sure man invented the potter's wheel and the lathe, and then carried on patterns which woman had conceived in the first place. As I have said before, the male of the human species has an innate tendency to streamline and mass-produce.

Leonardo's drawings show us how far man had got by the time of the Renaissance in the way of transmitting power by cogwheels and directing it at right angles by bevelling the cogs. There was no dearth of ingenious engines but the power was wanting. The eighteenth century was all ready for an access of power beyond that of wind and falling water when James Watt made steam drive an economical engine which was capable of doing more than pump water out of mines in Cornwall.

The Industrial Revolution was on immediately, the biggest factor of change the world has known. Steam applied to locomotion created a half-mobile world and might have detracted from the craft of the sea had not the engineers of the Clyde braved those incredible difficulties of making steam piston engines drive ships. But coal was cumbrous stuff and greater efficiency was constantly sought. Hydrocarbon oil could be won more easily than coal and Benz made the technical step forward of devising an internal combustion engine which made use of the almost academic researches of Faraday and his kind in electricity. Technology and invention run ahead, creating an inexorable momentum. But a momentum in a known, appreciated, desired direction; or a juggernaut spinning this way and that unpredictably? Of one thing we can be almost sure: each inventor in every field would be convinced that his idea put into practice would be for human good.

Our Greek derivation in western civilization gave us the reason which has guided our science, but the Judaic-Christian background has given us a man-centred world. Our technology is a monument to the belief that Jehovah created us in his image, a belief which of course had to be put that way to express the truth that man created Jehovah in *his* own image. The resources of the planet were for man, without a doubt. They could have no higher end than to serve man at the behest of Jehovah. There could be no doubt of the rightness of technology. At least, that is the way we have interpreted Christianity, though in its earlier years there was more feeling of man for the natural world.

Science, as our perception of the natural laws of the universe which we are still discovering, is the basis on which technology advances. Science isn't easy, because it involves a highly intellectual approach and a capacity to lay aside earlier belief and to think anew. Science is neutral and distinctly impersonal when it is soundly conceived. Technology is not science but the application of scientific principles to physical problems, very much man-centred. There is nothing impersonal about technology. Moreover, technology is fascinating: it works. What a blessing it is!

I am not being sardonic, because I live in my era. But I am one of the least technical of men except that I do like to know what scientific principles are behind the new gadgetry of living, even if I do not use it all – quite. Yes, technology is a lot easier than science to understand, and it commands immense respect from the species that has created it. Its capacity for efficiency and still more efficiency as new materials are discovered or synthesized and new scientific discoveries applied, increases all the time. Once an advanced technology gets going it creates new demands in machines, things, and materials, so grows geometrically.

Then the whole modern background of technology begins to impinge seriously not only on the natural environment, whose only conscious guardian is man, but on the expanded and immense population of the species that created technology. A harassed minister of government may be perfectly convinced that some new industrial development will spoil something in the natural environment but – he will grimace apologetically and plead that we cannot afford to stand in the way of progress. That nineteenth-century conception of inevitable and absolute progress is still believed and it pushes us forward rather than leads on to that which we truly desire. Technology is apt to condition us psychologically so that man becomes its servant, no longer its creator and master. The automobile gets faster, trucks get larger, roads belatedly get wider, but country lanes are no longer for a pedestrian and the advance of mechanical agriculture has meant the loss of footpaths and removal of hedgerow trees. Efficiency demands it. The supersonic airliner *must* be produced simply because it can be. If you cannot sleep through it all, wear earcaps or something but do not grumble in the path of progress.

Jehovah has been steadily losing out since the Renaissance though he has fought a good rearguard action. In our century we have seen the mantle of Jehovah passed to Science with a capital S. But Science, as I say, is impersonal and is but truth and understanding as we see it at any one time. The pursuit of science still has humanistic qualities, and many scientists, though not subscribing to any notion of a Jehovah, nevertheless bow to the unknown and unknowable, the Divine Ground that the mystics of all religions and races acknowledge. Technology, on the other hand, is not impersonal; it is not of nature but of man, and now that it is showing power to direct man as a species, is becoming Technology with a capital T, the new god, man's creation of an extension of himself to which he seems inclined to relinquish his power of free will which we have prized so much and accepted as being part of our difference, our apartness, from the animal world. It is not thought impossible any more that a computer could be constructed which by thinking in its own amoral, rapid, electronic fashion could outwit us.

Leaving philosophy aside for a moment, let me take an example of an industry that illustrates what I have in mind – oil. And what I have to say is said in the realization that I contribute to whatever the oil industry is doing in shaping our world. Mine is a two-car family and I shall probably continue to go well over forty miles an hour when driving. This means I am using leaded petrol. I also fly an average of 50,000 miles a year in airliners, so I am well and truly committed to oil. Oil is now the great motive fuel, and supplemented by natural gas is becoming preponderantly our main heating fuel. The oil industry is truly international, either by the fortuitous geography of the oilfields or because the markets for the oil are often where there are no oilfields. The United States has a wealth of oilfields in the States bordering the Gulf of Mexico. There are many fields offshore from California. The Middle East is extremely rich; Russia has the Caspian and Volga fields and her own Arctic Ocean finds. The oilfields of South-East Asia were one of the hopes of Japan in the 1940s. Now there is the new and vast Arctic Ocean strike in Alaska.

The oil industry is a good example of what I have called the technological exponential. To build cars you need steel and aluminium, plastics and rubber. Rubber-growing used up a lot of tropical wilderness, and now petroleum itself is needed as a raw material in the manufacture of synthetic rubber. The oil industry takes over from the older chemical industry and gives us many other things, detergents and plastics.

The great car assembly lines create aggregations of people, new towns, new roads, services, recreational facilities and so on. Technological growth, as I say, is exponential. People call this the expanding economy and feel pretty smug about it. The gross national product looks better every year, but what of the other side of the coin?

We are taught that matter is indestructible, and the axiom

applies to the products of technology. Junk heaps may offend the eye, and because sight is the foremost of human senses, these may well be dealt with early in the approaching chaos. Worn-out automobiles in huge piles impress us with our capacity for producing waste, time waste, something which we are not prepared to recycle. Plastics seem indestructible. But there are substances left which are less obtrusive visually, the corrosive products of combustion and the soluble pollutants of water. Out of sight, out of mind can, however, be dangerous because pollution has insidious effects on human health, and on the persistence of ecosystems that have an unseen function in maintaining life and purifying environments.

Population and pollution are the two great problems of our age, and pollution is a function of population increase, though it need not necessarily be so. Most pollution comes from getting rid of wastes at the least possible cost. We are still using our rivers as sewers as were our forefathers tens of thousands of years ago, but there are more of us doing so many more complicated things. Some parts of the chemical industries that emitted noxious and corrosive fumes had to do something about it quite soon, but not before they had devastated many square miles of pleasant country. They installed 'scrubbers' on their effluent routes and some found there was value even in whatever it was they scrubbed out. But whenever wastes could be blown off or run off, the economic factor – a term ill-used in this sense – has been the criterion on whether pollutants of air and water were removed at source or released. We were not prepared to pay the price of our technology, the cost of cleaning up after ourselves. Those 250,000 acres of dereliction in Britain are just the bare bones of our degradation; the more subtle effects of air and water pollution have not been presented in any national balance sheet but they are dreadful in the real meaning of that word. Their acreage is far greater.

There are examples of some correction through the advance of technology, for do remember that if the will of the people is ultimately that the environment of man shall be clean and decent, it will be technology that will be our handmaiden in achieving it. In my young days the Pennine Chain was a region of small farms on sour soil trying to produce milk for the manufacturing districts. Here was initially calcium-deficient ground on the millstone grit, a bad start, but the farmers could get lime fairly cheaply from the kilns on the adjacent carboniferous limestone. But Manchester and its satellites and Sheffield and all the rest were belching out a huge tonnage of sulphur dioxide into the air, which, combining with the heavy rainfall, ultimately deposited on the land a quantity of sulphuric acid far greater than could be neutralized by agricultural dressings of lime.

Today there are good roads and milk tankers to move the milk quickly from areas much better fitted for milk production, to the centres of population. The distance between cow and consumer can be hundreds of miles now, and those Pennine farmers are less harassed men than they were. But no one will dispute that there is still too much sulphuric acid falling in the industrial north.

There are some forms of almost unrestricted pollution that are growing rather than declining and some of them are more dangerous than sulphuric acid. As the chemical industry expanded in the years after the Second World War many new products that pleased most of us were introduced. Synthetic detergents were an example of the welcome we gave to a cleanser more effective than soap, especially in hard water. Then those of us who lived in the country found the bacteria in our septic tanks were not doing their work any more. They did not like detergents. Public sewage works fared no better. Many of us remember the foam that covered the rivers in the fifties. The chemists had not thought far enough ahead. Detergent pollution of water became so bad that industry had to deal with the problem as an urgent *ad hoc* research. In a short time chemists reached a solution by developing a different molecular structure which could be broken down before the detergent reached the nation's water and, don't forget, the fishes' water. As little as one part per million of the detergents of the fifties reduced oxygenation of water by almost half, so that natural purification was set back seriously. The moral of this story is that indus-

174

trial chemistry could have thought ahead much better than it did. The profits were enormous both in anticipation and realization, and the research towards producing non-pollutant detergents could have been undertaken before the damage was done.

Water as a scarce commodity was never considered to be much of a problem in Britain, but the expanding demands of industry make us realize how careful we must be with it. Haphazard, unthinking pollution of rivers is something we shall soon be unable to allow. Upland water must be conserved and not used for industrial process that merely needs raw water rather than pure water. Happily, our growing dilemma is calling forth more coordination between water authorities and water-using interests. Water conservation will redound to the benefit not only of wildlife conservation, but to visual amenity and recreation. Our need will cause us to spend the money, some of which would have gone a lot farther in an earlier day.

One more aspect of water use in our technological world is causing us to think hard, namely as a cooling agent. The warmed water runs away in rivers and into the sea and is changing the ecosystems of these habitats. Further, have you ever thought of low-temperature heat as a prodigious item of waste in our economy? We do not seem able to recycle it.

Advanced technology would have been unlikely to escalate had there not been a large population to absorb it and the world population would not be what it is had not technology made it possible. Are we confronted, therefore, with the revolting pictures of the two serpents ingesting each other from the tail end? The nearer they come to what is presumed to be desired success, the more congested the picture becomes. What is going to happen? We do not know. The serpents must either unwind voluntarily, choke explosively, or wither gradually. I believe we are in this condition of the serpents, with very little time in which to take the first course. Choking seems to me more probable than withering. Choking is not a simple bit of physiology, for several systems of the body are involved. It is possible that the snakes could survive, but for a long time they would be very sick serpents. They might even learn not to do it again but to live in a non-selfconsuming harmony.

Concorde – The Case Against Supersonic Transport

Barclay Inglis

Forty years of progress had raised the speed of passenger-carrying aircraft from the 80 mph of the thirties to the 600 or more mph of the sixties, at which time a big step forward appeared to be within reach. Military aircraft had demonstrated that speeds not so long before thought to be unattainable now presented no insoluble problem, and indeed were achieved daily as a matter of routine. Why, then, shouldn't the airliner of the 1970s cruise at, say, 1,300 mph, and so halve the travel time between major cities?

This challenge to man's technical abilities and inventive genius was, as is well known, taken up by the British and French Governments in an agreement, signed in November 1962, to design and build jointly a supersonic passenger plane which was given the (hopefully symbolic) name 'Concorde', a word near enough common to both tongues. The research and development costs, then estimated at between £150m and £170m and to be shared between the two partners, seemed a small price to pay for the facility of day return trips between Europe and the United States, with the rest of the world also to span.

The scientists, the designers and the technicians broached the many novel problems with a will, and quite quickly a beautiful aircraft, a masterpiece of technological art, a triumph of man's inventive genius indeed, took shape first in sketches and in models, then on the drawing-board, then in the prototypes, 001 and 002, in the Toulouse plant of Sud Aviation and the British Aircraft Corporation's establishment at Bristol. The first of these flew early in 1969 and went supersonic in October of that year; the British 002 duplicated these achievements with a suitable time lag.

So, within ten years of first concept, and within seven years of agreement to proceed, the early stages of success appeared to be reached, and all that apparently remained to attain the objectives in full were further testing, further development, further expenditure. With so dazzling a goal in sight, and with so much expertise deployed towards its attainment, who could doubt the result?

And yet, there is good reason to question whether that result offers all the advantages it had been assumed to give: and still better reason to weigh the disadvantages, and even dangers, that are inseparable from supersonic flight. For these criticisms are criticisms of all heavy supersonic transport, and not of the Concorde alone; they apply also to the Russian TU-144, but less is known of this, and it is furthermore of less interest to the British reader and taxpayer. The latter has plenty of reasons of his own for concern: £250m has already been spent on each side of the Channel, and it was suggested in late 1970 that the eventual development cost of Concorde may well escalate to £1,000m, or six times the original estimate – and this at a stage when doubt still remains as to the performance of the aircraft in comparison with specification. Costs rise, and can be expected to rise; but with so many vital claims on Treasury funds it is a certainty that no British Government would have launched into this venture if the original proposals had carried what will be the final price tag, and if the doubts and drawbacks now emerging had been ascertainable – or had been given adequate attention – at the outset.

Take the fallacy of halved travel times. The saving of three hours on a trip from London to New York would produce a reduction of little more than 30 per cent in total journey time. The journey time using subsonic aircraft is about ten hours from central London to downtown Manhattan, and by supersonic transport is unlikely to fall below seven hours. In theory, of course, the day return trip between Europe and the United States might, if anyone thought it worthwhile, be accomplished, but at the price, inevitably, of severe physical exhaustion, and with little practical result, having regard to the time difference between

178

east and west. In short, dramatic reduction in travel time is not at all probable.

Some of the dangers and disadvantages of supersonic transport are now making themselves felt – and heard. Nothing speaks louder than a sonic bang. This is a shock wave (analogous to the bow wave of a ship) which is generated continuously throughout the entire length of supersonic flight (not, as is still believed by some, only at the instant of 'breaking the sound barrier'). The sonic bang follows in the wake of the supersonic aircraft, covering, on the basis of the generally accepted cruising height of 60,000 feet, a corridor fifty miles wide and as long as the supersonic flight itself. The bang is sudden and violent, a pressure wave which can damage buildings, frighten animals, shock the nervous, scare the very old and the very young, upset delicate surgery, invade the silence of the oceans and the islands, and, if it is permitted, the continents as well.

Take-off noise, already the subject of angry complaints the world over from persons residing near airports is, in the case of the Concorde, equal to, if not greater than, that of the noisiest subsonic jets, and there is little if any prospect of reduction to acceptable levels. Supersonic planes are thirsty machines, and carry, over and above their payload, an enormous weight of fuel. Large, heavy aircraft need a great deal of power to lift off, and power means noise – the more power, the more noise.

The more power, the more fuel – and the fear has already been expressed that there could be a major world shortage of oil by the mid-1980s if supersonic transport were to develop. To give a minimum acceptable return on the capital outlay, such aircraft will have to be worked for 14 hours out of every 24. The Concorde will burn, according to the British Aircraft Corporation, some 5,300 gallons of fuel per hour. In fourteen hours, then, this means 74,000 gallons, or upwards of 300 tons per aircraft per day – and the projected Boeing supersonic airliner is twice as heavy, and will demand more than twice as much fuel, as the Concorde.

On the basis of the manufacturers' estimates, by 1980 the supersonic fleet of aircraft would be consuming the equivalent of at least 180 million tons of crude oil (more than twice the 1970 UK demand) and by 1985, assuming that there are no more than 300 Concordes and that they have been joined by the planned output of Boeing 2707-300s, the combined need would be not less than 300 million tons of crude oil, or the equivalent of about one-ninth of the present total world demand – and this solely for supersonic airliners.

Pollution of the air on take-off and landing is the subject of local complaints along with the associated noise levels, but the possibility of a far worse danger has reached print. Dr V. J. Schaefer, world-famous atmospheric physicist, has expressed concern lest a fleet of supersonic aircraft should produce 'global gloom' through discharging into the upper atmosphere each day, as the product of combustion, huge quantities of water vapour, which will linger, suspended, in the form of clouds. The Supersonic Transport *ad hoc* Review Committee set up by President Nixon similarly reported that, by raising the humidity in the upper atmosphere, supersonic transport 'would alter the radiation balance and thereby possibly affect the general circulation of atmospheric components'. The truth is that no one knows; the question is whether, when no one knows, is it worth risking?

Of the remaining questions, there are perhaps two which especially deserve answers: questions that can be related to moral issues, to economic issues or to both. When far fewer than 1 per cent of the people of even the most prosperous nations are regular travellers on inter-continental flights, and few of these would travel by supersonic airliner, is the British Government justified in sinking as much again as has already been spent of the taxpayers' money to make possible the production of a facility for so tiny a minority? There is certainly no solid indication at present of potential sales outside Britain to provide this justification.

But, above all, can the side-effects, some known, some unpredictable, the intrusion of noise and of contamination, and the risk – indeed, the near certainty – of long-term damage to the environment ever be acceptable?

Unless the answer to each of these questions is a straight unqualified negative, no further proof is needed that technology may have become an end in itself, to the detriment, and ultimately the possible extinction, of its creator, man.

Motorway Madness

Terence Bendixson

Not long ago English pop singers Alan Wakeman and Michael Klein wrote a song called *Motor Car Madness*. It became the theme tune for a group campaigning for 'Homes Before Roads' in a London election, and its chorus went

> *A pedestrian is a man*
> *Made to stand in the rain*
> *A pedestrian is a man*
> *Made to suffer traffic pain*
> *A pedestrian is a man*
> *Driven under the ground*
> *A pedestrian is a man*
> *Made to walk the long way round.*

The song is an eloquent bit of reporting. Tens of thousands of Londoners can be seen in the predicament it describes every day. A notorious place is where one of the first stretches of the inner ringway erupts back on to the existing main roads at Holland Park Avenue. Two years ago it was a place of streets and houses and people walking to and fro to shop at Shepherds Bush or to take the Central Line to Marble Arch and Oxford Street. Even in those days the traffic was too heavy, but at least the streets were of a width that seemed crossable.

Now all that is gone. The Greater London Council's highway engineers have opened up a traffic-swept gulf between Shepherds Bush and Holland Park. *It is not a place.* It does not even have a name. And into the gulf the highwaymen have poured a Mississippi of black tarmac. Torrents of traffic roar along it day and night.

Street lights like gallows stand gawkily about this noisome place and the people who inhabit it are out of sight in hurtling metal boxes or underground in a maze of tunnels.

There is no place on the ground for humans when the city is redesigned for motoring.

The foot tunnels also say something about the men who design urban highways. The different parts of the warren are all lined with drab, oatmeal-coloured tiles. This uniformity was no doubt an administrative convenience but it increases the difficulties of finding your way out. In effect the tunnels are people-sewers into which pedestrians are flushed as if they were some kind of urban contagion that must be banished from the townscape with the utmost haste.

London's highway engineers had a trial run at this kind of torture when they rebuilt the Elephant and Castle over ten years ago. The criticism aroused by the tunnels there prompted a new approach at the southern end of Waterloo Bridge where an echoing concrete cockpit, open to the sky, was provided for walkers to go through. At Shepherds Bush the highwaymen have reverted to their old approach of spending a minimum of money on arrangements for pedestrians irrespective of the way that this produces a maximum of unpleasantness for those using them. It is hardly a way to improve a city.

The significance of this tale is that it will be repeated again and again all over London and Birmingham and Manchester and Bristol and Glasgow if it is decided to go on building urban motorways. It is part of a process of destruction that might be acceptable if it resulted in towns being speedily transformed into more convenient and civilized places. Yet as American experience shows only too clearly, greater convenience is gained for some only at great cost to others. Furthermore it is becoming clear that it is not possible to get rid of old towns merely by allowing cars to crawl all over them. For reasons connected with the vast investment tied up in buildings and drains and telephone wires, and with the tenaciousness of the social networks they sustain, people go on living in cities even when they have been rendered intolerable by the noise, danger and fumes of motor traffic.

Admittedly some people do escape from the older districts to more spacious neighbourhoods being built on the fringes of the city. And they are reinforced by new young families setting up house for the first time. But for one reason or another – whether to go to the dentist, to buy a hi-fi, to go to college or to work – these people either daily or occasionally find they still need to travel in and out of the older places. This is where the trouble gets acute, for as huge new roads are built into the heart of the city a further circuit in a vicious spiral of decline occurs. More houses and businesses have to be condemned, still further reducing the tax base of the inner districts and sending yet another wave of people off to the fringes in search of places to set up homes.

In the neighbourhoods they have left behind, the schools decline a little bit more, the rubbish lies in the gutters a little bit longer, and the buses and trains and undergrounds become a bit more intermittent and irregular. Congestion on the roads gets worse, notwithstanding the fall in the numbers of residents. This is because more people are taking to cars, as public transport declines, and creating demands for space to manoeuvre in that does not exist amongst buildings put up in the day of the horse-bus, the tram and walking.

Meanwhile out in the newer suburbs built during the past thirty years, life is somehow a bit thin, particularly for the women and children who live around the place all day. The shops at the local centres are doing very nicely but they are mostly branches of national chains and somehow the place lacks individuality. There is a golf course and a swimming pool at the local sports club but, useful as they are, they cannot be said to give the place any liveliness.

Fortunately for those who are beginning to grow tired of all this, the new minister for the transport industries has not been idle and his road construction unit has just finished a fine new inter-urban motorway which swings its way through four counties to another big provincial city over 100 miles away. And so the leap-frogging business begins again as those who can, often the more energetic and able members of the community, scuttle out to the small towns and villages beside the motorway in pursuit of some ever-receding mirage of the good life.

When the first of the newcomers arrive, the villages still have what the estate agents call rural charm. It does not take long for that to vanish as the bungalows multiply and the publican begins tarting up the public bar with wood-grain formica and boudoir lamp shades. Admittedly the infusion of new blood does the introverted old village society some good. The trouble lies further back down the highway where ever more people are now rushing across the older suburbs mindless of the noise and fumes they spread. All they are concerned with is to try and compensate with speed for the growing distance they have to travel to get away from the ever more depressed surroundings of the old city.

Presumably if this process was allowed to go on long enough a stage might be reached where the people remaining in the older parts of the city would have both enough space to live and work in and to use cars without loss of peace and quiet. In other words it is probably not beyond the wit of man to reshape a London or a Glasgow so that it took on the form of a Los Angeles. The trouble is of course the agony of discomfort for millions while the process is going on. Furthermore an increasingly immobilized minority of old and young and poor people without the use of cars would remain to the bitter end.

However, even the supposition that one day the vast majority of people would be able to drive about in a city region such as London, Birmingham, or Manchester is becoming increasingly untenable. In the United States it has been rejected altogether for the great urban groupings, despite the availability of four cents' tax from every gallon of petrol for highway construction, and the existence of what are by British standards almost limitless reserves of land.

Secretary of Transport Volpe said as much in October 1970 while discussing how to ensure the mobility and the rapidly increasing numbers of Americans being born in, or migrating to, places like New York and Southern California. 'To accommodate that many people, we are going to have to cut back on car use in our urban areas. This will not be an easy task by any means, but the best way to do it is with fast, convenient and reasonably priced public transit, a service in critically short supply at the moment,' he said.

Yet already a start is being made in this process of car disarmament. The Department of Transportation, to take just one example, has on order for Washington DC, a traffic management system that will enable buses to be given priority at 130 sets of traffic signals in the downtown area. One set of detector loops buried in the roads will monitor the flow of cars, while a second will enable commands for a green light to be passed back from a bus to a central computer. The object is to encourage people to use buses rather than cars.

Other reactions to Detroit-made urban America are a vote by the Congress to provide $10 billion of matching funds for investment in new and improved public transport services; a partial moratorium on freeway building in the State of Massachusetts, and a proposal for a community without cars on an island in Manhattan's East River. The Welfare Island project, which is due to get under way in 1971 at the behest of New York State Urban Development Corporation, will contain houses and flats for 20,000 people. As at Venice, cars will have to be left at a motorgate. People will be able to get about on the island on foot (and there will be beautiful walks) and by electric mini-bus and taxi. A station on a new subway line connecting the island to Manhattan and Queens will open on to the main town square.

Indicators of this sort suggest that Europeans should question very carefully whether they wish in the 1970s to build the sort of cheap and nasty urban freeways that were driven through American cities in the 1950s and 1960s. One thing they can be sure of is that fewer and fewer such roads will be built in America in the future.

Of equal significance is the fact that where further motorways are built in America's old-fashioned east coast cities, they will be more costly than ever before. This is the price of trying to reduce damage to the social and physical environment. In most cases such roads will be sunk in cuttings rather than raised on stilts. This will be done in order to soak up noise, reduce visual intrusion, and provide opportunities for building over the top of the highways. Such roads will also increasingly be routed through more expensive commercial and industrial property, despite the expense, instead of through obsolescent low-cost houses. The object is to reduce disturbance to settled communities. Alan Voorhees, a distinguished American transport planner, estimates, on the strength of the costs of an expressway project in Chicago, that this kind of environmental approach will push costs up to $40 to $50 million (£17–20 million) a mile.

No one has yet started saying that at this price urban motorways are uneconomic, but it would appear that the time cannot be far off. What is being said is that there is a need to investigate the pros and cons of a new kind of urban road with only one through and one emergency lane in each direction and with traffic signals instead of curlicues at junctions with other highways. Such miniways would have higher capacities than traditional town roads of similar width and could be fitted inconspicuously into the city by building the two small-scale carriageways some distance apart. Heavy goods vehicles and long distance traffic would use them to by-pass much-peopled places.

Miniways would not however permit a perpetuation of the sort of growth of private motoring together with its toll of accidents, noise and fumes, that European cities have witnessed during the past ten years. Bus, train, taxi and underground services would therefore have to be greatly improved to provide a higher level of convenience than today. At the same time many high streets inexpensively bypassed by miniways could be turned into precincts and many residential areas could be freed of short-cutting traffic.

At present this sort of public transport alternative to motorways and to ever-increasing volumes of car traffic is a possibility that few people can imagine. Their thinking is understandably dominated by the ever-more irregular buses and increasingly shabby underground stations of today. A result is that such alternatives have never been gone into seriously in any of the elaborate transportation studies that tend nowadays to precede policy making in this field. On the contrary the designers of these studies have started from the assumption that the growth of travelling by car would go on increasing at the rate it did in the palmy days when there were only half as many vehicles on the roads as there are now. Furthermore they have advocated motorways to accommodate this growth as if people on the move somehow had a divine right to dominate the lives of those who were not.

There was no logic in this. It was just that highway engineers turned computer programmers could not conceive of a future without highway building. In effect the highway planners of the 1950s and 1960s were as ill-equipped to shape urban transport policy as gas engineers are to advise on how to heat and conserve heat in a house. Their expertise was too limited.

Yet it is on the strength of inadequate advice of this sort that city councils, whose members are all too often part-time amateurs, embarked on the motorways that are now beginning to chop and cleave through the major cities of Europe.

The politicians were not told that the price of the thoroughly desirable objective of more door-to-door journeys by car would be divided neighbourhoods and increases in air pollution and road casualties. Nor were they advised that more roads or more motoring would mean the frustration of people on foot and the lingering death of public transport even though it would remain the sole form of conveyance for many, and for a number of years a majority of people.

Admittedly an estimate of the future use of public transport can usually be found tucked away in studies leading up to proposed motorway networks. In London's case it is estimated that half the population will still be without a car at its beck and call in 1981. Such a forecast throws significant light on policy, yet it was noticeably absent from the synopses of the studies prepared for councillors. Looking back, it now seems obvious that the figure should have been a signal for action to improve existing bus and underground services. For instance, work should have started at once on giving buses priority over other traffic. Had this been done in the mid-1960s, attitudes towards the prospects for public transport would by now be very different. Many transport undertakings would probably be gaining passengers and still making a profit instead of being caught in a downward spiral of congestion, poorer services, lower productivity, higher costs, fewer passengers, more congestion, and so on.

In the United States the incompatibility of mass motoring and the city as we know it has at last been recognized and after years of trying to adapt the city to the car, Washington is manoeuvring to try and adapt the use of cars to fit the city.

President Nixon's adviser on urban affairs, Mr Daniel Moynihan, reflected the new attitude in this way: 'More than any other single factor it is the automobile that has wrecked the twentieth-century American city, dissipating its strength, destroying its form, fragmenting its way of life.'

The same wrecking process has not yet proceeded so far in most European cities. Prosperity and pleasantness still linger in many of the inner parts of the cities such as Amsterdam and Paris, Edinburgh, and London. This character can be conserved or destroyed. Let loose the highway engineers and these good living conditions will be destroyed. Recognize that these tight-knit places are ideal for improved kinds of bus, taxi, train, and tram and they can be saved.

The Traffic's Roar

John Barr

from *The Assaults on Our Senses*

'Road traffic is unquestionably the most important individual sound heard by and bothering people when at home and when outdoors.' (At work places it takes second place to industrial noise.) This finding by the Government Social Survey, based on a sample of 1,377 adults in forty square miles of central London, would doubtless hold true for town or city dwellers anywhere, even for villagers unfortunate enough to find their High Streets transformed into race-tracks. Road traffic irritated 36 per cent of the Social Survey's sample when at home, 20 per cent when outdoors; 22 per cent mentioned noise as one of the principal things they disliked about their immediate environment and 6 per cent considered that noise would be the main reason for moving to another area.

'Traffic noise is steadily developing into a major nuisance, seriously prejudical to the general enjoyment of towns, destructive of the amenities of dwellings on a wide scale,' warned the Buchanan Report in 1963. Since then little more than lip-service has been paid to this warning, more than four million new vehicles have come on the roads of Britain (there are now fifteen million) and noise pollution has become an even greater de-civilizer of our environment. In March 1968, the then Minister of Transport, Barbara Castle, admitted that vehicle noise in our streets was increasing at the rate of 1dB a year.

It needn't have happened. D. W. Robinson of the National Physical Laboratory has traced the deplorable history of the Government's failure to control motor noise. As long ago as 1934 the Ministry of Transport set up a departmental committee on the subject. During the subsequent three years the committee published many well-intentioned

191

reports, and a large amount of valuable experimental work was done by the National Physical Laboratory. By 1938, says Robinson, 'the technical problems of measurement of motor noise had already been largely solved and the Minister of Transport had begun to frame legislation to curb the noise . . . but it was not pressed through.' With justification, the war was blamed; but postwar inaction is inexcusable. It was not until the early 1960s that the Minister of Transport (then Ernest Marples) began once more to look seriously at the noise hazard. In 1963 the Wilson Committee urged strict limits on vehicular thunder. Nothing happened. We were then promised that maximum noise limits for vehicles would be introduced in June 1965. They weren't. It was not until the summer of 1967 that the Government finally announced that it was to bring in spot checks of vehicles, lay down stricter noise maxima from July 1st, 1968; and, from April 1st, 1970, require new vehicles to meet yet more stringent limits.

Though in July 1968 Britain became the first country in the world to introduce roadside noise checks, it has so far proved to be that common British phenomenon, a mainly theoretical pioneering without the follow-through. Police claimed (are still claiming today) that there were too many technical problems in conducting noise checks or that they couldn't afford the meters (about £140 each) or simply that they had too many other things to do to bother with such trivial pursuits. One chief constable called the regulations 'a load of old rubbish.' Another claimed he would not buy 'one of those ridiculous boxes'. The motoring organizations refused to cooperate with the Minister of Transport, on the grounds that they could not afford the equipment to set up noise-testing centres. The impotence of the new law has delighted the motor industry, which continues to trundle high-performance, high-noise-making machines off its assembly lines; whether the 1970 noise limits on new vehicles will really be enforced in years to come remains to be seen. It is impossible to be optimistic.

Both central and local government have consistently capitulated to the nation's most powerful lobby: the motor industry, long overdue on the noise issue for the kind of indictment Ralph Nader gave some years ago to the American car makers on the safety issue. Millions upon millions of pounds are spent by the industry each year on styling and high-speed performance, a negligible amount on noise reduction. Indeed, the Motor Industry Research Association is unable to give any figure for noise research, although it says that it is being done. The association says that the research priorities in the industry are (1) safety, (2) air pollution, (3) noise. No one would quibble with this order of things, but it is clear that the majority of what resources *are* being devoted to noise research is concerned with noise inside the vehicle – important in view of driver fatigue that could contribute to accidents. But what about the people in homes beside busy roads and the pedestrians half blasted off the pavements by the fortissimo cacophony of passing traffic?

A car, in a civilized society, should be designed for safety, ergonomic qualities, mechanical reliability, and quietness – not flashy styling and power. But it is unusual to see quietness stressed in car advertisements. Instead we have the four-seater Triumph Vitesse which equals the 'hot performance' of two-seaters or the Hillman Minx that 'out-accelerates some of our famous rivals' or the Ford Escort whose gear change 'may even give it an edge on 2 or 3-litre jobs' and which 'looms out of the blue at 80 mph' or the Vauxhall Victor in which you can 'sweep on to 70 in just 19.6 seconds and feel jetaway'. And these are shouts for family, not sports, cars. When noise is mentioned, the references are usually to noise as experienced by passengers, not pedestrians: 'Road noise, already minimized by fine engineering, will be lost in the soft meshes of the deep pile carpet and thick felt' (Jaguar); 'At 60 miles an hour the loudest noise comes from the electric clock' (Rolls-Royce). Quietness clearly doesn't sell motor cars; for that the customer stands indicted alongside the manufacturer.

Many foreign countries have not only imposed tougher controls on motor vehicle noise, but they enforce their controls. Paris has banned motor horns, without any measurable increase in accident rates; French law limits car noise to

83dB, and French police simply confiscate the cars of repeated violators. Switzerland imposes a daytime maximum of 70dB, a night limit of 60dB on main traffic arteries; Swiss law even makes it a punishable offence to slam a car door loudly. Major Japanese cities have designated noise zones, where large hoardings display the permitted noise levels; motorists who exceed the limits (50dB in residential zones, 70dB elsewhere) are prosecuted.

Diesel-engined goods vehicles, buses and coaches – of which there are about two million on Britain's roads – are the most objectionable noisemakers; any one of them can easily exceed 90dB. The road haulage lobby incessantly moans that it is ill-treated by the Government, yet at least on the noise issue the Government has repeatedly succumbed to the hauliers. The Wilson Committee recommended an 85dB maximum for heavy vehicles. The Noise Abatement Society has long pressed for an 80dB limit. But the Government's 1970 law allows 89dB. The Ministry of Transport's apologia is that 'more powerful heavy goods vehicle engines have come into production since the Wilson Committee reported'. They would not have (unless effectively silenced) had not the Government procrastinated for years. In terms of total noise production, a heavy commercial vehicle is equivalent to ten cars, a bus to sixteen cars. According to R. J. Stephenson and G. H. Vulkan, scientific advisers to the Greater London Council, the noise level in traffic at 1,200 vehicles per hour, with less than 20 per cent heavy vehicles, goes up seven decibels when the proportion of heavy vehicles increases to 50 per cent: 'This corresponds to almost a doubling in the loudness.' If there is an even slight up-gradient, the increase is much more severe. Such findings underline the imperative need for greater control of heavy vehicle noise and for measures to keep them out of town centres and residential areas.

The difficulties in controlling heavy vehicle noise are the variety of noise sources, the incessant emphasis on increased power and the simple fact that goods vehicles in use are increasing at the rate of about 50,000 yearly. A commercial vehicle produces noise from its engine and its fan; from its

194

intake, exhaust, transmission, and braking systems; there are combustion noises and various mechanical noises; the bodywork often clatters and there is frequently inexcusable racket from loose, inadequately secured loads or from miscellaneous junk like chains and timber baulks hurtling about in an otherwise empty lorry. G. H. G. Mills and D. J. Aspinall of the Motor Industry Research Association have concluded that 'the trend today is to extract more power from engines and make them lighter; this exaggerates the noise problem.' At the same time, commercial vehicle makers are reluctant to spend enough money on effective exhaust silencers and other noise-reducing elements; nearly all the emphasis in noise-abatement has been on designing quieter cabs. By time and again raising the maximum permitted weights for lorries, the Government has positively collaborated with this emphasis on noisy power, and as motorways spread and trunk roads are improved to near-motorway standards, commercial vehicle manufacturers scramble to create ever more powerful engines to keep abreast of road improvements.

The motor industry can be compelled to develop quieter car, lorry, and motorcycle engines if pressure is brought to bear on them by the public and the motoring correspondents. The science correspondent, John Davy, has suggested a purchase-tax concession on cars meeting stricter noise standards. Obviously the Government does not yet take motor vehicle noise seriously enough: it should impose stricter noise limits on new 1971 and 1972 vehicles. Exceptionally noisy vehicles now on the roads can be required to meet lower noise limits than those brought in in July 1968 – but even those limits must actually be enforced. So far they seldom have been.

The design and landscaping of roads can also mitigate noise. Existing roads and motorways which disturb large populations can be shielded by trees or barriers. Future urban motorways, if we must have them, should, wherever possible, be submerged. This is expensive but, as H. J. Purkis of the Building Research Station argues: 'It is likely to be cheaper in the long run than having to insulate all the buildings which flank an exposed one.' Ideally no new homes should be built along busy roads, but if it is unavoidable, they should at least be built with backs, not fronts, to the traffic. New buildings liable to be severely affected by traffic or aircraft noise must be required to have adequate soundproofing, and occupants of existing buildings already affected by noise should be offered realistic soundproofing grants.

There is a case for low-noise zones, along the lines of smokeless zones, at the very least in residential areas at nights and on weekends. 'Noise-concerned' siting of roads and heavy industry well away from residential districts, cathedral precincts and schools and hospitals is essential.

Inactivity about traffic noise is often justified on the grounds that people will eventually grow to tolerate it – as they have with railway noise. Stephenson and Vulkan conclude that rail noise is a minor problem 'because of the fact that the railway is probably the oldest established noise source and people have generally grown up with the noise.' This may be true, but it is a dangerous argument that could be appropriated by the newer noisemakers – the motor and aero industries in particular – as justification for their noise pollution: people will get used to the din in time. Maybe they will, but at what physical and social costs? At what costs to the quality of the environment?

By the end of the 70s we shall not only have to cope with nearly twice as many cars as there were in 1967, nine times as many as there were in 1950, but the increases in traffic volume and congestion will be greater than crude vehicle numbers suggest: as the popularity, indeed the availability, of public transport dwindles, people will use their cars more frequently, for purposes where in the past they have used bus or rail. With an increasing number of two-car households (about 13 per cent today, 25 per cent by the mid-80s) both vehicles will often be in use simultaneously; the 'kiss and ride' custom, part of twentieth-century folklore – wife dropping husband at railway station – will decline.

In urban areas, this intensifying use of cars will lead axiomatically to 'motorized cities' where – whenever the conflict arises, which will be often – environment will be sacrificed to the movement and parking of vehicles, where the very shape of settlements will be dictated by traffic – and Noisescape will replace Townscape.

This Noisescape – shaping up as yet another of Britain's glorious defeats, a Dunkirk of the ear – will presumably be peopled with Stiff Upper Lips on Brave Enduring Faces. Premature presbycusis may be the price for the pleasures of urban life in tomorrow's Britain. And for those who cannot bear the racket, there are always earmuffs. Might they become a fashion item, featured in the Sunday colour supplements, sold in the trendy shops? Why not embroidered earmuffs in psychedelic colours? Or why not earmuffs with built-in transistor radios, the Noisescape swamped in the Top Twenty?

One Man's Waste

Walter C. Patterson

from *Your Environment*

What's the difference between 'raw material' and 'waste'? Most people would agree that 'raw material' is what you can use, and 'waste' is what you can't. By this criterion, a large proportion of current human activity consists in making the usable into the unusable: metal ore into abandoned cars, trees into litter, petroleum into squeezebottles washed up on beaches. Man the maker is now situated between a dwindling supply of the usable and an overflowing midden of the unusable. If present attitudes continue to prevail, the inevitable denouement will be exhaustion of resources or suffocation with detritus, probably both.

In 'advanced' countries like Britain people are considered 'consumers'. But a cursory inspection of the nearest dustbin will remind you that much of what you consume remains very much in evidence after you have 'consumed' it. Furthermore the industrial processes which proclaim Britain's 'advanced' status are pouring out an avalanche of cast-off materials to compound the problem. Pollution, dereliction and destruction of amenities are the disturbing consequences of the accumulating unwanted unusables.

But what is usable depends very much on who is using it: bacteria find sewage delectable. Much of what finds its way into domestic and industrial dustbins could serve as the beginning of further natural or technological processes of value to us. What we too easily dismiss as 'waste' should rightly be regarded as 'secondary raw materials'.

The problem of effective and responsible management of waste has three aspects: technological, economic, and social. The technological aspect looks encouraging. The economic aspect is a matter for vehement debate: the traditionalists ask 'does it pay to reclaim?'; the reclaimers retort 'Does it pay not to?' But both these aspects arise in a social context which can only be called stultifying. When you think for instance of scrap metal the chances are you think of Steptoe and Son and Any Old Iron. When you consider domestic refuse you think of My Old Man's A Dustman. The whole field of waste-management has to the layman a faintly sordid air, as if it were beneath the concern of clean-living upright citizens. If it's mentioned at all it's usually with a snigger, as a music-hall joke. The most important problem now confronting the waste-managers is how to achieve public recognition and acknowledgement of their valuable contribution to society.

Consider again the contents of that household dustbin. In it you will probably find animal and vegetable refuse, paper, tins, glass, plastics, and possibly other materials. If you are a gardener you will be well aware of how easily you can enlist the cooperation of nature to make the animal and vegetable refuse into compost, to return the material to the productive cycle of natural growth: you'll probably have a separate dustbin for this organic material, reprocess it yourself. If you belong to the older generation you'll probably recall that during World War II it was standard practice to store waste paper separately, for separate collection, to be salvaged for re-use in Britain's paper and board mills, whose supplies of imported vegetable and animal fibre were severely curtailed by the war.

If you thus recognize the value of these two classes of material alone, you have already more than half-emptied the dustbin. You have also illustrated the fundamental principle of waste-reclamation: don't mix wastes of different kinds. If they're kept separate at the source their future usefulness is enormously enhanced. Unfortunately, as far as domestic refuse is concerned, for the great majority of British households such advice is a pious impossibility. Both housewives and local authorities find it easiest to mix refuse of all kinds: the housewife tosses everything into one bin, and the local authority dumps this bin on to one collection-lorry for processing as mixed waste.

As raw material, mixed waste leaves a great deal to be

desired. Its final destination in most cases is a tipping site. By judicious choice of site and observation of certain basic engineering principles the waste can be compacted into a suitable landfill for levelling derelict mine- and gravel-workings or for other landscaping. But it is an indiscriminate and low-level use of waste, and the opportunities for actual benefit from tipping and landfill operations are limited, perticularly by the economics of transport. Far too much tipping is done where it's most convenient for the tipper, with minimal regard for short- and long-term effects on the surroundings.

Some local authorities take a more sophisticated approach to mixed waste. Instead of tipping it directly they subject it to various processes, which may involve manual sorting, magnetic extraction of ferrous metal, incineration, pulverization, or composting, or combinations of these. To give a few examples: Bradford, Birmingham and the GLC separate waste before incineration; Worthing and Leicester separate waste before composting; Basingstoke, Derby, Exeter, Lichfield RDC, and Sutton Coldfield extract metal after incineration; Bristol, Manchester, Southend, Stoke, and Sunderland salvage waste paper; and so on.

The question at once arises: if it can be done, say, in Worthing, why not elsewhere? Why is the 'refuse utilization' approach not universal standard practice? Several factors contribute. The capital outlay required to establish a plant so complex is considerable, and must be justified to ratepayers who may well feel that straightforward tipping suits their pockets better. Staffing may present difficulties. Buyers may not be readily found for the various classes of reclaimed materials, the prices anticipated may not be sufficiently attractive, or the supplies may be uncomfortably unpredictable. Plant siting may be awkward, as may the related logistics of transport to and from the plant. But in the final analysis the decision seems to depend on the philosophy of waste-management espoused. If the philosophy is one of 'waste disposal', the aim will be to remove the waste from further consideration, as cheaply as possible. If, on the other hand, the philosophy is one of 'waste reclamation', the aim will be to make the best use of the waste, taking into account not only short-term economics but also long-term planning: considering waste not as an embarrassment but as a resource.

Most local authorities in Britain seem to feel that their responsibility to ratepayers is to ensure waste-disposal. Reclamation is of very secondary interest, undertaken only if immediately convenient and remunerative. As a rule little effort is made either to assess public opinion or to educate it. Within the terms of reference accepted by the local authorities their attitude is entirely reasonable; the question is whether their terms of reference should be altered. The issue is controversial among the professionals themselves, and hotly debated. The problem will not be quickly resolved; but it's evident that the public, who foot the bill, would be well advised to take serious note of the pros and cons, and make their views apparent to the office of the local borough engineer.

Domestic waste arises as relatively small amounts of a wide variety of materials. Trade and industrial waste, on the other hand, frequently arises as considerable amounts of a particular material, and presents a different problem. Local authorities generally make special provisions for collection of trade and industrial waste, according to its type. But at this point a new factor enters the picture: large amounts of a given waste may be so obviously valuable that they attract commercial interest. Whereas local authorities are likely to make a charge to a trade or industry for removing its waste, commercial waste-handlers may well offer to buy the waste to collect for their own further use.

The scale of the operations of the specialist reclaimers is astonishing; the value of reclaimed resources to the national economy should be much more widely recognized. For example: the British Scrap Federation's annual report for 1969–70 indicates that more than half of the 26.42 million tons of crude steel produced in Britain last year was reprocessed scrap. Of this 14.4 million tons, about half was purchased from the scrap industry. 4.106 million tons of scrap was used in iron foundries. Still more iron and steel scrap was exported. All told the cry of Any Old Iron? was answered with some 14½ millon tons of reusable ferrous metal.

Again: member companies of the British Waste Paper Association collect, process and return to the paper and board industry some 1.5 million tons of waste paper annually. When you remember that virtually all supplies of virgin fibre for the industry must be imported from countries whose forests have survived longer than Britain's, the value of salvaged waste paper becomes impressively evident. More than £66 million saved from the import bill in 1969. The waste paper dealers are working now almost to the limit of their usual supplies from trade sources; any major increase in amount salvaged will have to come from domestic refuse, with the cooperation of the local authorities. The waste paper dealers suggest that their efforts essentially complement those of the local authorities: the dealers supply 'quality' waste, graded and sorted, whereas the local authorities supply the more low-grade waste arising from old newspapers, magazines and containers. Whatever the form of agreement reached, it's to be hoped that the public and private sectors can collaborate for the benefit of all.

One of the more curious imbroglios in current waste-management surrounds the question of cast-off tyres. According to Mr George Lane, passionate advocate of reclamation of rubber, spokesman for the Rubber and Plastics Reclamation Association, some 300,000 tons of tyres are removed annually from vehicles in Britain. Of these, some 100,000 tons are collected and transported to the two remaining manufacturers of 'reclaim rubber'; another 100,000 tons are sorted and exported by waste rubber merchants as 'used' tyres. But the remaining 100,000 tons are accumulating at such a rate that serious support is being given to the financing of expensive incineration facilities. Mr Lane is doing his utmost to convince the decision-makers that these funds would be better used to assist the operations of rubber reclaimers, whose numbers have shrunk drastically in the past six years. Without attempting to unravel the intricate complexities of the intensely competitive wrangle between purveyors of natural rubber and purveyors of artificial rubber, it seems obvious that the large-scale incineration of a valuable and versatile resource like reclaimable rubber is indefensible by any criterion. The situation is a prototypical example of the need to replace 'disposal'-oriented attitudes with 'reclamation'-oriented attitudes.

Throughout the waste-management field a new awareness of social responsibility is growing. Self-interested convenience is no longer acceptable; it's no longer considered sound economy to dump your dustbins on your neighbour's doorstep, however metaphorically. The social awareness is coupled with an intensified community of interest; on every side the waste-managers are teaming up, to pool their experiences and establish guidelines for the most effective treatment of the outpouring flotsam and jetsam bobbing in our collective wake. Private disposal firms have now formed the National Association of Waste Disposal Contractors, to strengthen their voice in the community; they have laid down emphatic strictures against practices such as casual tipping which were all too prevalent in the past, and aim to make membership of the NAWDC a symbol of socially responsible waste-management.

The British reclaimers are planning their Confederation; while on an international level the Bureau International de la Récupération – which means just what it sounds like – held its annual conference in London in 1970, with some 550 delegates from twenty countries. As well as discussing matters of finance, technology and general policy the various sections devoted considerable time to discussion of the present and future of the world's resources, and to control of the environment.

The growing awareness on the part of the waste-managers should be matched by a similar awareness on the part of the rest of us, who keep them busy. (See Check List for Reclaimers, pp 227–9.) One man's waste is all too often another man's poison; but if we can develop a responsible and farsighted attitude we'll find that one's man's waste may well be another man's raw material.

Eco-Catastrophe!

Paul R. Ehrlich

from *Ramparts*

In the following scenario, Dr Paul Ehrlich predicts what our world will be like at the end of the 1970s if the present course of environmental destruction is allowed to continue. Dr Ehrlich is a prominent ecologist, a professor of biology at Stanford University, US, and author of The Population Bomb (*Ballantine*).

The end of the ocean came late in the summer of 1979, and it came even more rapidly than the biologists had expected. There had been signs for more than a decade, commencing with the discovery in 1968 that DDT slows down photosynthesis in marine plant life. It was announced in a short paper in the technical journal, *Science,* but to ecologists it smacked of doomsday. They knew that all life in the sea depends on photosynthesis, the chemical process by which green plants bind the sun's energy and make it available to living things. And they knew that DDT and similar chlorinated hydrocarbons had polluted the entire surface of the earth, including the sea.

But that was only the first of many signs. There had been the final gasp of the whaling industry in 1973, and the end of the Peruvian anchovy fishery in 1975. Indeed, a score of other fisheries had disappeared quietly from over-exploitation and various eco-catastrophes by 1977. The term 'eco-catastrophe, was coined by a California ecologist in 1969 to describe the most spectacular of man's attacks on the systems which sustain his life. He drew his inspiration from the Santa Barbara offshore oil disaster of that year, and from the news which spread among naturalists that virtually all of the California seashore bird life was doomed because of chlorinated hydrocarbon interference with its reproduction. Eco-catastrophes in the sea became increasingly common in the early 1970s. Mysterious 'blooms' of previously rare microorganisms began to appear in offshore waters. Red tides – killer outbreaks of a minute single-celled plant – returned to the Florida Gulf coast and were sometimes accompanied by tides of other exotic hues.

It was clear by 1975 that the entire ecology of the ocean was changing. A few types of phytoplankton were becoming resistant to chlorinated hydrocarbons and were gaining the upper hand. Changes in the phytoplankton community led inevitably to changes in the community of zooplankton, the tiny animals which eat the phytoplankton. These changes were passed on up the chains of life in the ocean to the herring, plaice, cod, and tuna. As the diversity of life in the ocean diminished, its stability also decreased.

Other changes had taken place by 1975. Most ocean fishes that returned to freshwater to breed, like the salmon, had become extinct, their breeding streams so damned up and polluted that their powerful homing instinct only resulted in suicide. Many fishes and shellfishes that bred in restricted areas along the coasts followed them as onshore pollution escalated.

By 1977 the annual yield of fish from the sea was down to 30 million metric tons, less than one-half the per capita catch of a decade earlier. This helped malnutrition to escalate sharply in a world where an estimated 50 million people per year were already dying of starvation. The United Nations attempted to get all chlorinated hydrocarbon insecticides banned on a worldwide basis, but the move was defeated by the United States. This opposition was generated primarily by the American petrochemical industry, operating hand in glove with its subsidiary, the United States Department of Agriculture. Together they persuaded the Government to oppose the UN move – which was not difficult since most Americans believed that Russia and China were more in need of fish products than was the United States. The United Nations also attempted to get fishing nations to adopt strict and enforced catch limits to preserve dwindling stocks. This move was blocked by

Russia, who, with the most modern electronic equipment, was in the best position to glean what was left in the sea. It was, curiously, on the very day in 1977 when the Soviet Union announced its refusal that another ominous article appeared in *Science*. It announced that incident solar radiation had been so reduced by worldwide air pollution that serious effects on the world's vegetation could be expected.

Apparently it was a combination of ecosystem destabilization, sunlight reduction, and a rapid escalation in chlorinated hydrocarbon pollution from massive Thanodrin applications which triggered the ultimate catastrophe. Seventeen huge Soviet-financed Thanodrin plants were operating in underdeveloped countries by 1978. They had been part of a massive Russian 'aid offensive' designed to fill the gap caused by the collapse of America's ballyhooed 'Green Revolution'.

It became apparent in the early '70s that the 'Green Revolution' was more talk than substance. Distribution of high yield 'miracle' grain seeds had caused temporary local spurts in agricultural production. Simultaneously, excellent weather had produced record harvests. The combination permitted bureaucrats, especially in the United States Department of Agriculture and the Agency for International Development (AID), to reverse their previous pessimism and indulge in an outburst of optimistic propaganda about staving off famine. They raved about the approaching transformation of agriculture in the underdeveloped countries (UDCs). The reason for the propaganda reversal was never made clear. Most historians agree that a combination of utter ignorance of ecology, a desire to justify past errors, and pressure from agro-industry (which was eager to sell pesticides, fertilizers, and farm machinery to the UDCs and agencies helping the UDCs) was behind the campaign. Whatever the motivation, the results were clear. Many concerned people, lacking the expertise to see through the Green Revolution drivel, relaxed. The population-food crisis was 'solved'.

But reality was not long in showing itself. Local famine

207

persisted in northern India even after good weather brought an end to the ghastly Bihar famine of the mid-1960s. East Pakistan was next, followed by a resurgence of general famine in northern India. Other foci of famine rapidly developed in Indonesia, the Philippines, Malawi, the Congo, Egypt, Colombia, Ecuador, Honduras, the Dominican Republic, and Mexico.

Everywhere hard realities destroyed the illusion of the Green Revolution. Yields dropped as the progressive farmers who had first accepted the new seeds found that their higher yields brought lower prices – effective demand (hunger plus cash) was not sufficient in poor countries to keep prices up. Less progressive farmers, observing this, refused to make the extra effort required to cultivate the 'miracle' grains. Transport systems proved inadequate to bring the necessary fertilizer to the fields where the new and extremely fertilizer-sensitive grains were being grown. The same systems were also inadequate to move produce to markets. Fertilizer plants were not built fast enough, and most of the underdeveloped countries could not scrape together funds to purchase supplies, even on concessional terms. Finally, the inevitable happened, and pests began to reduce yields in even the most carefully cultivated fields. Among the first were the famous 'miracle rats' which invaded Philippine 'miracle rice' fields early in 1969. They were quickly followed by many insects and viruses, thriving on the relatively pest-susceptible new grains, encouraged by the vast and dense plantings, and rapidly acquiring resistance to the chemicals used against them. As chaos spread until even the most obtuse agriculturists and economists realized that the Green Revolution had turned brown, the Russians stepped in.

In retrospect it seems incredible that the Russians, with the American mistakes known to them, could launch an even more incompetent programme of aid to the underdeveloped world. Indeed, in the early 1970s there were cynics in the United States who claimed that out-doing the stupidity of American foreign aid would be physically impossible. Those critics were, however, obviously unaware

208

that the Russians had been busily destroying their own environment for many years. The virtual disappearance of sturgeon from Russia's rivers caused a great shortage of caviar by 1970. A standard joke among Russian scientists at that time was that they had created an artificial caviar which was indistinguishable from the real thing – except by taste. At any rate the Soviet Union, observing with interest the progressive deterioration of relations between the UDCs and the United States, came up with a solution. It had recently developed what it claimed was the ideal insecticide, a highly lethal chlorinated hydrocarbon complexed with a special agent for penetrating the external skeletal armour of insects. Announcing that the new pesticide, called Thanodrin, would truly produce a Green Revolution, the Soviets entered into negotiations with various UDCs for the construction of massive Thanodrin factories. The USSR would bear all the costs; all it wanted in return were certain trade and military concessions.

It is interesting now, with the perspective of years, to examine in some detail the reasons why the UDCs welcomed the Thanodrin plan with such open arms. Government officials in these countries ignored the protests of their own scientists that Thanodrin would not solve the problems which plagued them. The governments now knew that the basic cause of their problems was overpopulation, and that these problems had been exacerbated by the dullness, daydreaming, and cupidity endemic to all governments. They knew that only population control and limited development aimed primarily at agriculture could have spared them the horrors they now faced. They knew it, but they were not about to admit it. How much easier it was simply to accuse the Americans of failing to give them proper aid; how much simpler to accept the Russian panacea.

The Russian Thanodrin proposal seemed to offer the masses in the UDCs an opportunity to save themselves and humiliate the United States at the same time; and in human affairs, as we all know, biological realities could never interfere with such an opportunity. The scientists were silenced, the politicians said yes, the Thanodrin plants were built, and the results were what any beginning ecology student could have predicted. At first Thanodrin seemed to offer excellent control of many pests. True, there was a rash of human fatalities from improper use of the lethal chemical, but, as Russian technical advisers were prone to note, these were more than compensated for by increased yields. Thanodrin use skyrocketed throughout the underdeveloped world. The Mikoyan design group developed a dependable, cheap agricultural aircraft which the Soviets donated to the effort in large numbers. MIG sprayers became even more common in UDCs than MIG interceptors.

Then the troubles began. Insect strains with cuticles resistant to Thanodrin penetration began to appear. And as streams, rivers, fish culture ponds, and onshore waters became rich in Thanodrin, more fisheries began to disappear. Bird populations were decimated. The sequence of events was standard for broadcast use of a synthetic pesticide: great success at first, followed by removal of natural enemies and development of resistance by the pest. Populations of crop-eating insects in areas treated with Thanodrin made steady comebacks and soon became more abundant than ever. Yields plunged, while farmers in their desperation increased the Thanodrin dose and shortened the time between treatments. Death from Thanodrin poisoning became common. The first violent incident occurred in the Canete Valley of Peru, where farmers had suffered a similar chlorinated hydro-carbon disaster in the mid-1950s. A Russian adviser serving as an agricultural pilot was assaulted and killed by a mob of enraged farmers in January 1978. Trouble spread rapidly during 1978, especially after the word got out that two years earlier Russia herself had banned the use of Thanodrin at home because of its serious effects on ecological systems. Suddenly Russia, and not the United States, was the *bête noir* in the UDCs. 'Thanodrin parties' became epidemic, with farmers, in their ignorance, dumping carloads of Thanodrin concentrate into the sea. Russian advisers fled, and four of the Thanodrin plants were levelled to the ground. Destruction of the plants in Rio and Calcutta led to hundreds of thousands of gallons of Thanodrin concentrate being dumped directly into the sea.

At the UN Mr Potemkin, representative of the Soviet Union, was on the hot seat. Mr Potemkin heard his nation described as the greatest mass killer of all time as Mr Shankarnarayan, Indian Ambassador to the UN, predicted at least 30 million deaths from crop failures due to over-dependence on Thanodrin. Russia was accused of 'chemical aggression', and the General Assembly, after a weak reply by Potemkin, passed a vote of censure.

It was in January 1979 that huge blooms of a previously unknown variety of diatom were reported off the coast of Peru. The blooms were accompanied by a massive die-off of sea life and of the pathetic remainder of the birds which had once feasted on the anchovies of the area. Almost immediately another huge bloom was reported in the Indian Ocean, centring around the Seychelles, and then a third in the South Atlantic off the African coast. Both of these were accompanied by spectacular die-offs of marine animals. Even more ominous were growing reports of fish and bird kills at oceanic points where there were no spectacular blooms. Biologists were soon able to explain the phenomenon: the diatom had evolved an enzyme which broke down Thanodrin; that enzyme also produced a breakdown product which interfered with the transmission of nerve impulses, and was therefore lethal to animals. Unfortunately, the biologists could suggest no way of repressing the poisonous diatom bloom in time. By September 1979 all important animal life in the sea was extinct. Large areas of coastline had to be evacuated, as windrows of dead fish created a monumental stench.

But stench was the least of man's problems. Japan and China were faced with almost instant starvation from a total loss of the seafood on which they were so dependent. Both blamed Russia for their situation and demanded immediate mass shipments of food. Russia had none to send. On 13th October, Chinese armies attacked Russia on a broad front ...

A pretty grim scenario. Unfortunately, we're a long way

into it already. Everything mentioned as happening before 1971 has actually occurred; much of the rest is based on projections of trends already appearing. Evidence that pesticides have long-term lethal effects on human beings has started to accumulate, and recently Robert Finch, Secretary of the US Department of Health, Education and Welfare, expressed his extreme apprehension about the pesticide situation. Simultaneously the petrochemical industry continues its unconscionable poison-peddling. For instance, Shell Chemical has been carrying on a high-pressure campaign to sell the insecticide Azodrin to farmers as a killer of cotton pests. They continue their programme even though they know that Azodrin is not only ineffective, but often *increases* the pest density. They've covered themselves nicely in an advertisement which states, 'Even if an overpowering migration [*sic*] develops, the flexibility of Azodrin lets you regain control fast. Just increase the dosage according to label recommendations.' It's a great game – get people to apply the poison and kill the natural enemies of the pests. Then blame the increased pests on 'migration' and sell even more pesticide!

Right now fisheries are being wiped out by over-exploitation, made easy by modern electronic equipment. The companies producing the equipment know this. They even boast in advertising that only their equipment will keep fishermen in business until the final kill. Profits must obviously be maximized in the short run. Indeed, Western society is in the process of completing the rape and murder of the planet for economic gain. And, sadly, most of the rest of the world is eager for the opportunity to emulate our behaviour. But the underdeveloped peoples will be denied that opportunity – the days of plunder are drawing inexorably to a close.

Most of the people who are going to die in the greatest cataclysm in the history of man have already been born. Both worldwide plague and thermonuclear war are made more probable as population growth continues. These, along with famine, make up the trio of potential 'death rate solutions' to the population problem – solutions in which the birth rate-death rate imbalance is redressed by a rise in the death rate rather than by a lowering of the birth rate. Make no mistake about it, *the imbalance will be redressed*. The shape of the population-growth curve is one familiar to the biologist. It is the outbreak part of an outbreak-crash sequence. A population grows rapidly in the presence of abundant resources, finally runs out of food or some other necessity, and crashes to a low level or extinction. Man is not only running out of food, he is also destroying the life support systems of the Spaceship Earth.

PART THREE:

ACTION GUIDE

Until one is committed there is hesitancy, the chance to draw back, always ineffectiveness. Concerning all acts of initiative (and creation), there is one elementary truth, the ignorance of which kills countless ideas and splendid plans: that the moment one definitely commits oneself, then Providence moves too. All sorts of things occur that would never otherwise have occurred. A whole stream of events issues from the decision, raising in one's favour all manner of unforeseen incidents and meetings and material assistance, which no man could have dreamt would have come his way. I have learned a deep respect for one of Goethe's couplets:

Whatever you can do, or dream you can, begin it.

Boldness has genius, power, and magic in it.

W. H. Murray

'Me Save the Environment?'

'Environment! That's for highbrows,' I said. 'Me preserve and improve the environment?' I said. 'You must be joking,' I said. 'What's the environment got to do with me?' I said.

'Listen, friend,' he answered. 'You are the environment, or part of it, and you're certainly a product of it, just as I am. The environment is the room, the flat, the house where you live: the factory, the office, the shop where you work: your road, your parish, your village, town or city: Britain, Europe, the world – even the space the world sails through.

'It's the street where your children play, the park they take the dog in, the flowers, the trees, the animals and birds, the fields, the crops, the streams, the waterfalls. It's the fish, the cliffs, the seashore, the sea itself, the hills and the mountains, the pubs, the bingo halls, the lanes, the motorways, the highways and byways, the farms, the rows of shops and houses, the dustbins, the historical buildings, the trains and buses and cars.

'It's the music and dancing and peaches and cream. It's the insects, an empty tin can, aeroplanes, pictures, pollen, and the leaves that fall from the trees. It's the smoke from a fire, a wormcast on the lawn, a cigarette end in the gutter, books, papers, greenfly on the roses, the paint on your front door, unbreakable plastic, the rain on the roof, an empty beer bottle, the heather and the bracken and the butterflies. It's the air you breathe, the blue sky, peace and quiet, the clouds and the sun.

'Through ignorance, thoughtlessness, stupidity or greed, man has done, and goes on doing, an unbelievable amount of damage to his world. As new processes and new products are developed, and as the pace of what we call "technological advance" speeds up, so the danger to the environment (and to you and me) increases faster and faster. But it doesn't only snowball; there's a chain-reaction too, because nowhere will you find it so inescapable that one thing leads to another.

'So, if you enjoy some of the millions of things that make up the environment, and if you want your children and their children and their children's children to enjoy them too, now is the time to act. The crisis is on us already. The detergent in this week's washing-up water can mean no fish in the river next week.'

'Well I'll be damned!' I said, 'I—'

He stopped me with a wave of his hand, and looked me squarely in the eyes.

'If you sit on your backside and do nothing to help,' he said, 'we all will be.'

Barclay Inglis

218

Ideas for Action

Jon Holliman

In the past we gave our consent to those who provided goods and services that we felt were our needs and satisfied our aspirations. When we gave our consent we were as ignorant as the industrialist, politician, and businessman as to the ecological consequences of what we were doing. There is now no excuse. Pollution and degradation of the environment can no longer be accepted as the price for the dubious benefits of a full range of consumer goods and material comforts manufactured to satisfy artificial desires largely manipulated and created by those controlling the means of production. The environmental costs will be too great and we are rapidly approaching a situation where further increased production and economic growth brings diminishing social returns.

Some radical action should now result from a knowledge and understanding of this situation and of the ecological parameters which must guide our return to value systems which cannot be measured only in terms of the Gross National Product.

The preceding chapters have provided much of the evidence with which you can judge your actions. There are as yet no handy guidelines to judge in specific cases what is in the best interests of the environment. Nor is there enough time to design total solutions before action starts even if this were ever possible. This strategy and 'code of practice' must be developed as we search for a way out of the technological and social fix we are in. It is probably never possible to get 100 per cent agreement on many of the ideas advocated in this book but one thing is certain – the closer our actions get to the functional principles of the ecosystem the more likely we will be able to survive as a species on this planet.

The following list is a few suggestions for a start that you can make as an individual to help us all to develop a life-style more related to the potential of the earth than to our society's greedy and complacent desires. You can think of many more as you go along and send Friends of the Earth your ideas.

Consumers

We are all consumers. The trouble is we consume too much – too great a proportion of the world's limited resources – and too quickly without considering the long-term consequences. Most of us are constantly conditioned to buy what the producer wants us to, not what we really need. So consume less. Your household motto should be: make your wants your needs.

If it is advertised on the television it could mean they spend so much on advertising and packaging that the goods inside aren't worth the money.

Do you consider not only the qualities of the product that you buy but also the total environmental affects of its production, distribution and disposal?

As every housewife knows there is often more packaging than there are goods inside. Demonstrate your disgust at the local supermarket by opening everything and just leaving superfluous packaging behind on the counter.

Avoid throw-away goods – there is rapidly becoming no 'away' to throw them.

Do you really need an electric can-opener or an electric carving knife? Where are your muscles? Consume less electricity and avoid goods that 'electrify' unnecessarily.

Did your grandparents suffer more from eating an occasional wormy apple than we will suffer from pesticide residues on shiny, worm-free apples?

The annual cost of a complete ban on organochlorine chemicals has been estimated at less than $2\frac{1}{2}$ np per head of the population. This is a small price to pay to avoid a 'Silent Spring'.

The prime offender in detergent pollution is not suds but phosphates. Phosphates in the water encourage algae growth and eventually dead and stinking lakes and underground water by acceleration of a process called eutrophication. Ask how much phosphate there is in the detergent you buy. If in doubt use soap or soap flakes. Even if everyone just read the instructions on the packet and stuck to the right quantities, detergent pollution would be drastically reduced.

Population Control

If all unwanted children in Britain were not born then we would virtually have stabilized the population. Fight for the removal of *all* restrictions on provision of *free* birth control information and devices. Press your local authority to implement the Family Planning Act by setting up clinics in your area.

Make sex education available at all levels, stressing birth control practices and the need to stabilize the population.

If you want more than two children – adopt them.

Transport

The cycle of ever-increasing reliance on the motor-car with consequent reduction in quality and quantity of public transport must be broken. Mobility should be recognized as a public right and integrated means for long and short distance travel that do not pollute, eat up land, or kill people must be widely available.

If you do not really need a car don't buy one.

If you really need a car to commute don't only pollute for yourself – form a car pool with your neighbours or workmates and do not drive within the city.

Better still take a bus or train, bicycle, or walk.

Oppose legislation or plans for more motorways, especially in cities. Support improvements to public transport facilities.

Water

Look at your local pond, lake or river and ask yourself:

How polluted is it?
Can you drink from it?

Can you swim in it or use it for recreation of any kind?

Ask the local council what it is doing about it. Are you satisfied with the answer?

Save water.

Don't leave the tap on when brushing your teeth.

Check for leaky pipes and taps.

Noise

Much of it is excessive and unnecessary. If you don't like noise, don't create it for other people.

Keep radio and television low especially on summer days with windows open.

Get a noiseless dustbin if you haven't got one already.

If you like noise keep it to yourself, preferably in a sound-proof room.

Try and maintain at least one quiet room in your house as a retreat from noise or where noise can be created without disturbing others.

In the war against noise pollution arm yourself with a handy Noise Survey Meter – £10 from the Noise Abatement Society. Every amenity society should have one to lend out.

The Noise Abatement Society also has a useful book called *The Law on Noise*. Make sure you know the facts; then be prepared to take legal action.

You Can Help to Fight Aircraft Noise

The British Association for the Council of Aircraft Noise (BACAN) asks you to:

1. Maintain regular contact with your MP, either individually or through your local anti-air noise association or both. Do not give up because he appears to be unsympathetic or unwilling to help, at first. Ask him to deal with ministries and departments on your behalf, and persuade him to ask Questions in the House on your behalf.
2. Write or telephone your local airport whenever you are

affected by aircraft noise. As the Parliamentary Commissioner has clearly stated, the Board of Trade 'welcomes' complaints – do not let this invitation go unanswered, and make sure of the regulations applying in your own district so that you know when they are broken.

3. Write to the Press, both local and national, and send the BACAN Committee your press cuttings, so that we can follow up.
4. Persuade those who complain about aircraft noise not to complain to you but to their MP and to join BACAN or their local association.
5. Keep in touch with us and with your local association. We can help you by putting you in touch with areas with similar problems, by supplying you with technical information and contacts, by helping you form new associations and revitalize old ones, and by getting you publicity. You can help us by keeping us up to date with your activities; with expert help – from technical help to translating – with your time, and with funds.

Trees

Guard your local trees. Plant trees wherever you can. Trees are not only beautiful; they are vital for the oxygen and water cycles of the ecosystem and give shelter and food to wildlife. If you buy a Christmas tree make sure it has roots and plant it somewhere afterwards. Find out from your local council if any large beautiful trees near you have a Tree Preservation Order – if not they might be cut down overnight.

If you have a mature tree you must get rid of, the Civic Trust has a registry of those who want trees for landscaping; or get in touch with the local council who might want to plant it somewhere else.

Campaign for more deciduous trees and mixed woodland to be planted by the Forestry Commission. Persuade your council surveyor to carry out vergeside planting.

Wildlife

In order to do something about disappearing wildlife we have to know what we have, where it is and how fast it is disappearing. If you can help in this, the Biological Records Centre at Monks Wood Experimental Station, Abbots Ripton, Hunts, coordinates many of the projects which collect the vital information.

If you are a farmer, the future of wildlife depends to a large extent on you. The Society for the Promotion of Nature Reserves has a Farming and Wildlife Advisory Group and produces a handy leaflet on what you can do to promote wildlife and farm economically at the same time.

At least 861 species and races of mammals, birds and reptiles are now in danger of extinction. All wild creatures are subject to increasing pressures from different sources; the loss of space to live; the loss of life itself through pollution, direct poisoning and hunting; the taking of specimens for zoos, the pet market and large-scale research. If you add to this the incredible demand for skins, fur and feathers, prompted by fashion and the interior decorating market, then the outlook for wild creatures is very grim indeed.

On principle don't buy the skin of anything that was once wild and this include crocodiles and snakes. Animals reared on a farm such as mink are a little bit better. Never buy any coats, clothes, bags or accessories made out of the skins of leopard – especially snow leopard and clouded leopard, cheetah, tiger, La Plata otter, and giant otter.

The International Fur Trade Federation has imposed a voluntary ban on all these skins. They have at last realized they are killing their own goose so help them – and perhaps after a few years' ban people will have realized that only a leopard really needs a leopard skin anyway.

It is no excuse to say 'it was dead before I bought it'; as Gina Lollabrigida said about her tiger skin coat. You encourage poaching, which is a serious problem in the sanctuaries and national parks of many countries like India, Kenya and Ethiopia which are becoming more and more interested in their wildlife heritage and are getting more and more of their foreign exchange by showing it to foreign visitors. So here is something constructive you can do to help some developing countries and it doesn't cost you anything.

If you want to help more in saving wildlife and natural areas in this country and abroad get in touch with:

'Wildlife'
WWF British National Appeal
7/8 Plumtree Court
London, EC4
Tel: 01-353 2615

and send them the money you decided not to spend on that leopard skin coat.

What We Gardeners Can Do . . .
The World Wildlife Fund offers the following
suggestions for home gardeners:

We tend to speak of 'farmers and landowners' as some other-than-us-group, yet every garden-owning one of us has a responsibility for management and encouraging wildlife. Let's run through a simple checklist of things *we* might be doing:

(1) planting things attractive to butterflies, such as the 'butterfly plant' (*Buddleia davidii*) or one of the many shrubs whose berries the birds like: Elder (mainly *Sambucus nigra*); Hawthorn (mainly *Crataegus monogyna*); Blackberry (*Rubus fruticosus* agg.); *Cotoneaster simonsii, horizontalis*, and *waterii*; Rowan (*Sorbus aucuparia*); Barberry (*Berberis darwinii*); Firethorn (*Pyracantha coccinea*); Holly (mainly *Ilex aquifolium*).

(2) leaving a bit of wild at the bottom of the garden. Perhaps your garden backs on to a neighbour's, and you might be able to coordinate planting trees and leaving a small haven for animals and plants.

(3) sparing dead trees, perhaps for a nature study project.

(4) refraining from clipping quite so much. Even stinging nettles, for instance, might be left if they're not really in the way – they are food for the caterpillars of the peacock and small tortoiseshell butterflies, which in turn are sought after by several birds.

(5) allowing undergrowth to accumulate at the base of hedges and around bushes, and leaving foliage at the base of trees, the leafy bowl of elm trees, for instance.

(6) creating a pond – even the smallest of home-made ponds, lined with butyl rubber or even polythene sheeting will teem with water-life in no time.

(7) feeding, housing, watering birds. The RSPB have a very practical leaflet 'Feed the Birds' (RSPB, The Lodge, Sandy, Bedfordshire). They warn us to give a bit of variety to the traditional white bread, which tends to become doughy and swell inside the birds' crops.

(8) thinking very long and hard about using pesticides and even herbicides. Read the labels. The Ministry of Agriculture and Fisheries has stated that *Aldrin* and *Dieldrin* should not be used in gardens, and the less poisonous but persistent chemicals DDT and BHC should be used with restraint. Products containing only *Pyrethrum* and *Derris* (='*Rotenone*') as the active ingredient can be used without fears of accumulation; but note that *Derris* is dangerous to fish. HMSO have a booklet 'Chemicals for the Gardener', 1s. 3d., which lists all products including weed-killers and their chemical make-up, and the pests against which the chemicals are effective.

Footpaths

There are thousands of miles of footpaths and rights of way in Britain. Most of these are now shown on definitive maps by county councils but their condition is sometimes poor and they may be ploughed up or overgrown. If you want to do something to conserve the paths while you are walking in the country get in touch with the Ramblers' Association for their excellent 'How to do it' leaflets on Parish Path Surveys, Footpath Clearance, and Waymarking.

> Ramblers' Association
> 1–4 Crawford Mews
> York Street,
> London, W1
> Tel: 01-262 1477

Country Codes

When walking, climbing, or studying in the countryside make sure you know The Country Code:

> Avoid damaging fences, hedges, and walls
> Leave no litter
> Keep to paths across farmland
> Fasten all gates
> Keep dogs under proper control
> Protect wildlife, wild plants, and trees
> Safeguard water supplies
> Guard against all risks of fire
> Go carefully on country roads
> Respect the life of the countryside

There are more specialist codes such as: Outdoor Studies Code, Water Sports Code, The Mountain Code, and 'Safety on Mountains' obtainable from the Central Council of Physical Recreation, 26 Park Crescent, London W1. Tel: 01-580 6822.

Check List for Reclaimers

Animal and vegetable refuse: can you compost it? All you need is a square yard or so of space and some hungry plants to use the results. See any good garden manual; better still, join the Henry Doubleday Research Association, 20 Covent Lane, Bocking, Braintree, Essex, telephone Braintree 1483. For the £2 membership fee you'll gain access to all kinds of relevant information.

Paper: does your local authority collect it separately for salvage? If not, do any community groups – schools, churches, youth clubs – run 'paper drives'? Does your local newspaper have any suggestions? Some newspapers themselves sponsor the salvaging of paper. For more information query Thames Board Mills Ltd, Purfleet, Essex, telephone: Purfleet 5555, Europe's largest users of waste paper.

Unwanted 'consumer durables' (cookers, refrigerators, furniture, etcetera): does your local authority operate a free collection service to forestall 'dumping'? If not, why not?

Abandoned motor vehicles: does your local authority collect these under the provisions of the Civic Amenities Act 1967, Part III? Report abandoned vehicles to the Street Inspectors' Department of your local Borough Engineer, who has a statutory obligation to remove them. They're valuable scrap metal, and plants like London's Proler-Cohen unit in Hammersmith, and the Bird Group Unit in St Helens, Lancashire, grind them into fist-sized fragments, ready to re-enter the steelmakers' furnaces.

Metals: each year disposal by tipping is burying useful metals valued at more than £7 million ('Public Cleansing', January 1970, p 21). Does your local authority make any attempt to salvage metals from domestic refuse? If not, why not?

Non-returnable bottles: why? You pay for them through your refuse disposal rates, and can't even get your investment back. They're a nuisance in domestic refuse, and the valuable glass is lost. Avoid them, and maybe the bottlers will notice.

Industrial waste: is your firm a member of the National Industrial Materials Recovery Association? Its services, including the excellent monthly journal, *Industrial Recovery*, cost only £5 per year. It's difficult to imagine a better value for money; yet according to Mr Holden, NIMRA secretary, some large firms terminated their membership when the fee was recently raised to this figure, a sorry commentary on the economic thinking of too many firms. Quite apart from the trivial nature of a £5 debit on the balance sheet of a healthy business, it seems highly probable that firms capitalizing on NIMRA experience and services will recoup their subscription many times over. For more information contact

Mr A. W. V. Holden, NIMRA, Carolyn House, Dingwall Road, Croydon CR9 2YU, telephone 01-686 7318.

Public Cleansing, the monthly journal of the Institute for Public Cleansing is another excellent guide to current activities and developments in waste-management, especially those involving local authorities. Many industrial waste-managers would benefit from the reports and discussions it publishes. Reprints of past articles contain much valuable information. It is available from the Institute for Public Cleansing, 28 Portland Place, London, W1, for 42s. per year or 3s. 6d. for a sample copy.

Is there derelict land in your vicinity – abandoned mine-workings, disused industrial areas, etcetera? Would it benefit from landscaping with landfill? Mention the matter to your local authorities and local newspapers.

If, like some of our readers, you wish to petition your local authorities to make better use of their takings, you'll want to refer to the Public Cleansing Costing Returns, to see where your local authority comes in the waste-reclamation league table. The Returns are now, alas, available only up to '65–'66, from HMSO, 9s. 6d.; but enlightening.

Walter C. Patterson

Action Suggestions for Organizations

There are a great number of voluntary and professional organizations contributing to the growing movement against environmental pollution. If your organization is not doing anything then there are some questions which should be asked.

First make a list of the phone numbers of local government departments which deal with complaints on noise, exhaust pollution, smoke, etc., and circulate them to your members.

Keep a chart of local politicians' statements and actions on environmental issues. Give a booby prize to the most contradictory person – preferably just before local elections.

Don't overlook the possibility of legal action.

Professional institutes. If you are an architect, surveyor, engineer, etc., find out if your institute includes environmental standards within your code of practice. If not ask for this to be investigated. Some institutes are making progress in this field and they need your support and ideas. Also ask for more inter-professional cooperation for agreement on standards. The standards of many British professional institutes are accepted all over the world. If our institutes can adopt high environmental standards based on ecological understanding then this will have an effect in many other countries.

Amenity Groups. They are doing a great deal. Join them and radicalize them with the help of this book.

Industry. If you work in a factory discuss environmental problems with your workmates. If your factory is polluting find out how much and why. Does your factory produce substances hazardous to your health or are conditions noisy? Write to your house magazine and let management know what you feel.

Unions. Unions in the USA and Australia, for instance, are urging the adoption of environmental control measures for the long-term benefit of their members. The US United Auto Workers Union is supporting a total ban on the internal combustion engine by 1975. They know that if they don't urge a changeover to other forms of quiet, pollution-free transport, then they will be redundant anyway. Is your union thinking ahead, not just in terms of the next wage packet?

Youth

Young people should be the ones most concerned about what happens to the environment since it will be they who have to live with the ecological catastrophe their parents are creating. Most environmental problems form part of a condition which you can recognize in many other forms – poverty, alienation, irrelevant education, etc. They have their root causes in a recklessly expanding population, a blind faith in technological solutions and a worship of economic growth and convenience. There is as yet no political group or system which does not implicitly accept these symptoms as inevitable, and many consider the environment an issue diverting them from their only true goals – more publicity and more votes.

Ministries may come and go, but don't be impressed that the British Government is doing anything. Beneath the veneer is chaos and apathy and to urge a public official merely to 'do something' about the environment is to leave it up to him to find the most impressive way of doing nothing. We must find out for ourselves what must be done and start kicking and pushing for action.

You will also surely hear that before we can worry about the environment we should find solutions to the immediate problems of people, such as housing and poverty. However, to wait for the advent of the next social revolution while man's habitat is destroyed is no solution either, nor will we be permitted the luxury of solving our problems one at a time.

It is mostly young people that see the connexion between their own problems and the system which creates environmental pollution and degradation in the name of progress. The young are not yet trapped in a system of vested interests which prevents them from seeing a way out of the crisis. We have no faces to save and have freedom to act.

Radicalize your school, youth organization, friends, university, and workplace to the environmental issues because here is something you can fight *for* and achieve the downfall of what you may be against. Yet at the same time you are putting a constructive rational and viable alternative – to live more ecologically.

How to Organize

Be as subversive, clever, radical yet constructive as you possibly can. Beware of being controlled to the point of suffocation, especially by adults, as this can kill any youth inspired project. Individual and small group action against pollution or in defence of the environment is a stronger weapon than most people realize. A loose association with clear objectives is much better than an organization with committee, procedures and annual general meetings. If you do form a group put your objectives in simple language. Don't bother with statutes – a manifesto is better. A useful example is the following from a young group called ECOS in the USA:

'We of ECOS believe that a crisis exists which endangers the future of (America), of mankind, and of life itself. We believe that all of us as human beings share the responsibility for this crisis.

We hold that these are the root causes:

> *an exploding population, which consumes vast and ever-increasing quantities of the entire world's energy and material resources, with little thought of the consequences ...*
> *an aggressive technology and economic system, which, in a rush to provide for and to profit from the human population, destroys other forms of life and contaminates our environment to a degree unprecedented in human history ...*
> *a burgeoning military establishment equipped with and committed to employ from its arsenal both nuclear and biochemical weapons in defence of this system ...*
> *a set of traditional values which may have sustained the human species in the past but which have led instead to the above problems and now inhibit us from responding to the present crisis.*

Against this dark picture is the individual man or woman, increasingly alienated from others and impotent to act, confronted by large, unresponsive institutions and the collapse of meaningful, human communities.

We believe that this crisis will not be resolved solely by traditional conservation activities, obstructionist tactics, force of arms, unilateral government action, or independent or uncoordinated efforts; nor will the solution be found in new scientific discoveries or technological advances within the present system.

232

We propose to create a fresh ethical response to our environment; a self-sustaining way of life in which man views himself as part of and as dependent upon the natural ecosystem.

We reject as unacceptable:

a world in which unlimited population growth and unlimited economic expansion are accepted uncritically as beneficial . . .

a world in which any person lives in luxury and privilege while many others live in hunger or oppression . . .

a world in which men and women view themselves as separated from the earth and the inspirations of nature . . .

a world in which the individual is victimized by the impersonal machinery of his technology . . .

a world in which people turn to violence, anarchy, or totalitarianism to resolve their dissatisfaction with government, technology, or society.

In coming together to meet these problems we understand that the greatest enemy of mankind at present is man, and that our source of hope in averting this environmental/social/ecological crisis rests with the community of concern and action which we are building together.

We see at least three tasks before us:

making the human population at large, and its political leaders in particular, aware of the crisis and the fact that it does affect them . . .

undertaking constructive campaigns to halt, or, at least, delay the excessive growth of our population, the depletion of our resources, and the pollution of our water, earth, and air . . .

developing basic alternatives to our present way of life and view of the world which will be more functional, more adaptive, and more stable in the future.

The time for decision and action is now. The responsibility cannot be left for future generations – we may be the last generation able to choose an effective course of action.'

The Project Approach

It helps to think of activities in terms of a project – you can even give it a name like Pollution Probe, the name of a massive student project in Canada. The project should have a well-defined and specific objective which should be made clear to everyone participating. The main purpose might be education, publicity, rehabilitation, etc., but do not try to make projects all-embracing. The project can also be related to a wider objective, although there must be seen to be a direct relation – for example, a project on a motorway can be extended to the role of the car in our society. Don't only demonstrate against, for instance, water pollution – pick a near-by stream and wage a clean-up campaign. Analyse the water; find out who is polluting it and why.

The project approach also has advantages in that it can involve other groups and attract financial and moral support more easily than a continuous programme. Try and pick as a first project one that involves improvement to your local area, that indicates solutions to a variety of other problems or can easily inspire people for further activities.

With a project it is also easier to evaluate your success. If the project is successful try not to institutionalize it but tell others how you did it. British life is full of institutions that have long outlived their purpose or meaning.

Avoid violence.

It is not that you are never justified, but the message of why something is done is often buried and lost by the public and the media. They often do not understand that the central problems may really be much more violent than any number of violent acts you could ever commit.

There are situations which require action beyond lawful tactics. The law does not yet recognize the right of every individual to a clean, quiet and healthy environment. For instance if you want to save a tree from being cut down, be prepared to climb up it and wait for the police to pull you down. Such illegal but *non-violent* tactics can generate support among young people and students who would not otherwise become involved.

Don't overlook other ways of getting the message across. Design and print posters and if they are good enough you can sell some. Prepare spots for local radio, hand-out leaflets in the streets, on the Underground, and to people in traffic jams. Tell the local press about what you are doing and tell the Friends of the Earth so they can tell the rest. Good luck.

Active Conservation

Many young people are willing to spend a great deal of their time and energy on ways to improve their immediate environment. This may involve an incredible range of things to do such as management and landscaping of parks and derelict areas, creation and repair of public footpaths and hill tracks, construction of nature trails, signs, bridges, and fences, and survey and census work in conservation, recreational, and land-use studies.

Many of these individual tasks may be relatively small but collectively they can make a real difference. The Civic Trust for the North East provides a leaflet *How to Organize Volunteer Work*, which is reproduced here:

How to Organize Volunteer Work

The appearance and amenities of our surroundings are not only spoiled by the major eyesores – the pit heaps, derelict factories and disused mine workings – but also by the acres of minor dereliction. The ramshackle and long forgotten allotments, broken down fences, neglected village greens, overgrown churchyards and countless other small eyesores when all added together create an impression of extreme neglect and decay. In addition, there are opportunities for adding to the amenities of an area by voluntary effort by providing additional grassed areas, clearing footpaths, preserving sites and structures of historic or archaeological interest and many other worthwhile jobs.

It is on these relatively small, but no less significant, tasks that volunteers can work to good effect.

Choosing the Project

Projects should be worthwhile improvements to the appearance or amenities of a locality and should be of benefit to the whole community.

The work must be capable of being carried out by largely unskilled volunteers and should therefore be limited to simple elements. As well as being feasible, simple landscaping for example often looks better and is more resistant to vandalism than more elaborate treatment.

It is important that the site is maintained afterwards, otherwise the work will be wasted. See that there are no future plans for the development of the site and that the local authority or some other body will undertake to maintain it once the work has been completed.

Be careful to ensure that volunteers are not used as cheap labour. Projects should be chosen so that volunteers are doing a job that would not otherwise be done.

Obtaining the Owner's Permission and Help

Sites may be owned by the local authority or some other public body. It is on public property that the local authority will be most likely to help with tools, materials, supervision, etc., and it is this land which is likely to be of most benefit to the community. If, however, the property is privately owned, the owner's full permission and cooperation are essential.

Seeking Professional Guidance

The Borough Engineer, Planning Officer, or a local landscape architect will usually give advice with method of treatment, materials, trees, etc., and should be consulted at an early stage.

Planning the Work

A reasonably accurate estimate of the amount of work involved, materials and equipment required, and the number of volunteers who can be usefully employed is required at an early stage. A list of priorities can then be drawn up, together with suitable dates for execution, taking into account such factors as weather, and availability of site and resources, including volunteers. It is often useful to have a 'master-plan' showing the envisaged scheme and the programme of work although this is not essential on simple projects.

Gathering Resources

The cost of the work can be kept down by:

(a) Simplicity of treatment.

(b) Re-use of material on the site or unwanted materials upon other derelict sites, e.g. soil, paving, bricks, shrubs, and even trees.

(c) Obtaining discount on goods purchased. The fact that work is being done for nothing often encourages others to be charitable.

(d) Obtaining gifts, in kind or cash from public bodies and private people.

(e) Obtaining grant aid from local authorities where this is applicable.

Tools and equipment can usually be borrowed, but it is necessary to be sure that they will be forthcoming before fixing a date for commencing work. Make sure that they are of the necessary type, strength and number.

Materials should be available in the right quantity and the right quality. Seek professional advice if required.

Volunteers usually require food and transport, and local people may help with these. Young people often prefer to work away from their own neighbourhood, but costs can be kept down by recruiting local volunteers whenever possible. If transport is required, it is preferable to arrange it privately, since sporadic arrival by public transport wastes time and is disruptive of the tempo of work.

There are many potential sources of volunteers. Personal contact to explain the project and its relevance is usually better than a letter, although this may be used to make an initial contact. When recruiting from schools it is necessary to inform the Director of Education before contracting individual headmasters. Remember to make sure that there is a sufficient number of older volunteers to act as leaders and take responsibility for seeing that the work is carried out.

Organizing the Work

Insurance is vital, both for personal and public liability. The Civic Trust can arrange this, but otherwise it can be arranged quite cheaply through a good insurance company.

First-aid kit is essential, and the nearest nurse, doctor or hospital should be known.

Inform the police well beforehand if any traffic control is going to be necessary, or to protect half completed work.

The key to a successful project is timing. Make sure that the right quantities of tools, materials, and volunteers are at the right place at the right time.

Publicity can be useful, but newspapers must be given accurate information regarding the time and place of a project.

The work should be timed to the stamina of the volunteers, allowing due time for tea and meal breaks. Remember that volunteers will usually wish to enjoy themselves on the job, and a relaxed approach is preferable to a highly regimented method of working. Similarly, leadership by example is usually more effective than an authoritarian approach.

Residential Workcamps

The foregoing applies to work carried out on single days, volunteers returning home in the evenings. A concentrated effort can, however, be made by organizing a residential workcamp in which volunteers are provided with food and simple accommodation. Such camps may involve any number of volunteers, the cost being about £2 per head per

238

week. This may be reduced if gifts of food and accommodation are received. In addition to these items already mentioned there are a number of further points to note:

Accommodation may be very simple. Typically a church hall, community centre, or even a camp under canvas will be suitable. The main requirements are separate dormitory for male and female with mattresses and blankets, washing and toilet facilities, a common room for eating and social activity, and cooking facilities.

A responsible residential leader should be appointed who may then delegate responsibility for specific functions to other members of the camp, e.g. cooking and catering, work leadership, social functions, etc.

The camp will wish to work as a team and have a social life of its own but a minimum of forty hours of work per week should be expected.

Sources of Projects

Your local Planning Office, or Borough Engineer's Department, Local Councils, Churches, Civic and Amenity Societies, Council for Nature, National Parks Authorities, National Playing Fields Association, National and Civic Trust, Rotary & Lions Clubs, Round Tables, and Inner Wheel Clubs, Women's Institutes and Townswomen's Guilds.

... of Materials, etc.

Local Engineers, Surveyors and Cleansing Departments, Local Industry, and help in kind from a variety of sources.

... and of Volunteers

Local Schools, Youth and Boys' Clubs, Toc H, IVS and CMP Groups, and Boys and Venture Scouts. Police Cadets, Church Lads Brigade, YMCA, YWCA. Girl Guides, Conservation Corps, Junior Civic and Amenity Societies, Local History and Industrial Archaeology Groups, University and College Societies, etc.

Where the Action is

Conservation Corps,
Zoological Gardens,
Regents Park,
London, NW1
Tel: 01-722 7112

The Conservation Corps started in 1959 and is now part of the British Trust for Conservation Volunteers. It organizes a wide variety of conservation work for young people throughout the year and provides an advisory and information service for anyone interested in working in their area. It will also provide you with a list of weekend projects and all the spring and summer work camps in various parts of Britain. Training courses will be started for youth leaders and a nationally recognized certificate of proficiency is being considered. The Conservation Corps has a booklet about their last ten years' work available at 38 np.

The regional Civic Trusts organize very similar activities, but more in the towns than on nature reserves and national parks.

Youth Enterprise,
Civic Trust for the North East,
34–5 Saddler Street,
Durham
Tel: 0385 61182

Rhondda Youth Action,
Civic Trust for Wales,
Snelling House, Bute Terrace,
Cardiff
Tel: 0222 33131

Civic Trust for the North West,
Century House, St Peter's Square,
Manchester 2
Tel: 061 236 0333

Also the following have active conservation programmes, including camps:

Enterprise Youth,
Conservation Projects Officer,
29 Queen Street,
Edinburgh 2.

National Trust – Junior Division,
The Old Grape House,
Cliveden,
Taplow,
Maidenhead,
Berkshire

Youth organizations for study projects, camps and other activities in conservation and environmental studies:

Conservation Youth Association,
London Road School,
London Road,
Mitcham,
Surrey

Young Ornithologists Club,
The Lodge,
Sandy,
Beds.

Wildlife Youth Service,
Marstons Court,
Manor Way,
Wellington,
Surrey

INTERNATIONAL:
International Youth Federation for Environmental Studies and Conservation,
c/o IUCN,
1110 Morges,
Switzerland

This Federation brings together 27 national or regional youth groups concerned with conservation or environmental studies from 15 countries, mostly in Europe. It has an international programme of projects, study camps, work camps, conferences, etc., all of which are run entirely by young people. It provides advice and information to young people and youth organizations who wish to set up conservation programmes and produces an information bulletin for Europe and one for North America. Any young person under twenty-eight can join in.

Conservation Activities in Schools

Here are two examples of action taken by staff and school-children at schools in Wales which both received the Prince of Wales Countryside Awards, 1970.

Recipient: Gwendraeth Grammar School Conservation Club.

Project Details:

Inspired by Sir Frank Fraser Darling's Reith Lectures in 1969, pupils at Gwendraeth Grammar School, Drefach, near Llanelli, Carmarthenshire, entered fully into the spirit of European Conservation Year in Wales.

In deciding what to do they looked outward from their school. They saw pylons, open-cast coal workings, pasture, houses, hedges, cars and people. However, they decided that as a first task they would 'put their own house in order'.

'Their own house' was translated into an area of land in the centre of the school campus, used in recent years for general waste burning. Many fine trees have scars from this burning.

Viewing their project in terms of improving amenity and providing environmental teaching facilities, the young people helped by the art master, Mr Nicholas, surveyed their site, consulted experts, made recommendations, undertook the implentation of their proposals. Positive change is now to be seen on the ground.

In June, the school was declared joint winners of the 'Wales in Bloom' Competition sponsored by the Wales Tourist Board. The fine presentation of their survey and proposals are models of how to sell your project.

The future looks very hopeful, awareness has been created throughout the school via the Conservation Club. *Conservation* is not enough; the youngsters of Gwendraeth have shown that by putting their own house in order, *conservation in practice* involves getting things done, and that one's own doorstep is where it should begin. From this base they become outward-looking to wider horizons.

Contacts: D. W. Nicholas, Gwendraeth Grammar School, Drefach, Llanelli. Wendy Phillips, Head Girl, and Adrian Rowlands. Tel. No. TUMBLE 322.

Excellent report has been prepared by Miss W. Phillips. Documentation is good.

Subject has considerable merit for television and radio purposes.

Recipient: The children and staff of Newport Primary School.

Project Details:

Fired by the urge to escape from the classroom, the children of Newport Primary School, Pembrokeshire, undertook an environmental study of their township. Stories and poems were written, photographs taken, maps and sketches drawn. The children aged from 7 to 11 amassed a considerable amount of material, and realizing their town was in a very popular tourist area, they decided to write a guide and publish it. This they did, and now they are just about to undertake a second reprint, having sold a first edition of 1,500 copies.

The guide book is remarkable. It is a publication of high quality showing the pride which the youngsters have in their home area and the obvious enjoyment the children had got through preparing the guide and waymarking the walks in and around the town.

As a practical conservation project they undertook to clean and renovate a famous local feature known as the 'Treacle Well'. This is now complete. Work in the out-of-doors is continuing, the school has projects in hand relating to the sea-shore and other areas nearby.

Contacts: D. Islwyn Jenkins, BA, Headmaster, Newport County Primary School, Pembrokeshire. Private telephone number: NEWPORT (Pembs) 554.

This project would afford excellent material for television or radio programmes.

Students for
Environmental Action

Graham Searle

This is not a eulogy about student involvement in the growing conservation movement. Nowhere near enough students
are involved – yet. Nowhere near enough is being done on
the campuses – yet. But in the late 1960s and early 1970s a
start has been made to focus student attention on the threats
to our environment. This summary isn't complacent. It is a
summary of some of the action taken by some students, a
pointer to other students for schemes of action they might
adopt in their own colleges. In the Appendix (pp. 302–8)
there is a list of contacts for student groups actively involved in environmental work. If you're a student, contact
them for advice and information about what they're doing.
If your college has such a group, join it; if not why not set
one up? There is abundant scope for participation and originality.

The history of the National Union of Students' involvement in conservation work is short. In August 1969
HRH the Duke of Edinburgh wrote to the then President of
NUS, Trevor Fisk, asking him whether the Union wished to
take part in the European Conservation Year programme
by contributing to the Countryside in 1970 conference in
October 1970, and by sponsoring what environmental projects it could. Mr Fisk replied that the Union would give its
support to the campaign. Consequently the incoming President, Jack Straw, met with the Secretary of the Standing
Committee of the Countryside in 1970 Organization and
representatives of the Nature Conservancy to discuss what
sort of contribution NUS could make. It was decided that
NUS should convene a committee made up of students
from member-colleges and universities of the National
Union, having as its terms of reference the stimulation of

interest in the environment on the part of students, and the preparation of a number of documents to be presented to the Countryside in 1970 Conference which would voice the opinions shared at least by some members of this section of society. The 600 or so member-organizations of NUS were circulated, and fourteen students from colleges up and down the country, having different but complementary interests and fields of study were invited to form this working group.

The committee produced three reports on Refuse Disposal; Agriculture, Forestry and Land Management; and Relations with Industry, which were presented to the Countryside Conference. Growing out of this involvement came the appointment of an NUS Conservation Officer and the establishment of an NUS department, the main job of which is to propagandize and to assist local student groups in their efforts to improve and to safeguard the environment.

However, NUS was not the only organization recently to become aware of the urgent need for a sane environmental policy. In March and April 1970 many clubs and societies at colleges throughout the country, which had never, prior to the launching of European Conservation Year, interested themselves in environmental management, suddenly became active in this field. In April 1969 the Department of Foundation Studies at the Maidstone School of Art organized and ran what they termed 'Earth Day'. There were obvious analogies, though of course vast differences in scale, between the aims of the organizers of Earth Day in Kent and those running Earth Day in the United States; first and foremost the purpose was to educate the public to realization of the dangers inherent in just 'carrying on as we are'. The students distributed pamphlets the main message of which was 'Give Earth a chance' and which highlighted the dangers associated with over-population, air and water pollution, land waste, and noise. The document also stated the objections to germ warfare research establishments and nuclear tests. The main tenet of the arguments was embodied in two sentences: 'Too many people produce too much waste for the earth to survive. Too many people and their waste are killing you', and the reader was asked to 'Send this letter to your MP'.

Unlike the approach of Maidstone School of Art, the students of Farnborough Technical College decided to aim their criticisms and demands for action at local targets. In a magazine called *Nothing but Smut*, the students (first year OND Engineers) complained of the state of the oil-laden Cove Brook, derelict buildings and the Basingstoke Canal which, they claimed, constituted a considerable hazard to health. The project received good coverage in the *Surrey and Hants News*, the local paper, where it received support in an editorial which declared: 'In Farnborough the students have given a lead ... Let's join them and make European Conservation Year something more than just another fancy title. Let's hope for action on a local level to clean up our black spots. And is it asking too much for a strong lead from the local councils?'

This local newspaper proclaimed the students' aim as being 'to stir the apathy, currently lying thicker than the slime on the Basingstoke Canal' [sic] and the extent of the apathy was amply illustrated by a survey conducted by the Farnborough students, the conclusion of which was that local people simply don't care what sort of a mess their immediate environment is in. But the students' protests are having repercussions in the Borough. A representative of the Thames Conservancy Board visited the Cove Brook to examine the extent of the oil pollution. The Basingstoke Canal Co. was in receipt of the students' complaints which were brought to the attention of the Hampshire and Surrey County Councils, currently negotiating with the Canal Co., over the future of the waterway. Finally the councils are aware of the objections of the young people of the town to the common practice of unauthorized tipping of refuse and abandoning of cars at a variety of locations throughout Farnborough. Since the initial publicity the Thames Conservancy Board decided to bring forward their starting date for dredging the Cove Brook from Christmas 1969, the clean-up being commenced in August. Farnborough Council threatened legal action against anyone dumping rubbish in the Brook, and has issued warnings to children about the danger of playing with mortar bombs slowly being revealed by the falling water level in the Canal. Whilst a 'strong lead from the local councils' might be an exaggeration of what has occurred, it is to be hoped that this sort of pressure applied by the columns of a widely-read local press will have the result of awakening them to the need to clean the place up.

At both Maidstone College of Art and Farnborough Technical College, the accent has been on the dissemination of information to a public which appears extremely disinterested in the basic issues of conservation and survival. At other colleges emphasis is currently placed on detailed examination of the problems which confront mankind, and an attempt to ensure that students at least are both interested in the issues and well-informed. At the University of Durham, staff and students came together to organize a teach-in on the subject of 'Population, Starvation, and their Political Impact', and at that university there has been established an active ecology action group named CATER (Comprehensive Approach to Earth's Resources) which devotes its attentions to the study of the feasibility of solutions advanced to cope with the growing pressures put on the environment. Members of CATER also erected in the centre of Durham a 'population thermometer' and painted in the daily increase in world population in an attempt to stimulate local recognition of one of the major problems which we each face, and of which we are each a part.

At Cambridge University the responsibility for this task is undertaken by an organization called Ecology Action which is a section of the Cambridge Society for Social Responsibility in Science. This group is currently considering the effect on society of the automobile and is attempting to monitor the associated noise pollution in the Cambridge area. There is also at Cambridge an extremely active branch of the Conservation Corps: this national organization is associated to the Council for Nature and was founded in 1959 to 'arrange volunteer youth labour for national conservation projects', and includes many student members. In Cambridge the local branch, since its inception about ten years ago, has played an important role in the management of the Cambridgeshire and Isle of Ely region. It works in close cooperation with the Cambridgeshire and Isle of Ely Naturalist Trust (which meets its expenses), and also sends helpers to assist in London Conservation Corps projects. The sort of work it performs varies from path clearance and bridge construction to ragwort-pulling and coppice maintenance, and the number of man-hours devoted to such tasks is impressive. In the first two terms of the last academic year, for instance, volunteers gave a total of 1,500 hours of their time to participation in these projects.

It will already be obvious that work connected with environmental conservation and improvement is, at different colleges up and down the country, undertaken by different bodies and organizations which themselves place the emphasis on different forms of activity. At the University College of Wales, Aberystwyth, it is the United Nations Student Association which provides the vehicle for such involvement. In January 1969 a series of study groups were set up, each consisting of between five and twenty students, to examine various aspects of environmental conservation. These groups have concerned themselves with aspects of pollution control, wildlife and conservation, the economics of pollution control, pesticides, domestic and industrial waste, and the public propagandizing of the problems to be faced. In addition to this more theoretical and academic attack, many students, as in other colleges, are themselves involved in practical work through such organizations as the Royal Society for the Protection of Birds, and these students are coming together to form a 'watchdog' committee to protect the local environment from thoughtless despoliation.

That the environmental brief should fall to the UNSA group in Aberystwyth is far from unique in that the national UNSA programme recognizes the need for such action, and consistent with this has run a seminar in Yorkshire entitled 'Armaments and Environment: Threats to Survival', and a conference on the environment at the City of Liverpool (C. F. Mott) College of Education.

That care for the environment is not confined to the

preservation of rural beauty is well illustrated by the Social Action Group at Bradford University. Last summer this group constructed an adventure playground for local children on a formerly derelict urban site. This year they plan to extend the idea by converting a disused goods yard into a fairground-cum-open-air theatre at which to stage a Wakes Festival. In order to achieve such results, the group has kept in close touch with the local council, which (in common with most other councils in the UK) welcomes such constructive application of the students' ideals.

Increasing attention is also being paid to studies in Ecology and Conservation in the Universities. Currently there are four universities in Britain which offer MSc courses in this field. At Aberdeen and Bangor the course is regarded as a 'broadening year' particularly designed for students going into teaching. At Durham the emphasis is placed on population and production studies and the aim is to provide useful training especially for overseas students who will later return to their own countries. The course at University College, London is geared to graduates who will take up work in such fields as wild life conservation, rural land use planning and the management of reserves and national parks.

At the University of Wales Institute of Science and Technology in Cardiff, Prof. Edwards has developed a scheme of staff-student involvement in useful and applicable environmental research. The Taff Project Group is financed by the Senates of the University College of Wales and UWIST, Glamorgan County Council, and the River Authority. It employs about ten students per year during the long vacation (at about £12 per week) to assist staff who are engaged in monitoring pollution in the Taff and assessing conservation requirements, as well as to construct nature trails in the locality. The Taff Project is of great value to undergraduates and research fellows alike, and involves a cross-section of the academic community in work of an extremely important nature. UWIST has shown that when researchers apply for grants to the NERC, the Council is prepared to include in its grant due provision for the payment of undergraduate assistants.

Grants made by NERC also support students studying for their PhD in matters related to ecology. The total cost of grants made by NERC to research fellows, MSc, and PhD, students of ecology was about £530,000 in 1968–9. Subjects for theses currently being prepared include studies of the tolerance of plants to heavy metals (at Bristol), aluminium and iron (Sheffield), and the effects and speed of the build-up of cadmium and mercury in ecosystems (Swansea). At Cambridge post-graduates are currently investigating vegetational history and its relation to agricultural practices, and at Sheffield post-graduates are engaged in studying tree mortality rates and population histories. Other important pieces of research include investigations into the adaptations one can apply to colliery spoil (York) and the extent of the accumulation and concentration of pesticides in food chains (Westfield).

Thus, there is a considerable amount of good and appropriate work currently being undertaken in colleges and universities. But the tragedy is that unless a student's work is mentioned subsequently in books or articles, then the findings of the researcher can too easily be committed to oblivion. PhD theses have a worse record even than government reports when it comes to dust-gathering. NERC does not require a copy of the completed thesis; instead two copies are printed, one going to the University at which the research is carried out and the other being retained by the individual. Hence there is no central library of NERC sponsored theses. It is true that NERC keeps an index of what work has been undertaken, but there are few students aware that information is available from this source. Perhaps if NERC published an annual list of what research topics have been sponsored by them in the past five or ten years and where the resultant theses can be obtained, then circulated this information to University departments and interested organizations, the communications difficulty could be overcome. The provision of this information would be extremely useful to bodies active in the environmental field in that they would then more easily be able to base their proposed policies on recent and up-to-date research.

UNIVERSITY OF THE AIR, EARTH, FIRE, AND WATER

B. All. Special Honours Examination 1971
Three hours

Answer all questions with a 'yes' or 'no'. Marks will be awarded for correct use of English and for orderly presentation of material.

1. Does your University contribute to the pollution problem by discharging untreated waste into local waterways or by disposing of chemicals (liquid or gaseous) in such a way as to constitute a danger to the environment?

2. Does a study of Environmental Management of Pollution form a part of the appropriate courses at your University?

3. Does your department seem more concerned with, and infinitely better informed on, aspects of sand-dune migration in the Sahara than in the Ministry of Agriculture's attempt to produce dust-bowls in East Anglia? (In these days of enlightenment students should feel free to delete these two references and to insert any analogous alternatives – for instance, the World Food Problem and the construction of motorways on agricultural land.)

4. Is there a society/group/organization/club at your University/college/institution for staff and students who wish to involve themselves in environmental conservation and improvement?

5. Does your society just talk about the crucial, all-embracing, and disheartening problems faced by mankind, or does it actually concern itself with activities which improve the local environment?

6. Are you aware that if any individual or group wishes to get advice on how to engage in activities of an ecological nature (be they identifying prime polluters, taking out injunctions, lobbying councils, or clean-up campaigns), they should write or phone the NUS conservation officer?

Teaching Environment
in Schools

K. S. Wheeler

Teaching by means of environmental studies is a well-established practice in British primary schools. The pupils use their interest in their local surroundings to follow up lines of inquiry set them by the teacher, or arising out of their own curiosity. Such a method of teaching is based on an understanding of child psychology which recognizes that young children learn best through direct experience rather than by the imposition of abstract knowledge, and that through such experience a wide range of study and communication skills is developed. Young children are holistic in their outlook, and their inquiries naturally take them across the traditional subject boundaries. Consequently, environmental studies replace more formal lessons in geography, history, general science, and natural history. As a result, too, the timetable is not parcelled up into small units of subject time, but teacher and taught are able to use the schoolday in accordance with the way their interests develop. The Plowden Report of 1967 (published by the Central Advisory Council for Education) gave influential recognition to this method of teaching.

Arising from the success of environmental studies in the primary school, educators have sought to apply the method to the teaching of older children. Unfortunately, much confusion has arisen because environmental studies is not solely a method of teaching about the environment, but rather a means of using the environment for the purposes of education. Environmental education in the more exact sense is concerned with finding a new approach to teaching about the environment, i.e. the social, biological, and physical milieu in which man lives. Indeed, the movement towards environmental education has to a large extent developed out

253

of the dissatisfaction, felt by many secondary school-teachers, with the inadequacy of the traditional subjects as a vehicle for teaching children about the problems confronting the modern environment. Hitherto, geography teachers believed themselves mainly responsible for this, but the academic content imposed by the universities on the schools has until recently taken the form of rigid learning about regions; and the value of fieldwork, pioneered by geographers, has tended to be of a rural and descriptive kind. A further complicating factor comes from those teachers of the non-academic secondary pupil who regarded environmental education as any project which takes the child out of the classroom and introduces him to the reality of the world outside. The Newsom Report of 1963 (also published by the CACEO) endorsed this kind of approach.

The recent upsurge of concern about the quality of the man-made, and the biological, environment has given great impetus to the need for communicating environmental awareness to the mass of young people growing up in Britain today. The curriculum objectives of such a movement are aimed at not only using environment for the purposes of education, but also directed towards educating about the environment. Again, many opinions exist as how best such education may be accomplished, and the argument is further bedevilled by there being as many definitions of environment as there are educationists! In secondary school education, so far, little consensus of opinion exists concerning the syllabus content of such courses. In Colleges of Education the same lack of agreement is found, although the central core of the work is invariably an amalgam of field biology, local history and geography. There are some colleges where a Bachelor of Education degree in Environmental Studies is offered.

In 1967 the Society for Environmental Education was founded in Leicester for the purpose of bringing together teachers interested in ways and means of educating about the environment. The Society organizes conferences which seek to explore the methodology of such teaching. For some years now the Field Studies Council has provided accommodation in numerous rural areas where fieldwork in the environmental sciences can be followed by older children. In 1965 the conservationist movement convened the second 'Countryside in 1970' Conference which led to the formation of the Council for Environmental Education 'to provide a focal point for coordinating and disseminating advice on environmental education, and to promote appropriate policies.' Three committees have been set up, and these are a Committee on Schools, a Committee on Higher Education and Training, and a Committee on Resources. Other important organizations concerned with developing environmental education are: the National Rural and Environmental Studies Association, the Geographical Association, and the Schools Council. In particular, the latter has an Environmental Studies project operating to help in the teaching of the 5–13 year olds. Other Schools Council projects include certain aspects of environmental education, too. This year the Town and Country Planning Association has set up an Environmental Information Centre aimed at providing a 'wide range of material to assist in teaching schoolchildren about their surroundings'; and the Department of Adult Education, University of Leicester, held an important conference to decide on the definition and content of Environmental Education.

At present, there are three General Certificate of Education Examination Syllabuses at 'O' Level which reflected the need for environmental education, but these have a bias towards the rural and the biological. In other syllabuses not specifically dealing with environmental education, such as geography, there is an opportunity to deal with aspects of urbanization. In some areas work is going ahead on the preparation of Advanced Level syllabuses for environmental education, but none of these have been published to date. In the case of the Certificate for Secondary Education, catering for the less academic pupil, there are nine examining boards offering in environmental studies.

There are many interesting cases of schools independently undertaking environmental projects. In Wiltshire, for instance, there is the M4 Project involving many schools in the

255

study of the motorway as it is built across the county. In Bolton, schoolchildren took part in the preparation of the town's area redevelopment scheme. In this connexion, it is interesting to note that the Skeffington Report: People and Planning (HMSO, 1969) has emphasized the need for schools to educate for participation in planning. The Countryside Commission is using schoolchildren to undertake a survey of rights of way, and there are many examples of schoolchildren taking part in conservation schemes.

Perhaps the first to connect the quality of environment with the method and content of education was Sir Patrick Geddes in his now famous educational laboratory he established in the Outlook Tower, Edinburgh, as long ago as 1887. It was the intent of his Regional Survey methods to develop in young persons a creative attitude to the improvement of environment. Today, although there are many voices speaking for and against different methods of educating about the environment, nevertheless educationists are more united than ever in the common aim of producing a school curriculum related to the way children learn, and whose purpose is to inculcate an awareness of environment, both urban and rural; local and worldwide.

Civic Societies:
Protest and Create

Fifty years ago the spoliation of Britain's countryside by ribbon development and the unplanned growth of towns became the rallying point for a civic society movement – local groups of concerned citizens determined to prevent the further deterioration of their environment. By the outbreak of the Second World War there were about 100 such local organizations. Today there are more than 750, and not all of them are in historic towns or rural beauty spots; some are in unlikely places like the Potteries where their battlecries are less the traditional ones about preserving this or protecting that, more about positively improving environments intolerable in 20th century Britain. In the past these amenity protestors have been almost entirely middle-aged and middle-class. Today this is less true: many young people are joining up, though only a few societies have broken through the class barriers – the masses have not yet taken up verbal arms against the highway engineers, airport planners, pylon erectors, military despoilers, all the devisers of ugliness, noise, pollution.

Letters to the editors of local papers, petitions, posters, leaflets, exhibitions, mass meetings, objections at public inquiries, arm-twistings of councillors and MPs, education of the local public: these are the weapons used by local civic societies. And, more and more, they are becoming more than protesters; they are becoming creators, they are making positive contributions to the quality of town and country planning in Britain. Less and less are they bands of crankish amateurs; more and more they are well-briefed professionals. The planners of Britain's cities, towns and countryside now take local civic societies seriously – if not yet seriously enough.

Does your community have a civic society? If so, join it.

Is it alert, progressive, professional? If not, couldn't you help to make it so? If your community doesn't have a society, oughtn't it to? Why not start the ball rolling yourself? The Civic Trust and its four regional associate trusts (addresses in Appendix, pp. 291–2) can tell you whether your community already has a society (though if you haven't heard of its activities yet, it can't be much of a society) and give you guidance on the formation and operation of a local group. The Civic Trust publishes a useful booklet (*The Civic Society Movement*, price 4s, post paid) which outlines the history, objectives, organization, failures and successes of local societies. From that booklet we reprint below the Civic Trust's guidelines on starting up a new society, a draft constitution for a society registered as a charity, and advice on alternative registrations as a trust, limited company or housing society.

Starting a new society

A society is best brought into being by getting a few people together and arranging to hold a public meeting. Half a dozen people who think in the same sort of way are enough to start the ball rolling. A key figure in the new society will be a competent and energetic Secretary. He or she should be included in the group from the very start. The editor of the local paper should be seen and told what the group proposes to do. If his interest is aroused he may refer to the group's plans in his editorial, or make them a news item. The meeting must be publicized as widely as possible by means of posters and leaflets. If local residents have been notified of a threat to some cherished amenity, they will probably come to the meeting anyway. A well-known speaker is always an additional draw and a good chairman is essential.

If it is decided to form a society, a Steering Committee should be appointed to work out aims and objects. Use can then be made of the Civic Trust draft constitution (see page 262). This has widely based aims and objects which should prove sufficiently elastic to cover any or all of the likely activities. This constitution has already received the approval of the Charity and Inland Revenue Commissioners and as little alteration as possible therefore should be made to it. Subscriptions to existing societies vary from 2s 6d to £1 1s per annum, but 10s 6d is generally found to be the most that members are prepared to pay. It is useful to hand out duplicated sheets at the inaugural meeting setting out the objects of the society. The name and address of anyone wishing to become a member can be filled in at the bottom of the form and handed in to the Secretary at the end of the meeting. If copies of the constitution itself can be duplicated and distributed to members before the meeting, so much the better as this will save valuable time. Alternatively, a draft constitution can be posted up by the door of the hall.

If a local society is to get off to a good start, it must provide for the interests and employ the energies of a wide range of members. Its activities will include: education in planning, design, and architecture; the preservation of the best from the past; action occasioned by current development; and, most important of all, thought and study for the future. It will often be found useful to work at these activities through a separate committee for each.

Lectures, meetings, publications, exhibitions, films, competitions, group expeditions to places of interest should all feature fairly soon in the programme of a lively new society. And the more the themes of such activities can be coordinated, the greater will be their cumulative effect. There is also tremendous scope here for collaboration with other groups. If a series of lectures is being organized, students and staff from the local art school, or Workers' Educational Association classes, might be invited. If a guidebook or an exhibition is planned, the photographic society can be called in to help. When a tree-planting week is undertaken, schools can be persuaded to cooperate and members of the Chamber of Commerce to join in with a window-box scheme. The local film society might be induced to devote a whole programme to architecture and design. If there is some controversy about redevelopment, an essay competition in schools may be a good idea, or a public debate with the Townswomen's Guild, or an exhibition in the biggest store, where there will be a large captive audience.

Architecture and civic design are not normally part of the curriculum of secondary schools but local societies can do much to change this by providing posters, small exhibitions, prizes for essay competitions and notes to form the basis for talks. Head teachers generally welcome initiative of this kind. Some societies as we have learnt follow this up by forming Junior Sections and these can do useful work on their own or in collaboration with the parent society.

By looking after archives, taking and collecting photographs and by preparing detailed technical reports on the most important old buildings and monuments in the area, a society can make itself the accepted repository of local knowledge. The Department of the Environment compiles lists of buildings of special architectural or historic interest after consultation with informed local people.

The conservation of areas, which contribute markedly to the character of a town, presents opportunities for valuable work. A local society can help to ensure by its vigilance that nothing of real value is destroyed and that such areas are designated as Conservation Areas by local planning authorities under the Civic Amenities Act.

A view across the hills, an avenue of trees leading into the town, an old market square, the approaches to a famous building may often be threatened by new additions to the scene as well as by demolition. Unsightly development in all its forms, from street lamps to wayside cafés, from badly designed buildings to ugly fencing round a park, should be a major concern of the local society.

Apart from dealing with such specific outrages as may threaten or occur, positive work should be initiated. Surveys of street furniture, tree-planting, tackling the litter problem, arranging for young people to tidy up beauty spots, clearing derelict urban sites for use as gardens, playgrounds are all actions worth a great deal more than words.

Constant watchfulness together with a realization that no detail of the civic scene, however small, is unimportant are

260

needed to combat the 'creeping mildew' of subtopia.

Cooperation with other bodies having similar aims is essential if needless overlap and waste of efforts are to be avoided and concerted action made possible. There are, for instance, many Residents' and Ratepayers' associations, and Rural Community Councils or Councils of Social Service, which are concerned with amenities. Many of the latter are particularly active in organizing 'Best Kept Village' competitions. Almost every county in England and Wales has a branch of those experienced bodies, the Councils for the Protection of Rural England and for the Protection of Rural Wales. In some counties societies have themselves formed county federations which act as central clearing houses for information. Such a grouping form a logical basis for the discussion of planning matters with the County Council as planning authority.

A society will best secure its objects through friendly discussion and cooperation with the local authority. Councillors may welcome the existence of a society; on the other hand its members should not be discouraged if the local authority remains aloof. The society's work can be judged by its results. For a society to find itself in opposition to its local authority at a Public Inquiry is often a confession of failure at an earlier stage.

Local authorities are liable to regard amenity societies – not, it must be admitted, always without reason – as interfering busybodies. It is up to a society to show that it criticizes only when sure of its facts and when supported by sound advice and a substantial body of local opinion; hence the importance of having members, not only professional people such as architects, surveyors, planners, and solicitors, but also representatives of local industry and of the trade union movement.

It is vital that members of a society should thoroughly understand the work of their local council. Nothing but good can come of inviting the chairman of county or district committees and the council's technical officers – architects, surveyors, engineers and, particularly, planning officers – to address meetings of the society from time to time. Informal discussions with councillors who know the work of the society often achieve far more than correspondence. When the council carries out work of particular value, the society should be quick to express its appreciation.

Staffs of local authorities are busy people who have to work within the bounds of financial restrictions. Imaginative ideas arising from surveys made by local societies may start a completely new train of thought. A society should not claim more than is justified for any report submitted, but it can at least suggest lines for consideration. It will often render useful service merely by pressing the local authority itself to prepare a comprehensive redevelopment plan for an area that is losing its character by piecemeal change.

Development and redevelopment of town and countryside is a continuous process. Buildings are constantly being altered, adapted, pulled down and rebuilt to suit different purposes and varying needs.

It is of little use creating a row at a late stage in the planning process when much time, effort, and money have already been spent in preparing development schemes. A society should keep itself well informed of development proposals from the earliest stages by scrutinizing the planning register on a regular basis. The majority of owners, developers, and local authorities will listen sympathetically to sensible ideas about their schemes when they are at the formative stage. What can be infuriating is ill-informed last minute criticism.

DRAFT CONSTITUTION FOR A LOCAL CIVIC SOCIETY

Charitable Status

The constitution which follows has been prepared with the object of satisfying the Charity Commissioners and the

Inland Revenue Authorities that any society constituted with these rules is a legal charity. Societies wishing to apply for charitable status must submit their constitutions or Deeds of Trust, together with a completed form of application (form RE1), to the Secretary, Charity Commission, 14 Ryder Street, London SW1, from whom any other information may be obtained. It is emphasized that each application will be individually considered. Registration under the 1960 Charities Act is recognized by the Inland Revenue.

The principal advantage of such recognition is that charitable bodies, unlike non-charitable organizations, are exempt from income tax. For a society or other body to constitute a charity, its objects must, by law, embrace one of the following four purposes:

1. The relief of poverty;
2. The advancement of education;
3. The advancement of religion;
4. Other purposes beneficial to the community not falling under any of the preceding headings.

Clearly the objects of amenity societies can generally come under heading 2 and certainly come under heading 4. The objects referred to under heading 4, in order to be legally charitable, must be analagous to those mentioned in one of the first three divisions; evidently both the Inland Revenue Authorities and the Charity Commissioners consider that the objects of Amenity Societies do so come within this definition.

Draft Constitution

1. NAME The name of the Society shall be the . . . .
2. OBJECTS The Society is established for the public benefit for the following purposes in the area comprising . . . . which area shall hereinafter be referred to as 'the area of benefit'.

   (*a*) To stimulate public interest in the area of benefit.

263

(*b*) To promote high standards of planning and architecture in the area of benefit.

(*c*) To secure the preservation, protection, development, and improvement of features of historic or public interest in the area of benefit.

In furtherance of the said purposes but not otherwise the Society through its Executive Committee shall have the following powers:

(1) To promote research into subjects directly connected with the objects of the Society and to publish the results of any such research.

(2) To act as a coordinating body and to cooperate with the local authority, planning committees, sanitary, drainage and all other local and statutory authorities, voluntary organizations, charities, and persons having aims similar to those of the Society.

(3) To promote or assist in promoting activities of a Charitable nature throughout the area of benefit.

(4) To publish papers, reports and other literature.

(5) To make surveys and prepare maps and plans and collect information in relation to any place, erection or building of beauty or historic interest within the area of benefit.

(6) To hold meetings, lectures, and exhibitions.

(7) To educate public opinion and to give advice and information.

(8) To raise funds and to invite and receive contributions from any person or persons whatsoever by way of subscription, donation, and otherwise; provided that the Society shall not undertake any permanent trading activities in raising funds for its primary purposes.

(9) To take and accept any gifts of property, whether subject to any special trusts or not.

(10) To sell, let, mortgage, dispose of, or turn to

account all or any of the property or funds of the Society as shall be necessary.

(11) To borrow or raise money for the purposes of the Society on such terms and on such security as the Executive Committee shall think fit, but so that the liability of individual members of the Society shall in no case extend beyond the amount of their respective annual subscriptions.

(12) To do all such other things as are necessary for the attainment of the said purposes.

3. MEMBERSHIP   Membership shall be open to all who are interested in actively furthering the purposes of the Society. No member shall have power to vote at any meeting of the Society if his subscription is in arrears at the time. Junior members shall be those aged less than 18 years at the time their subscription is due; and they shall not be entitled to vote at any meeting of the Society. The subscriptions of a member joining the Society in the three months preceding..................in any year shall be regarded as covering membership for the Society's year commencing on.....................following the date of joining the Society.

4. SUBSCRIPTIONS   The annual subscription shall be:

      Life members   £......................

(the joint life subscription of a married couple shall be   £......................)

      Full members   £......................

(The joint annual subscription for full membership for a married couple shall be   £......................)

      Junior members   £......................

or such other reasonable sum as the Executive Committee shall determine from time to time, and it shall be payable on or before...........................each year Membership shall lapse if the subscription is unpaid three months after it is due.

5. MEETINGS   An Annual General Meeting shall be held in or about..................................of each year to receive the Executive Committee's report and audited accounts and to elect Officers and Members of the Committee. The Committee shall decide when ordinary meetings of the Society shall be held and shall give at least.............days' notice of such meetings to all members

Special General Meetings of the Society shall be held at the written request of members representing not less than 10 per cent of the existing membership of the Society and whose subscriptions are fully paid-up. Members personally present shall constitute a quorum for a Meeting of the Society.

6. OFFICERS Nominations for the election of officers shall be made at or before the Annual General Meeting. Such nominations shall be supported by a seconder and the consent of the proposed nominee must first have been obtained. The elections of Officers shall be completed prior to the election of further Committee members. The Officers of the Society shall consist of:

Chairman
(Vice-Chairman)
Honorary Secretary
Honorary Treasurer

all of whom shall relinquish their office every year and shall be eligible for re-election at the Annual General Meeting. A President and Vice President may also be elected at a General Meeting of the Society, for periods to be decided at such a meeting. The Executive Committee shall have the power to fill casual vacancies occurring among the Officers of the Society.

7. THE EXECUTIVE COMMITTEE The Executive Committee shall be responsible for the management and administration of the Society. The Executive Committee shall consist of the Officers and not more than ... other members. The Committee shall have power to co-opt further members (who shall attend in

an advisory and non-voting capacity). The Officers and members of the Committee shall normally be resident or work in the area of benefit but the Committee shall have power to co-opt additional members from outside the area of benefit. The President and Vice-President may attend any meeting of the Executive Committee but shall not vote at any such meeting. In the event of an equality in the votes cast, the Chairman shall have a second or casting vote. Nominations for election to the Executive Committee shall be made in writing at or before the Annual General Meeting. They must be supported by a seconder and the consent of the proposed nominee must first have been obtained. If the nominations exceed the number of vacancies, a ballot shall take place in such manner as shall be determined. Members of the Executive Committee shall be appointed annually at the Annual General Meeting of the Society. Outgoing members may be re-appointed. The Executive Committee shall meet not less than six times a year at intervals of not more than two months and the Honorary Secretary shall give all members not less than seven days' notice of each meeting.

The quorum shall, as near as may be, comprise one third of the members of the Executive Committee.

8. SUB-COMMITTEES The Executive Committee may constitute such sub-committees from time to time as shall be considered necessary for such purposes as shall be thought fit. The Chairman and Secretary of each sub-committee shall be appointed by the Executive Committee and all actions and proceedings of each sub-committee shall be reported to and be confirmed by the Executive Committee as soon as possible. Members of the Executive Committee may be members of any sub-committee and membership of a sub-committee shall be no bar to appointment to membership of the Executive Committee. Sub-Committees shall be subordinate to the Executive Committee and may be regulated or dissolved by the Executive Committee.

9. EXPENSES OF ADMINISTRATION AND APPLI-
CATION OF FUNDS The Executive Committee
shall, out of the funds of the Society, pay all proper
expenses of administration and management of the
Society. After the payment of the administration and
management expenses and the setting aside to reserve
of such sums as may be deemed expedient; the remaining funds of the Society shall be applied by the Executive Committee in furtherance of the purposes of the
Society.

10. INVESTMENT All monies at any time belonging to
the Society and not required for immediate application
for its purposes shall be invested by the Executive
Committee in or upon such investments securities or
property as it may think fit, subject nevertheless to
such authority, approval or consent whether by the
Charity Commissioners or the Secretary of State for
Education and Science as may for the time being be
required by law or by the special trusts affecting any
property in the hands of the Executive Committee.

11. TRUSTEES Any freehold and leasehold property acquired by the Society shall and if the Executive Committee so directs any other property belonging to the
Society may be vested in trustees who shall deal with
such property as the Executive Committee may from
time to time direct. Any trustees shall be at least three
in number or a trust corporation. The Power of appointment of new trustees shall be vested in the Executive Committee. A trustee need not be a member of the
Society but no person whose membership lapses by
virtue of paragraph 3 hereof shall thereafter be
qualified to act as a trustee unless and until re-appointed as such by the Executive Committee. The
Honorary Secretary shall from time to time notify
the trustees in writing of any amendment hereto and the
trustees shall not be bound by any such amendments in
their duties as trustees unless such notice has been
given. The Society shall be bound to indemnify the
trustees in their duties (including the proper charge of

a trustee being a trust corporation) and liability under such indemnity shall be a proper administrative expense.

12. AMENDMENTS This Constitution may be amended by a two-thirds majority of members present at an Annual General Meeting or Special General Meeting of the Society, provided that.............days' notice of the proposed amendment has been given to all members, and provided that nothing herein contained shall authorize any amendment the effect of which would be to cause the Society at any time to cease to be a charity in law.

13. NOTICES Any notice required to be given by these Rules shall be deemed to be duly given if left at or sent by prepaid post addressed to the address of that member last notified to the Secretary.

14. WINDING UP The Society may be dissolved by a two-thirds majority of members voting at an Annual General Meeting or Special General Meeting of the Society confirmed by a simple majority of members voting at a further Special General Meeting held not less than 14 days after the previous Meeting. If a motion for the dissolution of the Society is to be proposed at an Annual General Meeting or a Special General Meeting this motion shall be referred to specifically when notice of the Meeting is given. In the event of the dissolution of the Society the available funds of the Society shall be transferred to such one or more charitable institutions having objects similar or reasonably similar to those herein before declared as shall be chosen by the Executive Committee and approved by the Meeting of the Society at which the decision to dissolve the Society is confirmed. On dissolution the minute books and other records of the Society shall be deposited with the Civic Trust.

Civic Societies as Property Owners

More and more societies seem to be contemplating the purchase of buildings or groups of buildings in order to ensure their preservation. The following notes therefore may be helpful.

To own property a society can register as a Trust, as a Limited Company or as a Housing Society.

1. If it decides to register as a Trust, a society's existing constitution, with certain clauses inserted, will often be accepted by the Charity Commissioners. It is, however, advisable to seek the aid of a Solicitor in drawing up a Deed. Trust Deeds are somewhat inflexible and any change of Trustees has to be entered formally by a Deed of Appointment. The main requirement is that the Trust shall have annually audited accounts.

2. The second method a society may adopt is to register as a Limited Company. A Solicitor should be asked to draw up a legal document known as a 'Memorandum and Articles of Association'. The society then has to have registered offices. In addition, its accounts must be audited annually in accordance with the Companies Act of 1948. Expenses involved in registration, printing and fees will generally amount to something between £25 and £75. Many Trusts register as Limited Companies at the same time and this is generally considered to be advisable, notwithstanding the additional expense. Charitable status can and should be applied for by both Trusts and Limited Companies. Both these forms of registration, in conjunction with charitable status, allow societies to buy and sell property provided that any profit made in the process is ploughed back into the funds of the society.

3. Finally, the simplest and cheapest way is for a society to set up, or itself register as a Housing Society under the Industrial and Provident Societies Act 1893. It should be noted, however, that the society would be expected to provide housing accommodation for letting and not for re-sale. Model rules can be purchased

from the National Federation of Housing Societies[1]; by their use, together with the payment of a £20 registration fee, the society automatically becomes a charity and has limited liability.

Any society so registered would of course be able to take advantage of the financial provisions of the Housing Act 1961, under which a fund of £25 million has been set aside for loan purposes to Housing Societies. The primary purpose of this fund is to encourage new buildings, although proposals to convert and improve existing property will not be excluded. Details of this loan fund are to be found in a Stationery Office free leaflet 'Building to Let'. Part I of the Housing Act 1964 also allows such societies to take advantage of current sources of finance available for cooperative housing schemes.

1. 12 Suffolk Street, London, London, SW1 from which a *Guide to the Formation of Housing Societies*, price 3s. can be obtained.

Use Your Laws

Parliament and Whitehall have only recently awakened to the environmental crisis facing this tiny island nation (a third the size of the American State of Texas, and with a population density one and half times that of India). While there has been sporadic legislation on environmental problems over the past quarter-century (and some before that), it was not until the late 1960s that 'environment', 'pollution', and 'ecology' became issues of national concern, issues which Parliament and Whitehall belatedly began to act upon. Now, in the early 1970s, it is all too clear that central government has still done much too little much too late. The environment has yet to become a genuine *political* issue of the importance of, say, industrial relations or inflation. Parliament and Whitehall still pay more lip service than real service, by way of legislation, to the critical problems of pollution, noise, a deteriorating environment in city, town, and country; and the root cause of all these problems – population growth – is clearly still too hot an issue to handle: no political party dares to put forward a policy to control the increase of people. Each day Britain's population swells by another 1,000 or so; as a direct result, each day the crisis of the environment becomes more desperate. Yet the Government's attitude can be summed up in the words of the Viennese wag who said: 'The situation is desperate but not serious.'

A start on legislating for a better environment *has* been made. It is a late start. It is not enough. But it is a start – and a pointer to the further and stronger legislation that is essential if Britain in 1970s and beyond is to be a place worth living in. Following is a summary of some of the major governmental actions now on the statute books. The summary may serve as a guide for citizens concerned about the environmental threats, discussed in the earlier pages of this book, citizens anxious to take direct action, to put pressure on local authorities and Members of Parliament to enforce and to strengthen existing laws and to fill the gaps in the statute books – now, before it is too late. The section SOME LAWS WE NEED suggests some of the gaps which urgently need filling. These are *your* laws. Use them!

Air Pollution

Alkali Act 1863. Established the Alkali Inspectorate, as industrial clean air inspectorate now controlling 56 'scheduled processes' in industry. The inspectorate has the right to prosecute firms which do not use 'the best practicable means' to prevent emissions of grit, dust, fumes, smoke, and gases. DO INDUSTRIES IN YOUR COMMUNITY KEEP THEIR POLLUTION TO A MINIMUM? IF NOT, COMPLAIN TO YOUR TOWN HALL OR MP. THE POLLUTERS MAY BE INFRINGING THE ALKALI ACT.

Public Health Acts 1874–1936. Provided that emissions of smoke could be dealt with by common law action as a nuisance. YOU CAN TAKE SMOKE POLLUTERS TO COURT.

Clean Air Act 1956. Introduced smoke control areas which could be established (but there was no compulsion) by local authorities under an order requiring ministerial approval. Provided for grants towards the cost of converting appliances for smokeless fuels and tightened up regulations on emissions of smoke, grit, and dust. Penalties for contravention of the Act were specified. DOES YOUR TOWN HAVE A SMOKE CONTROL ORDER? IF NOT, WHY NOT? IF SO, IS IT BEING ENFORCED? IF NOT, WHY NOT? PUT PRESSURE ON YOUR LOCAL COUNCIL.

Clean Air Act 1968. The result of a private member's bill (Mr Robert Maxwell), it closed some of the loopholes in 1956 Act. Gave minister power to compel local authorities to introduce smoke control areas. HAS YOUR COUNCIL ESTABLISHED SMOKE CONTROL AREAS? IF NOT, WHY NOT? IS THE COUNCIL DRAGGING ITS FEET? ARE THE TARGETS FOR SMOKELESS AREAS TOO FAR IN THE FUTURE? IF SO, COMPLAIN TO YOUR MP OR THE MINISTER FOR THE ENVIRONMENT, WHITEHALL, LONDON, SW1.

Dereliction

National Parks and Access to the Countryside Act 1949.
Provided 75 per cent reclamation grants in National Parks
and designated Areas of Outstanding Natural Beauty.

Industrial Development Act 1966. Provided 85 per cent central government grants to local authorities in Development Areas for reclamation schemes which will contribute
towards development of industry in the area.

Local Government Act 1966. Provided 50 per cent reclamation grants in all areas of the country.

Local Employment Act 1970. Provided 75 per cent rec-
lamation grants in the so-called 'intermediate' or 'grey'
areas of the nation, and in certain specified 'derelict land
clearance areas'. LOOK ABOUT YOU – IS THERE LAND LYING
DERELICT AND UGLY YEAR AFTER YEAR? AT LEAST ONE OF
THESE FOUR GRANTS SCHEMES APPLIES TO YOUR COM-
MUNITY. MAKE SURE YOUR LOCAL AUTHORITY IS APPLYING
FOR THE GRANTS. MAKE SURE IT IS GETTING ON WITH THE
JOB.

Local Authorities (Land) Act 1963. Authorized local councils to carry out reclamation works on land not in their
ownership, provided they got consent of all persons
having an interest in the land. IS YOUR LOCAL AUTHORITY
DOING THIS? IF NOT, PRESS YOUR PLANNING DEPARTMENT
TO GET MOVING.

Noise

Noise Abatement Act 1960. Established noise as a statutory
nuisance, offering citizen the right to complain to his local
authority, which is required to investigate the complaint;
if the public health inspector finds that the noise is a statutory nuisance, the local authority must take steps to abate
the nuisance, including, if necessary, legal proceedings
against the noisemaker. COMPLAIN TO YOUR COUNCIL
ABOUT NOISEMAKERS – DON'T JUST STICK COTTON WOOL IN
YOUR EARS AND BEAR IT.

Motor Vehicles (Construction and Use) Regulations 1969.
Required that all petrol-driven vehicles be fitted with

silencers; established maximum noise levels for new vehicles from April 1st 1970. IF YOU ENCOUNTER ANY VEHICLES WITHOUT SILENCERS, TAKE THE VEHICLE'S NUMBER AND REPORT IT TO THE POLICE.

Population Control

Abortion Act 1967. Liberalized law on legal abortion, introducing *social* grounds which admitted consideration of the well-being of other children in the family, e.g. the mother who feels she cannot cope with a further addition to an already large family. IS YOUR LOCAL HOSPITAL PROPERLY EQUIPPED TO CARRY OUT ABORTIONS? ARE SOME LOCAL DOCTORS REFUSING TO SANCTION ABORTIONS? IF SO, WHY NOT BOYCOTT THEM?

Family Planning Act 1967. Permitted (though not compelled) local authorities to establish adequate family planning services in their areas. HAS YOUR COUNCIL SET UP SUCH SERVICES? IF NOT, GO TO TOWN HALL AND DEMAND THEM.

Town and Country Preservation

Civic Amenities Act 1967. The result of a private member's bill (Mr Duncan Sandys) it made further provision for the protection and improvement of buildings of architectural or historic interest; for the preservation and planting of trees; and for the disposal of disused motor vehicles and other rubbish. Imposed fines for abandoning vehicles in public places. Provided for the protection of whole areas of towns ('conservation areas') as distinct from individual buildings. REPORT ANY ABANDONED VEHICLES TO YOUR POLICE. HAS YOUR PLANNING AUTHORITY SET UP CONSERVATION AREAS? IF NOT, ENCOURAGE YOUR LOCAL CIVIC SOCIETY TO AGITATE FOR SUCH AREAS.

Countryside Act 1968. Transformed National Parks Commission into the Countryside Commission, with wider powers for 'the conservation and enhancement of natural beauty'. Strengthened preservation controls over trees, woodlands, and public footpaths. Encouraged local authorities to acquire land near urban centres for 'country parks'. HAS YOUR LOCAL AUTHORITY ESTABLISHED COUNTRY PARKS? IF NOT, PRESS YOUR PLANNING OFFICER FOR ACTION.

Town and Country Planning Act 1968. Strengthened Town and Country Planning Acts of 1947 and 1962. Tightened up protection of historic buildings and conservation areas. Established 'planning inquiry commissions' to consider planning proposals of regional or national significance, e.g. the siting of London's third airport. Required that the public must be adequately informed and consulted before approval of plans. Emphasized greater citizen participation in whole planning process. IS YOUR LOCAL COUNCIL INFORMING CITIZENS ABOUT PLANNING DEVELOPMENTS AND ENCOURAGING CITIZENS TO PARTICIPATE IN DECISIONS? DOES THE COUNCIL STAGE EXHIBITIONS AND HOLD MEETINGS TO EXPLAIN PLANS? IF NOT, GET YOUR LOCAL CIVIC SOCIETY TO DEMAND THESE THINGS. IF YOU HAVE NO LOCAL SOCIETY, WHY NOT START ONE? (See pp. 258–62).

Water Pollution

Water Resources Act 1963. Constituted new river authorities responsible, among other things, for conserving water resources. River authorities charged with laying down standards for effluent discharges (though local authorities remain responsible for sewage treatment plants and outfalls). HOW POLLUTED ARE YOUR RIVERS? DOES YOUR RIVER AUTHORITY LAY DOWN HIGH ENOUGH STANDARDS? IS YOUR LOCAL AUTHORITY'S SEWAGE SYSTEM MODERN, EFFICIENT? ARE THERE FISH IN YOUR RIVERS? IF YOU HAVE A POLLUTION PROBLEM, COMPLAIN TO YOUR RIVER AUTHORITY AND TO YOUR LOCAL PUBLIC HEALTH INSPECTOR.

Some Laws We Need

At the third 'Countryside in 1970' conference, in October 1970, the Committee for Environmental Conservation (CoEnCo) representing fourteen national conservation bodies, presented a report based on study groups which had investigated pollution of inland waters, and sea and air; pollution by persistent pesticides; noise; and heavy lorries. The report called urgently for a wide range of new legislation to save the environment. Some of these recommendations follow. IF YOU AGREE THEY ARE URGENT, WRITE YOUR MP ASKING HIM TO SUPPORT LEGISLATION. ASK YOUR FRIENDS TO WRITE TOO.

POLLUTION BY PESTICIDES
A decision must be taken now to move quickly to a ban on all persistent organochlorines entering the environment. This should be coupled with immediate legislation to institute statutory controls on pesticides, including the setting of permitted residues in foods.

POLLUTION OF INLAND WATERS
So long as both producer and receiver of rectified sewage effluent are controlled by local authority members, any system of consent conditions, in practice, will not work, and the community as a whole will suffer a progressive deterioration of the quality of its water. Either sewage treatment plants and outfalls must come under the charge of river authorities or sewage treatment authorities must become contractors independent of local government.

SEA POLLUTION
A most urgent need is to ensure that smoke and fumes from domestic chimneys are reduced. This can be achieved by enforcing clean air legislation in all urban areas and by

ensuring that there are adequate supplies of smokeless fuels available.

Legislation should be enacted to ensure that the currently known means for the elimination of smoke from diesel vehicles and the substantial reduction of carbon monoxide from petrol vehicles are put into effect with as little delay as possible.

NOISE

The Civil Aviation Act 1948 (which expressly forbids legal actions for noise nuisance against airlines, airports, and pilots) must be altered to allow such actions.

The Noise Abatement Act 1960 must be tightened up to permit local authorities to take *instant* action (rather than, as now, give fourteen days' notice to an offender) to stop excessive or unnecessary noise.

Legislation must impose a maximum received noise level of 80dbA for an eight-hour day, with a peak noise level of 85dbA for one hour a day only for factory and other workers. The permissible noise level of vehicles should be lowered.

HEAVY LORRIES

No further increase in lorry load-carrying capacity or overall dimensions must be permitted in view of the damage even now being caused by heavy vehicles operating within the legal weight limits.

Any alternative in load-carrying capacity should be subject to international European consultation and agreement, with the heaviest categories of vehicles being confined to specified highways.

The use of Class B and unclassified roads by heavy traffic should be strictly limited to vehicles having business at premises on such roads, possibly being licensed by the county council, and a weight limit should be agreed for vehicles using roads of this type.

Legislation should be introduced to make mandatory the reporting of damage to property by vehicles.

In September 1970, the Council for the Protection of Rural England published the recommendations of working parties it had set up on mineral extraction and dereliction; loss of cover; power transmission; and road works. These recommendations include the following. JOIN PRESSURE GROUPS FOR THESE ESSENTIAL REFORMS OF THE LAW.

MINERAL EXTRACTION AND DERELICTION

Requirements for rehabilitation of mineral workings should be made statutory and embodied in a code of practice including obligation to submit with all mineral working applications a landscape architect's plans for restoration.

The Minerals Working Act 1951 (which requires ironstone extractors to restore their lands) should be extended to cover *all* extractive industries.

The definition of 'dereliction' should be revised and widened to include categories now excluded.

LOSS OF COVER

The Farm Improvement Scheme should be modified to ensure that the emphasis is shifted from short-term profitability to longer term values; that all applications for grant aid involving the reduction of hedgerows and/or felling of small coverts, should be examined in the light of cover loss and not accepted automatically; and that any application for grant aid involving more than an agreed maximum removal of cover should be dependent upon its replacement in an agreed form.

The Highways Act 1959 should be amended to make the planting of hedges or trees along highway/farmland boundaries mandatory on all highway authorities.

Ancient hedges should be protected by a new Hedge Preservation Order.

POWER TRANSMISSION

The existing obligation on the Central Electricity Generating Board and the area electricity boards to obtain landscape advice should be made much more specific than it is now.

Consultation with every authority which might be affected by a grid scheme should be mandatory *before it begins*.

In all Conservation Areas, at least, it should be mandatory to underground all new power lines, and make a programme for undergrounding all old lines within a fixed period.

The public advertisement of applications for planning permission for electricity sub-stations should be mandatory in all cases.

ROAD WORKS

There should be a mandatory obligation on the Road Construction Units to retain a landscape architect on all trunk and special roads. The 75 per cent central government grant for principal roads, now dependent on the proposed works reaching agreed engineering standards, should also be dependent on their reaching the approval of the Ministry of Transport landscape architects. The Road Traffic Regulation Act 1967 should be amended to permit the highway authority freedom to impose a *lower* speed limit on *all* roads where consultation with local residents and planning authorities suggest that environmental needs require it.

Planning authorities of national parks and areas of outstanding natural beauty should be given powers under the Countryside Act 1968 to create traffic-free zones (except for residents and services) in those areas.

At the annual conference of Labour Party women in 1970, these suggestions for actions against pollution were put forward. Check those you feel strongly about. JOIN PRESSURE GROUPS TO PRESS FOR THESE NEW LAWS.

POPULATION

—a comprehensive family planning service should be established under the National Health Service, backed by advertising of the facilities available and on the gravity of the population problem:

POLLUTION OF THE AIR

—the possibility of a small 'pollution levy' on household bituminous coal to be studied (to help finance production of smokeless fuel, speed up smoke control programme, finance research, etc.);
—place the smoke control programme on to a firm national base, backed by adequate Government aid, with deadline in mid-seventies for smokeless Britain;
—urgently review Alkali Acts to seek closing of loophole which allows companies to avoid restrictions by pleading 'poverty';
—overhaul procedures and practice of Alkali Inspectorate in enforcing restrictions;
—tighten these restrictions so that each firm uses 'best modern standard', and set deadline for industry to reach these standards;
—investigate possible imposition of 'pollution tax' on industry, e.g. where not possible (given existing technology) to clean up discharges;
—give police the power to order immediate return to home garage for attention if diesel has bad exhaust fumes, increase financial penalties on offending firms, and introduce new more stringent British Standard on fuel injection;
—give target date to car companies to remove most of carbon monoxide from car exhausts, and make use of lead-free petrol mandatory.

POLLUTION OF RIVERS AND LAKES

—treat expenditure on sewage facilities as priority for Exchequer cash, and early withdrawal of Circular 64/68;
—establish a three-purpose central executive agency (with

local three-purpose agencies in catchment areas) to deal
with sewage disposal, water supply, and river pollution;
—give this agency powers gradually to raise standards of
effluents discharged both into rivers and sewers, by industry (and/or to levy funds from them);
—give this agency powers to insist on industry either
undertaking research into the environmental side-effects
of new chemicals in effluents, or levying industry and getting research done on the funds raised;
—make 'accidental' spillages of toxic chemicals, etc., an absolute offence;
—ensure that farmers pay sewage authorities the full cost of
treating manure slurry and hence encourage use as fertilizer;
—urgent investigation into social costs of modern agricultural methods with reference to pollution of rivers by
chemicals leached from fields, and into methods of reducing this run-off;
—adopt a new water plan (through new central agency)
aimed at obtaining maximum re-use of water by industry.

POLLUTION AND THE SEA
—Britain to take lead in imposing strict controls (through a
new 'Sea Pollution Authority') on dumping of toxic
wastes at sea, and impose levy to finance research both
into effects and into methods of rendering waste harmless;
—need for some kind of 'Prevention of Pollution of Coastal
Waters Act' on lines of river pollution legislation, enforced by executive Sea Pollution Authority, with job of
laying down consent conditions for all discharges to
sea;
—bigger penalties on ships which break (UK) law by dumping oil close to land;
—British based companies, involved in oil production and
oil carrying, to finance research into methods of dealing
with oil slicks, and into long-term effect on ecology of
oceans, and into looking ahead for new dangers.

POLLUTION BY REFUSE AND LITTER

—the urgent overhaul of refuse disposal, to discourage tipping and encourage use of refuse for composting, or as a source of energy for district heating schemes, etc.

—investigate the costs and benefits of 'one-trip' bottles, excess packaging, etc., with a view to restrictions and/or a 'pollution levy' to recoup costs of disposal, and pay for priority research programme;

—set up national executive agency to coordinate and take initiatives in refuse disposal and reclamation (and research), and to encourage development of local government enterprise in this sector;

—make the collection of 'bulky' refuse a statutory duty on refuse authorities;

—need for better public standards of cleanliness, more litter-bins (and more frequently emptied), to be provided under law both by local authorities and by shops, public transport, etc.;

—adoption of recommendations of Working Party on Refuse Collection (e.g. phase out of kerb collection, more frequent refuse collection, etc.);

—national agency mentioned above – or the Ministry – to lay down 'standards' of general street cleanliness, number of litter bins to be required, etc., backed by an 'anti-litter inspectorate'.

POLLUTION AND DERELICTION

—increase the grants available to the poorest authorities to bring them up to 100 per cent, if necessary;

—where applicable, pay grants in full, and allow local authorities to refund the after-value, when the land is disposed of or developed;

—prepare a full survey of derelict land, a survey which would include all land still in active use, and land which does not have adequate restoration conditions, etc;

—set up a Land Reclamation Agency upon the nucleus of the Opencast Executive, with powers to draw up (in consultation with the planning authorities) a long-term plan for reclamation, and able to step in whenever needed to keep the plan on target;

—provide the coal industry with additional financial help from the Exchequer to expedite restoration of derelict land in its possession, while revoking the General Development Order allowing it to continue unrestrained tipping on any site so used in 1949;

—impose levies on industries which have created dereliction, where the dereliction is of a kind that is not amenable, with existing techniques, to reclamation, and use the money raised to finance the general reclamation programme, and, perhaps, provide the new Land Reclamation Agency with funds of its own;

—pass a 'Clean Land Act' imposing an obligation on all owners of land to restore and keep their land to amenity standards, laid down by the Ministry (or the new reclamation agency).

POLLUTION BY PESTICIDES

—replace the present voluntary system of control by a statutory one;

—impose a levy on the manufacturers of pesticides to finance research into the environmental factors involved, and to accelerate the search for selective pesticides;

—impose selective taxes to favour the widespread use of selective pesticides as opposed to the 'broad spectrum' type;

NOISE

—noisy processes in industry to be registered (as are processes under the Alkali Acts) and an Inspectorate to be created to encourage noise abatement in industry, backed by legislation designed to ensure that companies cannot plead 'poverty' as an excuse for inaction;

—the Inspectorate to help to enforce the Noise Abatement Act against contractors who use noisy concrete breakers;

—the urgent tightening of the restrictions on new vehicles to conform to the standards laid down by the Wilson Committee on Noise;

—the possibility of a 'noise levy' on vehicles to off-set the general impairment of the environment caused by the growth in the volume of noise;

—tighter restrictions on aircraft noise, and especially on new supersonic aircraft;

—the study of the overall costs and benefits of the existing pattern of air travel in this country, and the allocation of these costs to those who benefit.

PLANNING

—need for more positive approach, backed by cost and benefit studies of alternative schemes to allow effective participation in making judgements of value;

—the need for integrated government department to treat environmental problems as unities and especially the problem of transport in towns;

—the introduction of restrictions on cars and heavy through traffic in towns and specific Government initiative to encourage traffic-free zones and streets;

—powers for planning authorities to insist on improvements to external appearance of all private property;

—a study of the costs and benefits of alternative uses of 'agricultural' land, such as amenity, conservation, or recreation, and the need to look again at the assumption that land outside towns must be farmed.

PRIORITY

—the protection and enhancement of the environment to be treated as a major priority area for action and expenditure at all levels of government, and one that should not be deferred on the basis of untenable arguments concerning the balance of payments.

1970 WAS...

The year Concorde's sonic booms first assaulted the ears of Britons.

The year a sewage workers' strike set back river pollution control by months or years.

The year smoke-free zones in British cities were suspended because of a shortage of smokeless fuel.

The year Anthony Crosland served as 'pollution' overlord' but was given neither the powers nor staff to do the job.

The year when more than a million new motor vehicles came on the roads of Britain.

The year when mile after mile of urban motorways were completed, ripping the hearts out of a dozen British cities.

The year when another 40,000 acres of green Britain disappeared under bricks and mortar.

The year when tens of thousands of dead seabirds were washed up on Britain's coastline.

The year when Britain's population increased by another 300,000 or so.

The year when Britain and 18 other nations met in Strasbourg for a talkathon about...

...CONSERVATION YEAR

1970 WAS EUROPE AN *CONVERSATION* **YEAR
WHAT WILL 1971 BE? AND 1972 and 3?**

Appendix

Directories of Conservation Groups

1. *National Organizations Affecting Amenity*, prepared by the Civic Trust, 18 Carlton House Terrace, London SW1 (6s post paid): Lists objectives, addresses and telephone numbers of 197 national bodies in Britain concerned with the quality of urban and rural life. The Trust also publishes a shorter circular, *Joint Action for Conservation*, which outlines recent town and country planning legislation and discusses the aims and membership details of ten selected conservation organizations.

2. *Preservation in Great Britain: Societies, Organizations and Legislation*, published by the Society for the Protection of Ancient Buildings, 55 Great Ormond Street, London WC1: Gives details about 18 national conservation groups, including their histories, and a brief digest of legislation from 1900 to the present for the protection of buildings in Great Britain.

3. *Administrative Memorandum No. 16/69*, prepared by the Department of Education and Science, Curzon Street, London W1: Includes a directory of 33 organizations concerned with education in the fields of conservation, environment, and the wise use of natural resources. An appendix lists available films on ecology, population, soils and pesticides, pollution and nature conservation.

Some National and International Conservation Bodies

Ancient Monuments Society
> Concerned with the study and conservation of historic structures of all periods and all styles throughout the United Kingdom.

11 Alexander Street,
London W2
Tel: 01–229 5280
Secretary: Dr William Oddie

The Anti-Concorde Project
Part of a worldwide movement opposing all supersonic
airliners, the sonic boom and the economic and en-
vironmental consequences of such aircraft.
70 Lytton Avenue,
Letchworth, Herts
Tel: 046-26 2081
Organizer: Richard Wiggs

Arboricultural Association
Fosters appreciation of trees and seeks to maintain high
standards of practice amongst those professionally concerned with their care.
59 Blythwood Gardens,
Stansted, Essex
Secretary: D. R. Honour

Association for the Preservation of Rural Scotland
Organizes concerted action to secure the improvement,
protection, and preservation of the countryside in Scot-
land.
39 & 43 Castle Street,
Edinburgh 2
Tel: 031-225 8391
Secretary: K. Macrane

British Association for the Control of Aircraft Noise
Aims at a steady reduction in the level of aircraft noise,
active in lobbying MPs to this end. Many local anti-air
noise groups are affiliated to BACAN.
30 Fleet Street,
London EC4
Tel: 034–284–2382
Secretary: M. N. Jackson

Central Council for Rivers Protection

Representative of national bodies interested in maintaining the purity of rivers, the council considers proposals where there is a possibility of pollution.
Fishmongers' Hall,
London EC4
Tel: 01–626 3531
Secretaries: Commander S. M. Bayley and L. Millis

Centre for Environmental Studies

Serves as a forum for planners and researchers in the environmental field. It is an independent educational trust supported both by government and outside sources.
5 Cambridge Terrace,
London NW1
Tel: 01-486 3956
Director: Dr David Donnison

Civic Trust

Aims to encourage high quality in architecture and planning; eliminate and prevent ugliness, whether from bad design or neglect; stimulate public interest and inspire a sense of civic pride. Advises local amenity societies on organization and objectives.
18 Carlton House Terrace,
London SW1
Tel: 01-930 0914
Director: Michael Middleton

Associate Civic Trusts:

Scottish Civic Trust
24 George Square,
Glasgow C2
Tel: 041-221 1466
Director: Maurice Lindsay

Civic Trust for Wales/Treftadaeth Cymru
Snelling House, Bute Terrace,
Cardiff
Tel: 0222–33131
Director: Stanley Hall Cox

Civic Trust for the North West
Century House, St Peter's Square,
Manchester 2
Tel: 061-236 0333
Director: Graham Ashworth

Civic Trust for the North East
34–35 Saddler Street,
Durham
Tel: 0385-61182
Director: Neville Whittaker

Coastal Anti-Pollution League
Combats pollution of beaches by sewage; publishes list
of 'Golden Beaches' which are safe and clean because
of adequate sewage treatment installations.
'Alverstoke', Greenway Lane,
Bath, Somerset
Tel: 0225 64094
Chairman: J. A. Wakefield

Committee for Environmental Conservation (CoEnCo)
An alliance of fourteen national conservation organizations originated in 1969 'to consider matters of
national importance affecting the environment by providing a forum at which common problems, tran-
scending the terms of reference of any one body
represented, may be examined by representatives of the
major national voluntary amenity and conservation organizations; to promote concerted action by the voluntary bodies; to distinguish and, where possible, settle
points of conflict between the different environmental
interests; to identify areas of overlap or gaps in cover-

age and to encourage the best use of existing resources; to initiate such action and make such recommendations as may be necessary to further liaison between organizations at national, regional and county level.'
4 Hobart Place,
London SW1
Tel: 01-235 4771
Secretaries: A. F. Holford-Walker, Peter Conder; Information Officer: John R. H. Yeoman

Commons, Open Spaces and Footpaths Preservation Society

Protects footpaths and public commons. Offers advice on these matters to local authorities, commons committees, voluntary bodies, and the general public.
Suite 4, 166 Shaftesbury Avenue,
London WC2
Tel: 01–836 7220
Secretary: I. S. Campbell

Conservation Society

Aims to reverse 'increasing degradation of the environment' by population stabilization and more responsible use of technology. Promotes conservation of natural resources, animal life as part of man's natural environment.
21 Hanyards Lane, Cuffley,
Potters Bar, Herts.
Tel: 01–284 2517
Secretary: S. C. Lawrence

Council for Environmental Education

Aims to advance education in the importance of the environment and the status of man therein, by means of coordinating and disseminating advice on environmental education and training.
26 Bedford Square,
London WC1
Tel: 01-636 4066
Secretary: C. L. Mellowes

Council for Nature
> The national representative body of the voluntary natural history movement in the United Kingdom, acting on behalf of naturalists and others to further the study and conservation of nature. A major part of the council's function is to encourage among all a greater appreciation of wildlife.
> Zoological Gardens, Regent's Park,
> London NW1
> Tel: 01-722 7111
> Information Officer: Timothy Sands

Council for the Protection of Rural England (CPRE)
> Organizes concerted action to secure the improvment, protection, and preservation of the countryside and its towns and villages; acts as information and advisory centre; arouses and educates public opinion on matters affecting the visual amenities and usage of the countryside. Has 43 county branches.
> 4 Hobart Place,
> London SW1
> Tel: 01-235 4771
> Secretaries: A. F. Holford-Walker, M. V. Osmond

Council for the Protection of Rural Wales
> Same aims and similar organizational structure as CPRE (above)
> Meifod,
> Montgomeryshire
> Tel: Meifod 383
> Secretary: S. R. J. Meade

Countryside Commission
> Formerly the National Parks Commission, a statutory public body charged with keeping under review all matters relating to the provision and improvement of facilities for the enjoyment of the countryside in England and Wales, the conservation and enhancement of its natural beauty and amenity, and the need to secure public access for open-air recreation.

1 Cambridge Gate, Regent's Park,
London NW1
Tel: 01-935 5533
Chairman: John Cripps

Educational Advisory Section (Nature Conservancy)
A section of the Nature Conservancy set up to provide
advice and information on the use of land for environ-
mental education, particularly educational nature re-
serves, nature trails, field centres, and other outdoor
educational facilities for schools and the general
public.
Nature Conservancy,
Attingham Park,
Shrewsbury, Shrops.
Tel: 074–377–611
Director: Philip Oswald

Environmental Consortium
Concerned with the investigation and identification of
environmental problems, and with providing and im-
plementing workable answers to these problems. To
achieve this, the consortium works in temporary association with amenity groups, local and national
authorities, private business, artists, scientists, socio-
logists, etc.
27 Nassau Street,
London W1
Tel: 01-636 0726–8
Press Officer: George Hay

Field Studies Council
Encourages the pursuit of fieldwork and research in
every branch of knowledge whose essential subject
matters is out of doors. Has established field study and
research centres in England and Wales in localities
where unspoilt country affords opportunities for studying both general and specialized aspects of botany,
zoology, geology, geography, natural history, local history, archaeology and the landscape.

9 Devereux Court,
London WC2
Tel: 01-583 7471
Secretary: R. S. Chapman

Friends of the Earth (FOE), UK
A non-profit organization for aggressive political and
legislative activity aimed at restoring the environment
misused by man and at preserving remaining wilderness
where the life force continues to flow freely.
8 King Street,
London WC2
Tel: 01–836 0718
Director: Barclay Inglis

Henry Doubleday Research Association
Promotes gardening without the use of chemical ferti-
lizers or poison sprays.
20 Convent Lane,
Bocking,
Braintree, Essex
Tel: Braintree 1483
Secretry: L. D. Hills

International Union for the Conservation of Nature
Aims as title suggests.
1110 Morges,
Switzerland
Tel: (021) 714401
Directory-General: Gerardo Budowski

Keep Britain Tidy Group
A · voluntary organization aiming to make Britain
cleaner, tidier, and more beautiful.
86 The Strand,
London WC2
Tel: 01–836 6463
Secretaries: Miss Goodman and Miss Moss

National Society for Clean Air

Objects are to promote clean air in the United Kingdom by creating an informed public opinion on its importance.

134–137 North Street,
Brighton, Sussex
Tel: 0273-26313
Press Officer: Eric Hughes

National Trust for Places of Historic Interest or Natural Beauty

A charity incorporated by Act of Parliament. Its mandate is 'to promote the permanent preservation for the benefit of the nation of land and buildings of beauty or historic interest'. Owns or has protective covenants over 420,000 acres in England, Wales and Northern Ireland, including, as result of 'Operation Neptune', more than 100 miles of coastline.

42 Queen Anne's Gate,
London SW1
Tel: 01-930 0211/1841
Information Officer: L. E. M. Rich

National Trust for Scotland for Places of Historic Interest or Natural Beauty

Promotes the permanent preservation of places and buildings in Scotland of natural beauty or historic interest.

5 Charlotte Square,
Edinburgh 2
Tel: 031-225 2184
Secretary: J. C. Stormonth Darling

Nature Conservancy

A governmental body founded by royal charter in 1949 'to provide scientific advice on the conservation and control of the natural flora and fauna of Great Britain; to establish, maintain and manage nature reserves, including the maintenance of physical features of

297

scientific interest; and to organize and develop the research and scientific services related thereto.'
19 Belgrave Square,
London SW1
Tel: 01–235 3241
Information Officer: M. Blackmore

Noise Abatement Society

Aims to eliminate all excessive and unnecessary noise from all sources by taking all possible steps under the existing law to protect the public from assault by noise; to inform the public by every means of the dangers of noise to health and pocket and of their legal rights against those who create noise; to press for enforcement of present laws against noise and for new byelaws where existing laws appear inadequate.
6 Old Bond Street,
London W1
Tel: 01–493 5877
Secretary: John Connell

Pedestrians' Association for Road Safety

Safeguards the needs and interests of pedestrians; opposes increased weight limits for heavy goods vehicles.
4 College Hill, Cannon Street,
London EC4
Tel: 01–248 5116
Secretary: Mrs M. Gray

Ramblers' Association

Protects rights of public on country paths; preserves the beauty of the countryside; secures the right of public access to open country.
1–4 Crawford Mews, York Street,
London W1
Tel: 01-262 1477
Secretary: Christopher Hall

Royal Commission on Environmental Pollution
   Established by the Government in 1970 'to advise on matters, both national and international, concerning the pollution of the environment; on the adequacy of research in this field; and the future possibilities of danger to the environment.'
   Great George Street,
   London SW1
   Tel: 01-930 3324
   Secretary: Miss D. M. Wilde

Royal Forestry Society of England, Wales and Northern Ireland
   Aims to promote good forestry, encourages good management of private woodlands, and organizes professional examinations.
   102 High Street,
   Tring, Herts
   Tel: 044–282–2028

Royal Scottish Forestry Society
   Aims similar to those of the Royal Forestry Society of England, Wales and Northern Ireland.
   Drumsheuth Gardens,
   Edinburgh
   Tel: 031–229–3651
   Secretary: W. B. C. Walker

Royal Society for the Protection of Birds
   A registered charity which protects and conserves our national heritage of wild birds for the benefit and enjoyment of this and future generations; buys and maintains reserves to ensure permanent protection of bird habitats against the growing disturbance of the countryside by man's continuing needs for roads, housing, industry, power, and water supplies.
   The Lodge,
   Sandy, Beds.
   Tel: 076–78551
   Director: Peter Conder

Scottish Committee on Education and the Countryside
Similar aims to Council for Environmental Education (above)
c/o Scottish Education Department,
St Andrews House,
Edinburgh
Tel: 031-556 6591
Secretary: J. F. C. Neilson

Society for Environmental Education
Provides opportunities for meeting and discussing the role of the environment in education.
16 Trinity Road,
Enderby, Leicester
Tel: 053-729-4396
Secretary: G. C. Martin

Society for the Promotion of Nature Reserves
Aims to secure the protection of fauna and flora by the establishment of nature reserves. Sponsors the formation of county naturalists' trusts and represents their interests at a national level.
British Museum (Natural History),
London SW7
Tel: 01-589-6323
Secretary: A. E. Smith

Society for the Protection of Ancient Buildings (SPAB)
Founded by William Morris in 1877, its interests cover ecclesiastical and secular buildings both large and small, including also mills, barns, dovecotes, and bridges. SPAB advises on all problems affecting old buildings, particularly technical advice on their treatment and repair. It publishes information on the history and care of old buildings and circulates an index of threatened properties to prospective purchasers.
55 Great Ormond Street,
London WC1
Tel: 01-405 2646
Secretary: Mrs M. Dance

Soil Association

Brings together those working for a fuller understanding of the vital relationships between soil, plant, animal, and man. Initiates, coordinates, and assists research in this field. Collects and distributes the knowledge gained so as to create a body of informed public opinion.

Walnut Tree Manor,
Haughley, Stowmarket, Suffolk
Tel: 044–970–235/7
Secretary: Sir Ronald Garvey

Town and Country Planning Association

Fights for 'humanity in planning'; advocates national land-use policy to safeguard green belts and farmland; promotes policies of dispersal and growth of New Towns; informs public of planning issues.

28 King Street,
London WC2
Tel: 01-836 5006/7
Director: David Hall

Ulster Society for the Preservation of the Countryside

Safeguards the amenities of Northern Ireland; arouses and educates public opinion to this end. Acts, either directly or through the members of affliated bodies, as a centre for giving or obtaining advice and information on such matters.

West Winds,
Craigavad, Co. Down
Secretary: W. M. Capper

United Kingdom Federation Against Aircraft Nuisance

A federation of societies with the aim of reducing aircraft noise, air pollution and hazards to safety; attaches particular importance to the siting of airports as a means of attaining these ends.

9 Dover Park Drive,
London SW15
Tel: 01–788–4931
Secretary: Mrs M. St. A. Moore

World Wildlife Fund (British National Appeal)
Dedicated to saving threatened wildlife throughout the world.
7–8 Plumtree Court,
London EC4
Tel: 01-353 2615
Information Officer: Ted Scrope-Howe

University Eco-Action Contacts

University College of Wales, Aberystwyth
Tony Vann,
UNSA,
Department of Botany,
UCW, Aberystwyth,
Cards.

Alan Herbert,
Community Action,
SRC,
UCW, Aberystwyth,
Cards.

University College of North Wales, Bangor
Conservation Corps,
c/o Dr Geoff Gibbs,
School of Plant Biology,
UC of North Wales,
Bangor,
Caerns.

Bath University of Technology
Roy Long,
Students' Union,
University of Technology,
Claverton Down,
Bath.

302

University of Bradford
    Social Action Group,
    c/o Brian Green,
    18 Ethel Terrace,
    Lister Hills,
    Bradford.

University of Bristol
    United Nations Students' Association,
    c/o Steve Lawrence,
    Department of Zoology,
    Queen's Road,
    Clifton,
    Bristol 8.

    Prof. Dinely,
    Sabrina Project,
    Department of Geology,
    University of Bristol
    Bristol 8.

Cambridge University
    Conservation Corps,
    c/o John Booth,
    Junior Parlour,
    Pembroke College,
    Cambridge.

    Ecology Action,
    c/o Francis Arnold,
    JCR,
    Churchill College,
    Cambridge.

City of Liverpool (C F Mott) College of Education
    Alec Bray,
    United Nations Students' Association,
    Students' Union,
    C F Mott College of Education,
    The Hazels,
    Prescot,
    Lancs.

Durham University
> CATER,
> c/o Dr David Bellamy,
> 1 Windmill Hill,
> Durham.

University of East Anglia
> Victoria Newsome,
> Environmental Sciences Society,
> Students' Union,
> UEA,
> University Village,
> Wilberforce Road,
> Norwich.

Essex University
> Conservation Corps,
> c/o Graham Jenkins,
> School of Physical Science,
> University of Essex,
> Wivenhoe Park,
> Colchester.

University of Exeter
> Conservation Corps,
> c/o David Alexander,
> Devonshire House,
> Stoker Road,
> Exeter.

Farnborough Technical College
> Mrs Jo Hooley,
> Department of General Studies,
> Farnborough Technical College,
> Boundary Road,
> Farnborough,
> Hants.

University of Hull
>
> Conservation Corps,
> c/o Margaret MacDonald,
> 100 Cottingham Road,
> Hull,
> Yorks.

University of Leeds
>
> David Teal,
> Liberal Society,
> Students' Union,
> University of Leeds,
> University Road,
> Leeds 2.

> Roger Sweeting,
> Society for Social Responsibility in Science,
> Students' Union,
> University of Leeds,
> University Road,
> Leeds 2.

University of Liverpool
>
> Society for Social Responsibility in Science,
> c/o Dr Graham,
> Mathematics Department,
> University of Liverpool,
> Liverpool 7.

University of Manchester
>
> UNSA,
> c/o George Breeze,
> 11 Martin House,
> 4 Conningham Road,
> Manchester 14.

University of Manchester Institute of Science and Technology
> Julian Marrow,
> EAVP,
> Students' Union,
> UMIST,
> PO BOX 88,
> Sackville Street,
> Manchester M60 1QD.

Nottingham Polytechnic
> Conservation Corps,
> c/o A. Baldrey,
> Union of Students,
> Nottingham Polytechnic,
> Burton Street,
> Nottingham NG1 4BU.

Oxford University
> UNSA,
> c/o Graham Ashurst,
> JCR,
> St John's College,
> Oxford.

> Ecology Action,
> c/o R. Black,
> JCR,
> St Catherine's College,
> Oxford.

University of Reading
> Tim Ardill,
> Scout and Guide Club,
> Students' Union,
> University of Reading,
> Reading.

Pat Rubery,
Transport Society,
Students' Union,
University of Reading,
Reading.

Salford University of Technology
Conservation Corps,
c/o Keith Elder,
Davy Hall,
Oaklands Road,
Salford M7 0PX.

St Andrews University
UNSA,
c/o Mike Buchanan,
Andrew Melville Hall,
North Haugh,
St Andrews,
Scotland.

St Paul's College of Education
Anthony Stevens,
Student Community Action,
Students' Council,
St Paul's College,
Cheltenham,
Glos.

University of Southampton
c/o D. Goode,
JCR,
Students' Union,
University of Southampton,
Southampton.

Stirling University
UNSA,
c/o Malcolm Roome,
Students' Union,
Stirling University,
Stirling,
Scotland.

University College, Swansea
Conservation Corps,
c/o Jull Payne,
Neuadd Martin,
Mill Lane,
Blackpill,
Swansea.

University of Wales Institute of Science and Technology
Taff Project group,
c/o Prof Edwards,
Department of Applied Biology,
UWIST,
Cathays Park,
Cardiff.

University of Warwick
UNSA,
c/o Dave Dodwell,
Students' Union,
University of Warwick,
Coventry CV4 7AL,
Warwicks.

———————

National Union of Students
The Conservation Officer,
NUS,
3–4 Endsleigh Street, London W1.

Bibliography

THE CRISIS

Allison A. (ed.), *Population Control*, Penguin Books, 1970 (7s, 35np).

Barr, J., *The Assaults on Our Senses*, Methuen, 1970 (50s., £2.50).

Borgstrom, G., *The Hungry Planet*, Collier-Macmillan, 1967 (75s, £3.75); Paperback (25s, £1.25).

Borgstrom, G., *Too Many: A Study of the Earth's Biological Limitations*, Collier-Macmillan, 1969 (42s, £2.10).

Commoner, B., *Science and Survival*, Gollancz, 1966 (21s, £1.05).

Curtis, R., and Hogan, E., *Perils of the Peaceful Atom*, Gollancz, 1970 (52s, £2.60).

Dansereau, P. (ed.), *Challenge for Survival*, Columbia University Press, 1970 (72s, £3.60).

Dasmann, R. F., *The Destruction of California*, Collier-Macmillan, 1967 (7s 6d, 40 np).

Dorst, J., *Before Nature Dies*, Collins, 1970 (63s, £3.15); Paperback (38s, £1.90)

Ehrlich, P. and A., *Population, Resources, Environment*, W. H. Freeman, 1970 (84s, £4.20).

Fraser Darling, Sir F., *Wilderness and Plenty*, (1969 Reith Lectures), BBC Publications, 1970 (21s, £1.05).

Galbraith, J. K., *The New Industrial State*, Penguin Books, 1969 (8s, 40 np).

Hardin, G., *Population, Evolution and Birth Control*, W. H. Freeman, 1969 (50s, £2.50); Paperback (24s, £1.20).

King-Hele, D., *The End of the Twentieth Century?*, Macmillan, 1970 (36s, £1.80); Student Edition, (15s, 75 np).

309

Nicholson, M., *The Environmental Revolution*, Hodder and Stoughton, 1970 (84s, £4.20).

Rattray Taylor, G., *The Doomsday Book*, Thames and Hudson, 1970 (42s, £2.10).

Taylor, L. R. (ed.), *The Optimum Population for Britain*, Academic Press, 1970 (35s, £1.75).

ECOLOGY, CONSERVATION, WILDLIFE

Cox, W., *Readings in Conservation Ecology*, Appleton, Century and Crofts, 1969 (54s, £2.70).

Fisher, J. and HRH the Duke of Edinburgh, *Wildlife Crisis*, Hamish Hamilton, 1970 (84s, £4.20).

Goodman, G. T. (ed.), *Ecology and the Industrial Society*, Blackwell Scientific Publications, 1965 (reprinted 1970) (£5, £5.00).

Hardin, G., *Thirty-nine Steps to Biology Readings from 'Scientific American'*, W. H. Freeman, 1968 (84s, £4.20); Paperback (42, £2.10).

Hardin G., *Science, Conflict and Society* from *'Scientific American'*, W. H. Freeman (94s, £4.70); Paperback (48s, £2.40).

Kormondy, E., *Concepts of Ecology*, Prentice-Hall 1970, (50s, £2.50); Paperback (30s, £1.50).

Odum, E., *Ecology*, R. & W. Holt, 1963 (21s, £1.05).

Russell, E. J., *The World of the Soil*, Collins, 1957 (30s, £1.50).

Stamp, Sir D., *Man and the Land*, Collins, 1955 (32s, £1.60).

Stamp, Sir D., *Nature Conservation in Britain*, Collins, 1969 (36s, £1.80).

Stapledon, Sir R. G., and Waller, R., *Human Ecology*, Faber, 1964 (30s, £1.50).

Storer, J., *Man in the Web of Life*, V. Stuart, 1963 (25s, £1.25).

Vesey-FitzGerald, *The Vanishing Wildlife of Britain*, Macgibbon and Kee, 1969 (36s, £1.80).

THE HUMAN ANIMAL

Ardrey, R. *The Social Contract*, Collins, 1970 (45s, £2.25).
Ardrey, R., *The Territorial Imperative*, Collins, 1960 (36s, £1.80); Paperback – Fontana, 1969 (9s 6d, 50 np).
Dubos, R., *Man Adapting*, Yale UP, (£5 12s 6d, £5.63).
Dubos. R., *So Human an Animal*, Rupert Hart Davis, 1970 (45s, £2.25).
Hall, E. T., *The Hidden Dimension*, Bodley Head, 1969 (42s, £2.10).
Morris, D., *The Naked Ape*, Cape, 1969 (30s, £1.50); Corgi, 1969 (5s, 25 np).

COUNTRYSIDE AND COASTLINE

Bracey, H. E., *People and the Countryside*, Routledge and Kegan Paul, 1970 (63s, £3.15).
Christian, G., *Tomorrow's Countryside: The Road to the Seventies*, John Murray, 1966 (35s, £1.75).
Crowe, S, *The Landscape of Power*, Architectural Press, 1958 (20s, £1.00).
Steers, J. A., *The English Coast*, Collins – Fontana, 1966 (8s 6d, 45 np).

CITIES AND TOWNS

Cities, A 'Scientific American' Book, Penguin Books, 1967 (7s 6d, 40 np).

Cullen, G., *Townscape*, Architectural Press 1961 (70s, £3.50).

Eldredge, H. W., *Taming Megalopolis*, Praegar, 1967 (£7 14s, £7.70).

Hall, P., *London 2000*, Faber, 1969 (revised edition) (70s, £3.50).

Osborn, F. J., and Whittick, A., *The New Towns*, L. Hill, 1969 (second edition) (75s, £3.75).

Schaffer, F., *The New Town Story*, Macgibbon and Kee, 1970 (55s, £2.75).

Sharp, T., *Town and Townscape*, John Murray, 1968 (45s, £2.25).

ECONOMICS

Boulding, K., *Economic Analysis*, Harper and Row, 1966 (45s, £2.25); Paperback (30s, £1.50).

Galbraith, J. K., *The Affluent Society*, Hamilton, 1958 (21s, £1.05); Pelican (5s, 25 np).

Mishan, E. J., *The Costs of Economic Growth*, Staples Press, 1967 (36s, £1.80).

LAND USE

Arvill, R., *Man and Environment*, Penguin Books 1969 (revised edition) (10s 6d, 55 np).

Barr, J., *Derelict Britain*, Penguin Books, 1970 (revised edition) (7s, 35 np).

Best, R., *The Major Land Uses of Great Britain*, Wye College, Ashford, 1969 (10s 6d, 55 np).

Bracey, H. E., *Industry and the Countryside*, Faber for the Acton Society Trust, 1963 (36s, £1.80).

Brett, L., *Landscape in Distress*, Architectural Press, 1965 (40s, £2.00).

Colvin, B., *Land and Landscape*, John Murray, 1970 (84s, £4.20).

Crowe, S., *Tomorrow's Landscape*, Architectural Press, 1963 (second impression) (21s, £1.05).

Fairbrother, N., *New Lives, New Landscapes*, Architectural Press, 1970 (75s, £3.75).

Hawkes, J., *A Land*, Penguin Books, 1959 (3s 6d, 18 np).

Hilton, K. J. (ed.), *The Lower Swansea Valley Project*, Longmans Green, 1967 (80s, £4.00).

Stamp, Sir D., *The Land of Britain: Its Use and Misuse*, Longmans Green, 1962 (third edition) (£6, £6.00).

Thomas, D., *London's Green Belt*, Faber, 1970 (65s, £3.25 np).

PESTICIDES AND POLLUTION

Carson, R., *Silent Spring*, Hamish Hamilton, 1963 (25s, £1.25); Penguin Books, 1965 (5s, 25 np).

Graham, F., *Since Silent Spring*, Hamish Hamilton, 1970 (40s, £2.00).

Herber. L., *Our Synthetic Environment*, Cape, 1963 (25s, £1.25).

Hunter, B., *Gardening Without Poisons*, Hamish Hamilton, 1965 (25s, £1.25).

Mellanby, K., *Pesticides and Pollution*, Collins, 1967 (30s, £1.50); Paperback – Fontana, 1969 (8s 6d, 45 np).

Rudd, R., *Pesticides and The Living Landscape*, Faber, 1965 (35s, £1.75).

TRAFFIC

Buchanan, C. D., *Mixed Blessing: The Motor in Britain*, Leonard Hill, 1958 (45s, £2.25).

Buchanan, C. D., *Traffic in Towns*, Penguin Books, 1964 (10s 6d, 55 np).

Tetlow, J., and Goss, A., *Homes, Towns and Traffic*, Faber, 1968 (50s, £2.50).

NOISE

Bell, Dr. A., *Noise*, World Health Organization, Geneva, 1966 (10s, 50 np).

Burns, W., *Noise and Man*, John Murray, 1968 (50s, £2.50).

Noise Abatement Society, *The Law on Noise*, 1969 (21s, £1.05).

Rodda, *Noise and Society*, Oliver and Boyd, 1967 (7s 6d, 40 np).

JOURNALS

The Ecologist (monthly), Subscriptions Department, Darby House, Bletchingley Road, Merstham, Surrey (£3 pa, £3.00 pa).

Your Environment (quarterly), Subscriptions Department, 10 Roderick Road, London NW3 (30s pa, £1.50 pa).

Books on ecology and conservation subjects can be obtained from The London Ecology Bookshop, 45 Lower Belgrave Street, London, SW1 (Tel: 01-730 8603).

PAMPHLETS

Clean and Pleasant Land (35 np, 7s) from Conservative Political Centre, 32 Smith Square, London SW1.

Controlling Our Environment, by Lord Kennet (15 np, 3s) from Fabian Society, 11 Dartmouth Street, London SW1.

Man and His Environment (15 np, 2s 6d) from The Soil Association, Walnut Tree Manor, Haughley, Stowmarket, Suffolk.

Pollution and Our Environment (15 np, 3s) from The Labour Party, Transport House, Smith Square, London SW1.

Our Polluted Planet (free) from Ambassador College Press, PO Box 111, St Albans, Herts.

Film Bibliography

Agriculture/Soil/Pesticides

CF/RF/SS	*Look to the Land*	28 min
SA	*The Secret Highway*	30 min
PFB	*The Living Soil*	20 min
CFL	*World at Your Feet*	22 min
CFL	*Chemical Conquest*	25 min
CON	*Poisons, Pests and People*	60 min/bw
PFB	*Pests or Plenty*	20 min

Cities

CT	*New Face for Britain*	20 min
CT	*You Can Choose*	20 min/bw

Ecology/Population

RF	*Population Ecology*	11 min
RF	*Ecology Teaching Series* (seven linked films)	Each 11 min

Education/Voluntary Action

CEGB	*Learning by Discovery*	29 min
EF	*Lake Survey*	13 min
EF	*The Way to Adventure*	17 min/bw
CT	*The Big Clean Up*	28 min/bw
CT	*Breakthrough*	15 min/bw

Forestry/Trees

PFB	*The Changing Forest*	39 min
CF	*Greenwood Revived*	14 min
CT	*Trees on the Move*	19 min
CT	*Spare that Tree*	20 min/bw
CT	*Moving Big Trees*	13 min

Landscape Conservation

BH	Conservation and Balance in Nature	18 min
EFVA	The Face of Britain	21 min
RF	Against the Sea	17 min
PFB	The Vanishing Coast	29 min
BT	Between the Tides	22 min
PFB	People and Leisure	30 min
CEGB	The Lonely Places	23 min
PFB	The Wind on the Heath	30 min
BBC	The Peak	30 min
PFB	Beauty in Trust	23 min
SS	Who Cares for England?	30 min

Nature Conservation (General)

PFB	The Living Pattern	30 min
BBONT/SPNR	Wildlife in Trust	20 min
LTNC/SPNR	Nature in Trust	35 min
GTNC/SPNR	Today and Tomorrow	30 min
SS	Wildlife in Danger	23 min
WWF	Conservation Piece	7 min

Nature Conservation (Habitats)

RF	The Secret World	28 min
WTNC/SPNR	The Wealth of the Chalk	35 min
EFVA	Wildlife in the Marsh	20 min
RSPB	Ripples in the Reeds	21 min
SFL	Aberlady Task Force	11 min
RSPB	The Call of the Running Tide	18 min
RSPB	Reserves for Birds	83 min

Natural Conservation (Species)

RF	Where Have All the Butterflies Gone?	9 min
RSPB	Operation Osprey	14 min
RF	Deer Hunters	9 min
RF	Should We Kill the Seals?	9 min
EFVA	Waterfowl: a Resource in Danger	16 min
BT	Wild Wings	34 min

Water Pollution, Resources

MWB	*London's Water Supply*	29 min
PFB	*The River Must Live*	21 min
RSPB	*After the Torrey Canyon*	13 min

FILM DISTRIBUTORS

BBC   BBC TV
Television Centre, Wood Lane
London W12

BBONT   Berkshire, Bucks and Oxon Naturalists' Trust
Pednor Close, Pednor
Chesham, Bucks

BH   Boulter Hawker Films Ltd
Hadleigh
Ipswich, Suffolk

BT   British Transport Films
Melbury House, Melbury Terrace
London NW1

CFL   Canadian Film Library
Canada House, Trafalgar Square
London SW1

CEGB   Central Electricity Generating Board Film
    Library
Sudbury House, 15 Newgate Street
London EC1

CF   Central Film Library
Governments Buildings, Bromyard Avenue
London W3

CT   Civic Trust
18 Carlton House Terrace
London SW1

CON   Concord Films Council
Nacton
Ipswich, Suffolk

EFVA   Educational Foundation for Visual Aids in
    Education
Brooklands House
Weybridge, Surrey

EF	Explorer Films
	58 Stratford Road
	Bromsgrove, Worcs
GTNC	Gloucestershire Trust for Nature Conservation
	The Woodlands, St Briavels
	Lydney, Glos
LTNC	Lincolnshire Trust for Nature Conservation
	Manor House
	Alford, Lincs
MWB	Metropolitan Water Board
	New River Head, Roseberry Avenue
	London EC1
PFB	Petroleum Films Bureau
	4 Brook Street, Hanover
	London W1
RF	Rank Film Library
	1 Aintree Road, Perivale
	Greenford, Middx
RSPB	Royal Society for the Protection of Birds
	The Lodge
	Sandy, Beds
SFL	Scottish Film Library
	16 Woodside Terrace
	Glasgow C3
SPNR	Society for the Promotion of Nature Reserves
	Manor House
	Alford, Lincs
SA	Soil Association
	Walnut Tree Manor
	Haughley, Suffolk
SS	Sound Services Ltd
	Wilton Crescent
	London SW19
WTNC	Wiltshire Trust for Nature Conservation
	Tyning Wood, Gare Hill
	Frome, Somerset
WWF	World Wildlife Fund
	7 Plum Tree Court
	London EC4

Contributors

MICHAEL ALLABY has been a member of the Soil Association's staff since 1964, where he founded and edited the association's monthly newspaper SPAN. He is also associate editor of *The Ecologist*.

KENNETH ALLSOP is a writer and television broadcaster, a members of BBC TV's *24 Hours* team. He is the author of numerous books, the most recent of which is *Fit to Live in? The Future of Britain's Countryside*.

JOHN BARR is a freelance writer, formerly on the staff of *New Society* magazine, who specializes in environmental issues. He is the author of *Derelict Britain* and *The Assaults on Our Senses*.

TERENCE BENDIXSON was correspondent on urban affairs for *The Guardian* from 1964–69. Now a freelance writer, he is working on a book called *Can We Kill the Car?* to be published in 1971.

THOMAS L. BLAIR, an urban sociologist, is senior lecturer at the School of Planning, The Polytechnic of Central London. His articles have appeared in *Official Architecture and Planning* and *The British Journal of Sociology*.

KENNETH E. BOULDING is a member of the teaching staff at the Institute for the Behavioral Sciences, University of Colorado, US. He is the author of *The Meaning of the Twentieth Century*.

JOHN BRESLAW is a graduate student in the department of economics at the University of California, Berkeley, US.

DAVID R. BROWER has been active in conservation work since 1933. He is president of the Friends of the Earth, which he founded in the US in 1969, and is director of the John Muir Institute.

KENNETH BROWLER is a freelance writer who has edited seven volumes in the Sierra Club, US, Exhibit Format Series.

GARRETT DE BELL received a BS degree in biology from Stanford University in 1966. He now devotes his full time to ecological problems. He is the editor of the US edition of *The Environmental Handbook*.

RENÉ DUBOS is professor at Rockefeller University, New York City. Among his many books are *So Human an Animal* and *Reason Awake: Science for Man*. He has done research in microbiology and pathology.

PAUL R. EHRLICH is professor and director of graduate study in the department of biological sciences, Stanford University, US. He is a leading advocate of population control and author of *The Population Bomb*.

NAN FAIRBROTHER is a member of the Institute of Landscape Architects and lectures and writes on landscape and land use. She is the author of *Men and Gardens* and *New Lives, New Landscapes*.

JOHN FISCHER, the author of several books, is a contributing editor to *Harper's* magazine in the United States.

SIR FRANK FRASER DARLING, vice-president of The Conservation Foundation, delivered the British Broadcasting Corporation's 1969 Reith Lectures on *Wilderness and Plenty*. He was knighted in 1970.

GARRETT HARDIN is professor of biology at the University of California, Santa Barbara, US, and is the author of *Population, Evolution and Birth Control*.

SUZANNE HARRIS, who writes and sings conservation songs, is an American now living in Britain. She sang at the European Conservation Year Conference in Strasbourg in 1970.

JON HOLLIMAN is a geography graduate from University College, London. He now works for the International Union for the Conservation of Nature and Natural Resources.

TED HUGHES is a poet and advisory editor of *Your Environment*. His most recent collection of poems is *Crow*.

BARCLAY INGLIS, a Scottish chartered accountant living in Surrey, is a founder member of Friends of the Earth in Great Britain. He is coordinating the activities of FOE in this country.

WESLEY MARX is a freelance writer specializing in conservation, natural history and public affairs. He is the author of *The Frail Ocean*.

DR KENNETH MELLANBY is director of the Nature Conservancy's Monks Wood Experimental Station. He is the author of *Pesticides and Pollution*.

DR EDWARD J. MISHAN is reader in economics at the London School of Economics. Among his books is *The Costs of Economic Growth*.

WALTER C. PATTERSON, a graduate in nuclear physics, is a Canadian now living in Britain. A freelance writer, he is also co-editor of *Your Environment*.

LORD RITCHIE-CALDER, author and journalist, is a former president of The Conservation Society. He is the author of numerous books, including *Living with the Atom* and *Common Sense about a Starving World*.

GRAHAM SEARLE is chairman of the National Union of Students' Committee on the Environment. A geologist, he is on the executive of the UK World University Service.

ANTHONY SMITH is a freelance journalist and author, formerly on the staff of *The Manchester Guardian* and the *Daily Telegraph*. Among his books is *The Body*. In 1970 he was a member of 'Operation Seashore', a six-month expedition round Britain's coastline.

K. S. WHEELER is senior lecturer in geography, College of Education, Leicester. He is the author of several textbooks on environmental subjects and a founder-member of the Society for Environmental Education.

LYNN WHITE Jr is professor of history at the University of California, Los Angeles, US. He was formerly president of Mills College, US. He is the author of numerous books, the most recent of which is *Machina Ex Deo*.

Other Ballantine
Environmental Titles

THE POPULATION BOMB   *Professor Paul R. Ehrlich*
The book you can't afford not to read! Over-population is
with us now and will be the root cause of major world problems unless it is brought under control. This book tells what
is likely to occur – and what can be done.

(6s) 30 np

THE FRAIL OCEAN   *Wesley Marx*
'A fascinating and important book. The obvious comparison
is with Rachel Carson's *Silent Spring*, and I can only hope
Mr Marx's book will be as widely read, and have a comparable impact.' – *New York Times*

(8s) 40 np

MOMENT IN THE SUN   *Robert and Leona Train Rienow*
A powerful, provocative book for those who care about
what tomorrow might bring ...

(8s) 40 np

CONCORDE – THE CASE AGAINST SUPERSONIC TRANSPORT
A documented source book of supersonic transport. The
untold facts of the heavy cost to the environment ... the
unknown extent of the sonic bang ... the unpredictable pollution ... dangers in flight ...

(7s) 35 np

Friends of the Earth

Thomas L. Blair

The man-made environmental crisis which exists on this planet is only now being recognized as the ultimate threat to Man's survival. Something needs to be done at once in order to avert the final catastrophe.

There are in Britain many individuals, researchers, and conservation organizations working hard to protect the Earth from man's abuse. These people are deserving of the support of a wider public committed to stand up for the environment, its heritage and its future, and to be counted as Friends of the Earth.

Action is required to replace the throw-away consumer philosophy with a way of life based on sound ecological principles. To place our faith in an economic system which ignores the need to come to terms with our environment is foolhardy.

Friends of the Earth Ltd, founded in London in 1970, believe that the conservationist's cause is good and his heart is in the right place, but that he deserves more effective power. We also believe that the ecological researcher's cause is good, his head is in the right place, but that unless we act now on what he already knows, his work will have been in vain.

We are not just idealists, but we do have ideals. We place emphasis on practical action and we recognize the need for many new organizations to share the work. We are also aware of the need to give more help to existing conservation groups, which have been labouring long and hard. Our Earth is threatened and needs every friend it has.

FOE intends, firstly, to pursue an active publishing programme with Ballantine Books, to provide the best possible information, written for the intelligent layman, about the remedial action required to meet current threats to the environment. We intend to encourage further research aimed at a greater understanding of the impact on the Earth of Man and his technological society. We shall also urge action now, based on what is already known, to resist the use of a given technology without proof that it will not cause lasting harm.

We believe that the proper application of science and humanity will enable us to shun projects to which mere technological achievement lends attraction.

Unhampered by any party-political allegiance, FOE will undertake substantial legislative activity, including, lobbying and focusing public attention on critical issues. We will join other organizations in going to court to fight environmental abuse. We shall wage an all-out war on any interest which ignores the needs of the environment.

FOE's members will form specific task forces supported by teams of environmental experts and citizen's groups. The acronym FOE is appropriate: any friend of the earth must be the foe of whatever or whoever degrades the earth.

If these goals are yours, contact us by completing the form on the last page of this book and sending it to Friends of the Earth, 8 King Street, London WC2.

FRIENDS OF THE EARTH

London
Friends of the Earth
8 King Street
London WC2
Tel: 01–836 0718

France
Les Amis de la Terre
25 Quai Voltaire
Paris 7, France
Tel: 222–8140

Switzerland
Freunde der Erde
JM Bruggen 425
8906 Bonstetten
Zurich
Switzerland
Tel: (051)-95-53-58

New York
Friends of the Earth
30 East 42nd Street
New York, NY 10017
Tel: (212)-687-87-47

San Francisco
451 Pacific Avenue
San Francisco, California 94133
Tel: (415)-391-4271

Washington
917 15th Street, NW
Washington, DC 20005
Tel: (202)-638-25-25

European Representative
52 Avenue des Champs-Elysées
Paris 8, France.

Time is Short – Write Now – Your Chance to Act

If you want action now for sound ecological practices and an end to environmental destruction – make sure the politicians know how you feel. The Government has just announced at long last, a new Department of the Environment and a 'central capability unit' of experts to review central policy at Cabinet level. Following are two coupons which we urge you to fill up, tear out and send to Friends of the Earth, 8 King Street, London WC2, for forwarding to the Prime Minister, Edward Heath, and Peter Walker, the Secretary of State for the Environment.

Write also to your MP and to your local councillors; this is how your opinions can provoke action.

To:
 The Rt Hon. Edward Heath, MP,
Prime Minister,
c/o Friends of the Earth,
8 King Street,
London WC2.

Dear Mr Prime Minister,
   Having read in John Barr's *The Environmental Handbook* something of the threats to our environment, I write to urge you to ensure that your government deal boldly with environmental problems. I ask you to take active practical steps to make Britain worth living in.
   Will you please let me know how I can assist the Government's work in any way?

                              Yours sincerely,

NAME ....

ADDRESS   ....

           . . . .

           . . . .

           ....

To:

The Rt Hon. Peter Walker, MP,
Secretary of State for the Environment,
c/o Friends of the Earth,
8 King Street,
London WC2.

Dear Minister,

As the Minister charged with responsibility for the environment, please exercise your new office to give our earth, environment, and resources a new lease of life. I urge you to read and seriously consider John Barr's *The Environmental Handbook* produced by Friends of the Earth.

I am sure you would agree that people need to be involved in many aspects of your work, which concerns all of us on Earth. Can you suggest what I myself could do to assist your Department in its work?

Yours sincerely,

NAME . . . .

ADDRESS . . . .

. . . .

. . . .

. . . .

FRIENDS OF THE EARTH
8 King Street,
London WC2

—I should like actively to participate in specific projects.

—I should like to see FOE tackle such problems as

....

—I should like to be kept informed of other books by Friends of the Earth.

—I should like to contribute the sum of £   s.   d. to further your aims.

NAME ... ...

ADDRESS   .. . .

.. . .

... .

born to hunger

by Arthur Hopcraft

Never again, after reading this book, will anyone ask why rich countries should devote their time and earnings to bettering the poor ones.

Arthur Hopcraft visited many of the world's hunger spots to see what was being done to help the afflicted and lift their terrible burden. This vital and important book tells what he saw:

'These people are the poor and the threatened. The threat is hunger and they are born to it.'

Published by PAN at 25p

THE POPULATION BOMB

POPULATION CONTROL –
or RACE TO OBLIVION?

Overpopulation is now the dominant problem in all our personal, national, and international planning.

No one can do rational personal planning, nor can public policy be resolved in any area unless one first takes into account the population bomb.

Schools, politicians, and mass media only touch the edge of the major problem.

Paul R. Ehrlich, Professor of Biology and Director of Graduate Studies, Department of Biological Sciences, Stanford University, U.S.A., clearly describes the dimensions of the crisis in all its aspects – air, food, water, birth control, death control, our total environment – and provides a realistic evaluation of the remaining options.